PRAISE FOR BART D. EHRMAN

"A humane, thoughtful and intelligent historian... The great appeal of Ehrman's approach to Christian history has always been his steadfast humanizing impulse."

New York Times Book Review

"One of my absolute favorite biblical scholars, [Ehrman] stimulates the mind and charges the spirit."

Michael Eric Dyson

"Bart Ehrman has made a career of zeroing in on some of the most difficult questions at the intersection of faith and history."

Boston Globe

"Vigilantly persuasive."

Washington Post

"Ehrman's style is marked by the narrative thrust of a good story or even a sermon."

Christian Science Monitor

ALSO BY BART D. EHRMAN

Armageddon

Heaven and Hell

The Triumph of Christianity

Jesus before the Gospels

How Jesus Became God

The Other Gospels

The Bible: A Historical and Literary Introduction

Forgery and Counterforgery

Did Jesus Exist?

The Apocryphal Gospels: Texts and Translations

Forged

Jesus, Interrupted

God's Problem

The Lost Gospel of Judas Iscariot

Peter, Paul, and Mary Magdalene

Studies in the Textual Criticism of the New Testament

Misquoting Jesus

The Apostolic Fathers

Truth and Fiction in The Da Vinci Code

A Brief Introduction to the New Testament

After the New Testament

The New Testament: A Historical Introduction to the Early Christian Writings

Christianity in Late Antiquity

Lost Christianities

Lost Scriptures

Jesus: Apocalyptic Prophet of the New Millennium

· *The Orthodox Corruption of Scripture*

The Text of the Fourth Gospel in the Writings of Origen

Didymus the Blind and the Text of the Gospels

LOVE THY STRANGER

How Jesus Transformed Our Moral Conscience

BART D. EHRMAN

ONEWORLD

A Oneworld Book

First published in Great Britain, the Republic of Ireland and Australia
by Oneworld Publications Ltd, 2026

Copyright © Bart D. Ehrman, 2026

The moral right of Bart D. Ehrman to be identified as the Author of this work has been asserted
by him in accordance with the Copyright, Designs and Patents Act 1988

All rights reserved
Copyright under Berne Convention
A CIP record for this title is available from the British Library

ISBN 978-1-83643-182-4
eISBN 978-1-83643-183-1

Interior design by Wendy Blum
Printed and bound in Great Britain by Clays Ltd, Elcograf S.p.A.

No part of this publication may be reproduced, stored in a retrieval system, or transmitted, in any form or by any means, electronic, mechanical, photocopying, recording or otherwise, or used in any manner for the purpose of training artificial intelligence technologies or systems, without the prior permission of the publishers.

The authorised representative in the EEA is eucomply OU,
Pärnu mnt 139b–14, 11317 Tallinn, Estonia
(email: hello@eucompliancepartner.com / phone: +33757690241)

Oneworld Publications Ltd
10 Bloomsbury Street
London WC1B 3SR
England

Stay up to date with the latest books,
special offers, and exclusive content from
Oneworld with our newsletter

Sign up on our website
oneworld.co.uk

For Sarah

*She of scintillating intelligence
and an infectious passion for life*

CONTENTS

Acknowledgments	xi
A Note on Translations	xiii
Introduction: Strange(r) Altruism	1
Chapter One: Does Altruism Exist?	5
Chapter Two: The Ancient Quest for Happiness	13
Chapter Three: Love, Charity, and Forgiveness in the Greek and Roman Worlds	43
Chapter Four: The Jewish Roots of Jesus's Ethics	77
Chapter Five: Love, Charity, and Forgiveness in the Teachings of Jesus	99
Chapter Six: The Afterlife of Jesus's Ethics	137
Chapter Seven: Love after Jesus	163
Chapter Eight: Charitable Giving and Forgiveness after Jesus	181
Conclusion: Altruism in the Conscience of the West	217
Notes	223
Index	251

ACKNOWLEDGMENTS

One of the best parts of finishing a book is being able to thank everyone who has lent a hand (or two). After completing a draft of my manuscript, I consulted with scholars in the fields of Classics, Biblical Studies, and Christianity in Late Antiquity, each of whom has graciously read my manuscript, made incredibly useful comments, and saved my skin on multiple issues. The errors, flaws, and weaknesses that remain, alas, are all mine.

And so, I extend my deepest gratitude to:

- John Barclay, Lightfoot Professor of Divinity, Durham University
- David Brakke, Joe R. Engle Chair in the History of Christianity and Professor of History, Ohio State University
- Radd K. Ehrman, Professor of Classics, Kent State University
- Andrew Jacobs, Senior Fellow at the Center for the Study of World Religions, Harvard Divinity School
- James Rives, Kenan Eminent Professor of Classics, University of North Carolina at Chapel Hill
- Jeffrey Siker, Professor of Theological Studies, Emeritus, Loyola Marymount University
- Elizabeth Vandiver, Clement Biddle Penrose Professor of Latin and Classics, Whitman College.

ACKNOWLEDGMENTS

In addition, I am grateful to three members of my blog who have offered extensive and helpful comments. This will require a bit of explanation. For thirteen years now the Bart Ehrman Blog (www.ehrmanblog.org) has raised funds for charities dealing principally with hunger, homelessness, and disaster relief. I post five to six times a week on topics connected with biblical studies, the historical Jesus, the rise of Christianity, and most related things. Members have full access to the posts past and present and are allowed to comment and ask questions, all of which I answer. There is a small membership fee for the blog. Every penny goes directly to the charities we support (I don't get a dime, and we take out no overhead). This past year we raised over $580,000.

I provided my blog members with the opportunity to read and comment on my manuscript in exchange for a donation to our charitable work, and three very generously accepted. Their comments were insightful and extremely helpful. And so, many thanks to blog members: Giselle Ben Dor, John Merrick, and Michael Waddell.

I would also like to thank everyone at Simon & Schuster who has worked with me and made this book possible, especially my two editors, Priscilla Painton, vice president and editor in chief, who first brought me on at S&S and has been an advisor nonpareil over the course of four books; and my conscientious and devoted senior editor Megan Hogan, who worked over my manuscript with a fine-tooth comb that now, regrettably, has very few teeth left.

I am especially indebted to Sarah Beckwith, Katherine Everett Gilbert Distinguished Professor of English at Duke, a Shakespeare scholar who is knowledgeable, so far as one can tell, about nearly everything else as well, and is a famously insightful and engaging dialogue partner. I have dedicated this book to her on the occasion of our twenty-fifth wedding anniversary.

Translations of the Bible are from the New Revised Standard Version Updated Edition (NRSVUE) or are my own; those of other ancient texts are my own unless indicated otherwise.

LOVE THY STRANGER

INTRODUCTION

Strange(r) Altruism

Most people I know are moved by news of tragedy. A terrible earthquake, a drought, a famine, a flood, wildfires, displaced people, innocent victims of military aggression—we feel pity for those pointlessly suffering and a desire, even an obligation, to help. So we donate to disaster relief; we organize a collection for food, water, or first aid; possibly we volunteer. Almost never do we know the people in need: they are complete strangers, often in far-off lands, people we will never meet and possibly wouldn't like if we did. Yet we—at least most of us—want to help.

This sense of moral obligation to strangers in need is not written into the human DNA.[1] Nor was it found in the ancient roots of our cultural heritage in the West. Philosophers in the Greek and Roman worlds enthusiastically agreed that helping others was appropriate and often obligatory, but altruistic acts were focused almost exclusively on close genetic and social relations—family, friends, and, less frequently, others "like us" in the same community. The sense that anyone should help anonymous strangers in far-away places was simply not part of the moral equation.

Why then is it part of the equation today? Why does this urge to provide assistance—for some of us quite intense, for others admittedly faint—seem like moral "common sense," not just among religious folks but agnostics and atheists as well, a common sense that affects not only our individual psyches but also our views of social agenda and governmental priorities?[2] My argument in this book is that the impulse to help strangers in need is embedded in our Western moral conscience because of the teachings of Jesus. As Christianity spread throughout the ancient world, it revolutionized the understanding of ethical obligation, leading to a fundamental transformation in the moral conscience of the West.

I realize this is a bold claim, but the chapters that follow will provide the evidence.[3]

It is not that Jesus invented this kind altruism out of whole cloth. On the contrary, he based his teachings on his understanding of the Hebrew Bible, and similar views can be found among other Jewish teachers of his day. Unlike other religious traditions at the foundation of Western culture, Judaism had long emphasized the obligation to care for the poor, the needy, the outcast, and the oppressed. But, and this is an important "but," these obligations for the most part extended only to those who belonged to the Israelite community, either by birth, conversion, or immigration. Jesus universalized this obligation. Since it was the followers of Jesus—rather than adherents of other Jewish teachers—that converted millions of gentiles and eventually became the religion of the West, the shift in ethical concerns and practices is ultimately based on Jesus's own distinctive teachings.

The Christian church that emerged in Jesus's wake was never a monolith, advancing a single code of ethics, any more than it endorsed a single set of doctrinal teachings or ritual practices. On the contrary, "the" early church was startlingly diverse in nearly every way.[4] Very few Christians, even at the beginning, adopted the strict ethical injunctions of Jesus himself. Moreover, as soon as Christianity began to spread outside his native land, Christian converts faced new situations in unexpected contexts, completely different from those of their founder, an itinerant Jewish preacher in the sparsely populated hinterlands of rural Galilee. Christian leaders adjusted Jesus's teachings accordingly, often altering and almost always softening them for public consumption. Still, by the end of the fourth century, when Christianity became the state religion of the Roman Empire, the basic core of his teachings had begun to make a significant difference in the lives of thousands on the margins of society. Prior to the spread of Christianity, there were no public hospitals in the Roman world; no orphanages, poorhouses, or old persons' homes; no government assistance to help those in need or private charities to minister to the poor, homeless, and hungry.[5] These are Christian innovations that evolved from Christian understandings of what it meant to be a good person.

Would these values and institutions have arisen without Christianity? There is no way to know. It is possible, of course, that the religions and cultures of, say, Southeast Asia or China would eventually have influenced Western mores. But the developments in moral thinking I will be exploring arose internally in the West, not under Eastern influences.[6] Ultimately they derived from Jesus's distinctive teachings about what it means to love others. This kind of love is not strictly (or even necessarily) a feeling or emotion; it is directed toward the good of others, even at a cost to oneself. One very concrete expression of active love involves sharing material resources, for example through charitable giving; another, less often considered, involves nonmaterial kindness in personal relationships, graphically exemplified in acts of pure forgiveness extended to those who have harmed us (a different kind of "charity"). These are the issues we will be considering in the chapters that follow: the Christian revolution in ethics based on love, charitable giving, and forgiveness.

There can hardly be a more important time to reflect on these Christian moral principles. We live in a world of heightened hatred and hostility toward the "other." Much of the animosity is directed toward those who are not like us, and often our personal grievances lead to violent social action and governmental policy. In these times of power and dominance, it may be useful for all of us, whatever our religious commitments (or noncommitments), to consider the ethical principles that lay at the root of our civilization, and to consider what it would mean to love a neighbor, even if the neighbor is a stranger.

Before plunging into the matter, I need to explain some of the key terms and concepts I will be using throughout my study, and consider one key question in particular: Does altruism actually exist?

Chapter One

DOES ALTRUISM EXIST?

One might think that "altruism" is a straightforward term. It comes from the Latin word *alter*, which means "other," and so refers broadly to actions that benefit someone other than oneself.[1] That stands in contrast with "egoism," based on the Latin word *ego*, meaning "I" or "myself," and therefore referring to actions that benefit oneself.

This all seems simple enough. But as is so often noticed, in practice and in principle it is extremely difficult—maybe impossible—to establish clear boundaries between altruistic and egoistic acts.[2] Let me illustrate the problem by telling a strange personal anecdote. I'll leave you to judge whether it involved an act of altruism, egoism, or, somehow, both.

It happened in 1974, when I was a first-year student at Moody Bible Institute in downtown Chicago. On a late afternoon in February, while walking along Chicago Avenue, I heard a car horn persistently honking up the street. I didn't think much of it; it was rush hour. But looking up, I saw a car that was heading my direction run a red light and almost hit a pedestrian. As the car moved toward me, I saw a woman behind the wheel frantically screaming. When it came nearer, she looked straight at me and screamed for help.

My immediate reaction was to look away. What in the world could I do? Then I thought: *No, I've got to help her.* So I started running after the car.

I wasn't sure what I would do once I caught up to it. You can't exactly jump in front of a moving vehicle like Superman and stop it in its tracks. After a block or so, when I caught up to the car, I had a vague thought that I would—what? Grab the door handle? But the woman solved the problem for me. She threw the driver's-side door open. And I jumped in.

Whenever I tell this story I pause at this point to say: This really happened.

On the passenger seat next to the woman was a young boy. Her son? To make room for me, she jumped on him. He wrapped his arms around her from behind as she kept screaming and flailing her arms, and I immediately realized what the problem was. There were no brakes.

I tried the emergency brake. No good. I tried ramming the shift into park. Nothing. The car was in neutral, so at least it wasn't gaining speed. But cars were coming at us and I was weaving to avoid them as we approached State Street, a major intersection. I had a red light and I thought: *I'm dead.*

Given my other problems, I didn't notice something even more bizarre happening across the street. Another fellow had watched me run after a car and jump in, and now he saw a screaming woman and a child, and . . . he thought I was kidnapping them. As I was weaving the car in and out of traffic, he sprinted up to the passenger side, yanked the door open, and tried, on the run, to pull the child out.

Just then we came to the red light and I made a split-second decision. If we kept coasting straight ahead, we would hit crazily busy Michigan Avenue, and then, as we used to say, we would be toast. So I jerked the wheel to turn onto State Street.

Back then, next to the stoplight on the corner of Chicago and State, stood one of those large blue mail-collection boxes. The fellow who was trying to yank the child out of the car was not, rather obviously, watching where he was going. As a result, as I later found out, I ran him straight into the mailbox (and ran over his foot), thereby taking him rather decisively out of the equation.

The traffic was not as bad on State Street, but we were still in danger: coasting along with no brakes. Then our salvation appeared. Looking up the block, I saw a police paddy wagon parked on our side of the street, and I thought to myself: *I know how I'm going to stop this car.* And I did. I rammed it into the paddy wagon.

Unfortunately, there were two police officers *in* the paddy wagon, and, to put it mildly, they were not pleased that someone had just plowed into their vehicle. They burst out, cursing and screaming and ready to haul me off. I was out of breath, but eventually explained what had happened. By that time a crowd had gathered. One of the police officers took notes; the woman was in tears and incredibly grateful; the fellow I had run into the mailbox came limping up and was excited when he learned what he had been involved with; and I headed back to my dorm with my head spinning.

When I got there, I told a few guys in the floor lounge what had happened, and they didn't believe me. But the next day the story made the front page of the *Chicago Tribune*. It was a crazily mangled account. It said that the other fellow (the one I ran into the mailbox) and I were walking along Chicago Avenue when we saw the car out of control and we both sprinted after it and jumped in. I steered in and out of traffic while he was in the back seat shielding the child from injury. Up ahead, police officer so-and-so, detecting our distress, skillfully maneuvered his paddy wagon into our path to stop the car and prevent us from coasting all the way onto Michigan Avenue.

That's eyewitness testimony for you.

For a while I puzzled over where that bizarre account came from. But soon I realized: it must have been from the police officer, who had "skillfully maneuvered his paddy wagon" to save us all.

Once the report hit the paper, things went a bit crazy. My school found out about it and sent out a press release; over the next few days, talk shows on Chicago radio discussed the event and explained what to do if your brakes fail; my home newspaper in Lawrence, Kansas, got ahold of the story and ran it with my picture; my congressional representative read it and put the story in the *U.S. Congressional Record*; and a month later the Chicago Police Department held a ceremony to give me and the other fellow (no longer limping) placards for heroism, plus a commendation to valiant police officer so-and-so, who skillfully maneuvered his paddy wagon.

For fifty years, whenever I've thought about it, I've often wondered why I did what I did. Was it an act of genuine altruism? Obviously, I did something that benefited someone else. That's altruism, right? Or was it more complicated than that?

At the time I was a deeply committed Christian studying at a fundamentalist Bible college. I had devoted my entire life to God and was willing to give up everything in his service. Is it possible that I chased the car not only, or even mainly, to help a desperate woman but to please God? So that God would approve of me? Or perhaps because I wanted to be the kind of person who would do such a thing? Or maybe so I would be *known* to be the kind of person who did such a thing? Is it possible (I often think it is) that I did it mainly because, in the split second before I started running, I knew that if I didn't try to do something, I would feel horribly guilty afterward? Did I prefer doing something risky to playing it safe with a certainty of self-loathing later? If so, wasn't it really all about me? Wasn't it egoistic? But if that's true, can *any* action be considered purely altruistic?

In reflecting on these questions over the years, I have come to realize they involve three different but related issues: our *actions* (what we do), our *motivations* (why we do them), and our sense of *obligation* (why we think we should do them). The first two issues are widely debated among philosophers and psychologists, the third less commonly so. But it is the key to understanding the revolutionary effect of Jesus's teachings on the conscience of the West.

Let's consider the issues in turn.

Do people behave in altruistic ways beneficial to others and sometimes at a cost to themselves?

The obvious answer is yes, of course they do. But if I do something that benefits another, what if I also do it, in part, with myself in mind?

Here is where philosophers and psychologists love to propose thought experiments. Suppose the apartment I share with two others is cold and they both want me to turn up the heat. I'm the one who pays the utility bills and prefer to keep it cool. After a while, though, I start thinking it really is too cold, even for me, and so adjust the thermostat. In that case, I'm doing what benefits others, but I'm doing it mainly for myself. Is it an altruistic act? Or an egoistic act with altruistic results? Or should we simply consider it value-neutral?

Answers in this particular case could go any direction. The bigger problem is imagining any action that is entirely altruistic without any element of egoism. Take a commonly cited act of extreme self-sacrifice: a soldier who throws himself on a hand grenade to save his comrades. This is about as selfless as one can imagine, and one might consider it a purely altruistic act. Even so, one can also think of non-altruistic reasons for his split-second decision to sacrifice himself, for example, if he wanted to be the kind of person who would do such a thing or if in the moment he instantaneously and intuitively knew he would not be able to live with the guilt of not having done so.

These, though, are questions of motivation, and for this first issue I'm interested in actions. Some philosophers and psychologists maintain there is no conceivable action we can take only for others with no benefit (mental, emotional, or physical) for ourselves. If so, then "pure altruism" is not even theoretically possible. Many others, however, believe that any act that does benefit others—especially if it comes at some cost to the self—should still be considered altruistic, at least on some level.

Moreover, evolutionary biologists have maintained that whatever we might know, imagine, or suspect our motivations to be, we are programmed to *behave* in certain ways. The inclinations to act on behalf of others at a cost to ourselves is rooted deeply in our DNA.[3]

The biological issues have puzzled specialists at least since the nineteenth century. Natural selection necessarily entails the idea (or, rather, the reality) that those who perpetuate their genes are more evolutionarily successful than those who do not. That would suggest that selfless behavior benefiting only others, especially at a cost to the self, would be bred out of the gene pool. If members of a species had genes that led them to do that, they would eventually all die and not pass along their genes.

Yet people do behave this way. Darwin (who was not yet aware of genes) thought long and hard about the problem, for example, in connection with the honeybee that stings an invader to protect the nest, even though it will lead to its death. Why doesn't it simply fend for itself? Darwin's answers continue to be debated over a century and a half after the publication of *On the Origin of Species*, but there are indeed compelling explanations for this kind of self-sacrifice, even within a system that focuses on survival. As Darwin recognized, the individual bee dies, but its death benefits the community—that is, it makes possible the ongoing lives of others that share its genes.[4]

In more recent times, many readers have objected to Richard Dawkins's term "selfish gene," but usually because of a misunderstanding.[5] The term is a self-consciously anthropomorphic metaphor that explains why some genes manage to survive and outnumber other genes. Dawkins does not claim that selfish genes are "thinking selfishly" or necessarily create selfish *people*. On the contrary, selfless people often enable their genes to thrive, sometimes precisely by sacrificing themselves. If a mother saves her three children from a burning building but dies in the process, more of her genes will survive than if she had chosen not to do so, since each of her three offspring has 50 percent of her genes. It is not that she's thinking about things that way ("Oh, I have to save my genes!"); it is that within the history of a species, those individuals inclined to this pattern of behavior have passed on more of their genes to their descendants than those who did not.

There is no need to delve deeply into the complexities of evolutionary biology to make a basic point, that altruistic behavior on some level is indeed written into our DNA. It is part of what it is to be biologically human.

Even so, that does not address my ultimate concern of how to explain the ethical impulse found among people today to help *strangers* in need. Honeybees do not throw away their lives for nests other than their own. And throughout history very few people have felt a moral obligation to help strangers at a cost to themselves, let alone at the cost of their lives. That takes us to the question of motivation.

Do people ever have purely altruistic motives?
That is, do they ever have reasons for wanting to
help others with no thought for themselves?

Most of us probably already have an opinion about this. My view is that we do not and cannot know what motivates others, no matter how certain we are about it, since we can never crawl into their minds. Most of the time we can't even know our own minds fully. It is dead easy to deceive ourselves about why we did or did not do something.

Even so, my personal (cynical? realistic?) sense is that when all is said and done, there is always *some* kind of egoistic motivation for whatever we do. Sometimes I wonder if that is simply my (realistic? cynical?) reaction to the myriad excuses invoked for the awful political, military, social, and cultural activities we see all around us. Or possibly I've inherited and assimilated it from the age-old Christian claim that humans are born sinful and so remain incurably self-centered, even when born "again." Either way, it is a common view that came to philosophical expression in the decidedly rationalist world of the Enlightenment. Thus, we have the great English philosopher Thomas Hobbes in his 1651 classic, *Leviathan*:

> No man giveth but with intention of good to himself, because gift is voluntary; and of all voluntary acts, the object is to every man his own good; of which, if men see they shall be frustrated, there will be no beginning of benevolence or trust, nor consequently of mutual help.[6]

In other words, there is no genuine altruism; our motivations are egoistic all the way down. That seventeenth-century view has lived on in academic circles. The summary account of altruism in the *Stanford Encyclopedia of Philosophy* states that it was: "The dominant view about human motivation in the social sciences of much of the twentieth century."[7]

At the same time, philosophers and psychologists have considered the flip side of the motivational coin, pointing out that many actions also cannot be readily explained apart from some kind of altruistic motivations. Volunteers who risk their lives providing humanitarian aid in war zones; physicians who abandon swanky lifestyles to work in poverty-stricken regions of the globe; good-hearted people who take refugees into their own homes; those who serve meals at the local soup kitchen or give their weekends to construct affordable housing: there are millions of people in our world who act in ways that do not primarily benefit themselves, even if they do receive personal satisfaction from what they do as well. Surely these benefactors of humanity—may their tribe increase—engage in acts of altruism, even if their motivations are mixed. It makes no sense to say altruism does not exist unless one's motivations are purely altruistic, any more than to say that egoism does not exist if any part of one's motivation is a concern for the other.

Which leads us to our third question.

If people sometimes engage in altruistic behavior (acts) and do so because they want to do so (motivations), why do they sometimes want to do so for complete strangers?

This is the issue we will explore in the next eight chapters.

Chapter Two

THE ANCIENT QUEST FOR HAPPINESS

The question of how to live ethically became particularly urgent for me when I experienced a crisis of faith some thirty years ago. I was born a Christian, baptized a Christian, and confirmed a Christian. I was active in the Episcopal church as a child and teen. My entire higher education was in Christian settings, starting with the aforementioned Moody Bible Institute, followed by a bachelor's degree from Wheaton (an evangelical liberal arts college), and then a master of divinity and a PhD from Princeton Theological Seminary. That was twelve years in Christian environments. After leaving high school, the first time I even set foot in a secular classroom was the day I started teaching at Rutgers University.[1]

Years later I began having serious doubts about my Christian commitments. Leaving the faith was a daunting prospect, and I did not go eagerly or even willingly, in no small part because I had no clear idea of what life "on the outside" would be like. I was anxious about abandoning my beliefs and particularly anxious about the ultimate fate of my soul. (What if I had been right all along?) But I also had very practical worries. If I left the faith, how would I know how to behave? Without any direction from above, would I have no moral compass? Would I fall into meaninglessness, nihilism, anarchy, and despair? Would it be drunken revelry every night?

Despite these concerns, I felt driven to follow where I thought the truth led, and in the end, I didn't see an alternative. For reasons unconnected with my biblical scholarship, I began to recognize that I had become an agnostic.[2] One of my biggest surprises was that my deconversion had almost zero effect on my daily life. Anarchy and wild living never did arrive. Today, all these years later, I'm no less ethical than I was before. I'm not much *more* ethical, either, as it turns out, but I do seem to have a more refined sense of what it means to be a moral person, and I do work hard (often without much success) to do what is right both for myself and for others.

Some evangelical Christians tell me this makes no sense, that unlike believers in God, I have no reason to be moral. They think I'm deceived when I insist I feel a deep commitment to other members of a species that originated through time, matter, and chance. Without divine guidance, they say, I have no grounds for deciding what is right and wrong and no incentive to behave well.

What almost none of them realizes is that this notion that ethical behavior is or should be directed by one's faith is a relative latecomer in the history of the human race. It certainly would have seemed very odd in the ancient Greek and Roman cultures at the foundation of Western civilization.

Ethics and Ancient Religion

It is very difficult for most people today to imagine a religion not focused largely on how people should treat one another, but the idea that a divine being would care much about daily behavior would have made little sense to most people for most of human history. To explain, let me give a quick overview of how religion worked in antiquity.

There were countless religions in ancient Greece and Rome.[3] Scholars normally group them together as "pagan," not using the term in a derogatory sense, but simply to differentiate them from Judaism and then Christianity.[4] There were enormous differences among these various religions, but nearly all of them accepted the existence of numerous gods ("polytheism") and virtually none of them insisted it alone was the one true religion or that only its god should be worshipped everywhere.

On the whole, the gods were cooperative with one another. It may not seem that way from the ancient Greek and Roman myths we know today, but these tales were not Scriptural "authorities" the way the Torah was for Jews, or the Old and New Testaments for Christians. Myths were entertaining stories about the gods, and they could provide thoughtful material for reflection. Rarely were they taken as historical narratives or theological guidelines for what to believe, and they played only a distant role in ancient pagan religious practices. Outside of mythology, the gods were very much involved with human everyday life. They could be found in every place and were connected with nearly every human experience. There were gods of mountains, oceans, forests, streams, crossroads, homes, and hearths. There were gods of war, healing, weather, crops, childbirth, fortune, and love. In that context it made no sense to worship just one of the gods. You needed a whole lot of them, and the gods knew that as well as the humans who worshipped them.

Throughout Greek and Roman antiquity, nearly everyone worshipped the gods, but not to secure a good afterlife or avoid eternal punishment.[5] Ancient religions were consistently concerned about life in the here and now. Gods were worshipped because they could provide humans with what they needed in a brutal world where it was difficult to survive, let alone thrive. The vast majority of people then, even more than now, lived very much on the edge. In antiquity, a simple tooth abscess was often a death sentence. Many women died in childbirth and many babies died within months of being born. There were no modern agricultural technologies, no sustained methods of irrigation, no mass transportation systems: a drought in a village this year meant crop failure and starvation the next. No one could predict natural disasters or control even such quotidian matters as finding work and having happy relationships.

The gods, however, could provide what was needed and desired. Gods could ensure safety in childbirth; they could bring rain and sunshine, make the crops grow and the livestock reproduce; they could provide victory in war and success in business; they could procure the affections of the boy or girl of your dreams. And throughout antiquity, the gods were not understood to be particularly demanding. They mainly wanted to be acknowledged and worshipped. When they were, they would be inclined to provide their worshippers with the benefits they needed. When they were neglected, they could make life miserable.

The worship of the gods was not overly complicated. It principally involved saying prayers and making offerings. Pagans prayed much as Jews and Christians did and still do: praising the god for their greatness; thanking them for their assistance; asking them for what was needed. Offerings could include sacrifices of animals either at large communal festivals or with a small group of family and friends. These sacrifices were to honor the god, giving them what they desired by burning parts of the animal they preferred (the fat and bones). The rest of the animal would be cooked and served up at a festal meal in the god's honor. These were not the only kinds of offerings to the gods: more common were inexpensive and easily accessible items, such as flowers, grain, or wine given to show one's devotion and commitment.

To the surprise of many moderns—and particularly significant for our discussion—ethics did not play a large role in ancient pagan religions. If someone had neglected the god, then an apology or confession might be in order. But the gods were not focused on how humans treated one another, not all that concerned about whether you insulted your neighbor, stole their lamp, or slept with their spouse. There were a few exceptions: as a rule, gods did not approve of oath-breaking or patricide, for example. But by and large, ethics was not their principal interest, and the gods did not hand down codes of law to prescribe moral behavior. They were more concerned about whether you worshipped them properly.

That is not to say that the pagan world lacked ethical standards or that pagans were lawless and licentious. On the contrary, most ancient pagans were just as ethical as Jews and then Christians. They loved their families, took care of their kids, helped neighbors in need, and worked to promote the social well-being of their villages, towns, and cities. The human race had always been like that—but for biological and cultural reasons, not religious ones.⁶ Then, as now, there was a "common sense" about right and wrong, without which human societies would not have survived. Dominant social structures had always served to enforce proper behavior within a community: "Do not murder," "Do not commit adultery," and "Do not steal" are not distinctively Jewish or Christian ideas, but sensible regulations that allow humans to live together and thrive in a hostile world filled with predators, enemies, and other dangers.

In addition, ethical ideas were widely discussed and moral practices well-defined in the pagan world—just not in the context of religion. Ethical thinking lay within the realm of philosophy. That may seem odd today when, in our far more educated world, the number of people you know who have carefully read, say, Plato, Aristotle, Hume, or Kant is likely to be precisely none. But ancient philosophy was not important because people actually read it. For one thing, the vast majority of the population could not read. Those who could read were rarely digging into heady intellectual treatises. That does not mean, though, that philosophical discourse made little impact.

Think of an analogous situation today, in the realm of Christian thought. How many people in the pew have read the heady intellectual stuff produced by the world's leading academic theologians? It's been a long time since I met a nonacademic who has studied, or even just read, the books of Augustine, Anselm, or Aquinas (just to start with some of the *A*'s). Yet, Christian ethical views as developed by theologians and other thinkers over the centuries have certainly seeped into the conscience of the broader religious community. Consider it a trickle-down effect. That happened in antiquity too—particularly when it came to the ethical views developed by Greek and Roman philosophers, both in general and in relation to the key issues that we will be exploring: altruistic love, its material manifestation in charitable giving, and its important interpersonal expression in personal forgiveness.⁷

Ethics among Greek and Roman Philosophers

I begin our investigation with the great Greek philosopher Aristotle (384–322 BCE), almost certainly the most influential ethical thinker in the Western tradition.[8] There were, of course, important Greek moral philosophers before him; he himself was famously the student of Plato, who was in turn a follower of Socrates, before whom were others, most of them known today only by name or not at all. But it was Aristotle who made the greatest impact on ethical thinking. He continues to be read by ethicists today, over 2,300 years after his death.

Aristotle's best-known book is the *Nicomachean Ethics*.[9] He begins this ten-volume work with some essential questions that remain remarkably apt. What does it mean to live a good life, and how do we do it? All of us certainly want to enjoy what is good, and many of us want to *be* good. But what, actually, is the "good" that we want to have and to be?

Aristotle approaches the question with a brilliant twist: What does each of us consider to be the *ultimate* good we can have?

Many of us think we know the answer: we want health, wealth, a good job, a good marriage, a loving family, lots of friends, or . . . or pick your answer. But Aristotle argues that none of these things, singly or collectively, is what we ultimately seek. They are things we want so we can get something we want even more. You can see this simply by asking yourself, *Why* do you want more money? Or a good job? Or friends and family? It is always for some other reason. And so these various "goods" are what Aristotle calls "instrumental" desires, which is to say they are the means by which we acquire something further. But is there anything we want, not in order to get something else, but entirely because it is good to have in and of itself?

Let me explain with an example. I am talking to an undergraduate student and he tells me he wants to get an A in my class. I ask him why he wants an A. He says it's because he wants to have a high GPA. I ask why he wants a high GPA. So he can get into a top-level business school. Why does he want that? Because he wants a career as a major business executive. And why is that something he wants? So he can make a lot of money. Why does he want a lot of money? So he can buy and do anything he chooses. And why is that what he wants? Because that would make him happy. At precisely that point there is no longer any reason to ask why. We don't want happiness for some other reason. It's the ultimate reason. The other things we want—the entire string of them—are means to that end.

If Aristotle is right on this point (I happen to think he is), the obvious implication is that each of us needs to figure out how to live in the world, what to do, and how to *be* in order to be happy. Not in the simple, surface sense of being happy after someone praises us for doing a good job at work or when we watch our team win the Super Bowl. Those can indeed be happy moments, but a happy *life* is much fuller than that. It is not merely a sequence of random, periodic good experiences. It comes when we are flourishing and know it: when we are content with who we are, what we have done, where our life is right now, and where it looks to be going. That kind of "happy" is more like contentment or joy, a deep sense of well-being.

The Greek word for that kind of overall flourishing and life-satisfaction is *eudaimonia*, a term that's notoriously difficult to translate into English. You'll notice the word *daimon* in it. That's the Greek word behind our word "demon," but it doesn't mean demon in the sense of an evil being that invades a body to compel it to do nasty things. A *daimon* in Greek thought was a divine spirit, a divinity less powerful than the great gods of Mount Olympus, but closer to and more involved with us. Having a good *daimon* in your life was a bit like having a guardian angel.

The first two letters of *eu-daimonia* mean "good" (as in "eulogy"—a "good word" that is spoken in memory of the deceased at a funeral). And so having *eudaimonia* literally means having a good divine spirit in your life—not necessarily an actual *daimon*, but a sense of flourishing and inner peace. The word is usually translated (as the least unsatisfactory option) as "happiness," but again, this is not a reference to a fleeting emotion that strikes us on occasion. It is a broad and pervasive sense of living a good life and feeling satisfied because of it. The question raised by Aristotle and virtually all the Greek and Roman pagan moral philosophers after him was: How does a person attain *eudaimonia*?[10]

As you might imagine if you have ever dabbled in philosophy, the answer is decidedly not going to be: "A house in Malibu."

Aristotle stressed that no one can be "happy," in the sense I'm using it, in a chaotic and threatening environment. Ultimate happiness requires a stable, secure world that promotes individual well-being. This is where Aristotle's historical and social context becomes particularly important. He produced his writings in Athens in the fourth century BCE. Up to this time, there had been no great empires or nation-states ruling huge tracts of land in that part of the world. Greece had long consisted of individual city-states, each with its own government, economy, military, culture, and so on. Aristotle's city, Athens, was in competition with other city-states in the region (especially Sparta) and within living memory had been involved in a drawn-out and disastrous military conflict (the Peloponnesian War) that ended in Athenian defeat. Athens continued to exist, however, and its citizens' civic identity depended on their urban context. For Aristotle, a happy life could be found only in a well-functioning city, with security, opportunities for employment, public entertainments, and all the other elements of civilization. *Eudaimonia* thus depended on life in the context of a Greek city.

The word for "city" in Greek is *polis*. In the century before Aristotle, Athens had been the birthplace of democracy, a place where free adult males established and enacted civic policies. Aristotle considered such participation fundamental to individual and social happiness—which is why he famously said, in a comment often misunderstood, that "man is a *political* animal" (*Politics*, 1). By this he did not mean that humans necessarily ought to run for high office or even, as I once thought, that people are always in negotiation with one another in an attempt to acquire more individual power. Instead, for Aristotle, people (or at least "men") are "political" creatures because they are members of the *polis* and find their well-being in that context.

If happiness is the ultimate good and if people are happy only in the context of the *polis*, the *polis* must be good to allow people to obtain happiness within it. The *polis* thus needs to be run and populated by people with the abilities and personality traits that promote the welfare of others and of themselves. They must be the best humans they can be. The key to a happy life is to figure out what that might entail.

Aristotle points out that every kind of living being has qualities of excellence that distinguish it from other living beings. What makes a most excellent apple tree is not what makes a most excellent racehorse. The function of an apple tree is to yield good fruit. The most excellent apple tree produces the most and best fruit. The function of a racehorse is to run fast. The most excellent racehorse will therefore run the fastest. Speed is not an excellence of apple trees and fruit-bearing is not an excellence of racehorses.

What then is the ultimate excellence of humans? The word for "excellence" in Greek is *aretē*, a word that can also be translated as "virtue." In our day, virtue often carries unattractive connotations—it sounds a bit pious and unnaturally wholesome. Not so in antiquity. The English word does not come from the Greek, but from the Latin word *vir*, which means an "adult male" (think *vir*ile). Thus "virtue" in the ancient context (whether Greek or Latin) refers to the qualities that make a man—a *vir*—the best man he can be.[11] A virtuous *vir* is the manliest man there could be. For Aristotle's city-state, that would be a man whose personality and actions promote the wellness and happiness of the *polis* and of the individuals in it.

Specifically, men had to have courage, so as to fight bravely when their personal or communal safety was under threat. They had to promote justice, so that everyone was fairly treated both in private and by the law. They had to be self-controlled, rather than prone to uncontrollable fits of rage or wild debauchery that could lead to violence and social chaos. And they had to have wisdom (or prudence) to know how to behave in every circumstance. These were the four principal virtues of the Athenian man. For Aristotle, having them was the key to finding personal and communal happiness.

Since these virtues were closely connected with the *polis*, they were not purely inward-looking. No man or woman is an island, and to survive there must be social unity, social good. That alone would make *eudaimonia*—a full and satisfying life—possible. As a result, altruism was important to Aristotle.

Altruism in Ancient Greece

The ethical codes of the Greek and later Roman worlds encapsulated the understanding of altruism that had governed human societies for as long as societies had existed, written into the human genetic code before becoming an object of philosophical discussion. For Aristotle, his predecessors, and his successors, since the "good life" requires strong social bonds, and social bonds are strongest between those with the most intimate contact, doing "good for another" meant engaging in altruistic behavior toward those to whom one is most closely related biologically, socially, and geographically, more or less in concentric circles: family first, then friends, then others in the same social network, and then the larger community, the *polis*.

What about outsiders? Strangers? Foreigners?

Throughout the Greek city-states, if "others" who entered your world were much like you in terms of socioeconomic status and cultural heritage, it made sense to welcome them and engage with them on friendly terms. This hospitality was demanded of anyone who wished to be a good person, and for solid sociological reasons: a strong and like-minded ally could provide assistance to you and your community if the need arose. But that applied only to those "like" you. If anyone from a different social standing—say, someone who was poor or uncultured or with radically different values—should come into your ambit, there was no expectation that you would welcome them, even if they lived near you. As an important study by classical scholar Matthew Christ argues, "Athenians felt little pressure as individuals to help fellow citizens whom they did not know and, consistent with this, did not feel strongly obliged as a group to help peoples of other states through collective action."[12] In particular, distant "others" whom you never had met and had only heard about were none of your concern. If you knew they had resources your community needed, you might well attack them. If they came to you with aggressive intent, you were well within your rights to show no mercy in beating them off and destroying them.

And so, while there was certainly altruism in ancient Greece, it was of a limited kind. Aristotle was an outspoken advocate of altruistic behavior toward friends and potential friends,[13] but he would not have urged his readers to "love your *neighbor* as yourself," unless your neighbor was part of your social sphere. Would he have urged anyone to give away their resources to help social outcasts within Athens or those they had never met? Most certainly not. Would he have instructed someone to love their enemies? He would have thought it was a joke. In saying this, I am not denigrating his view. It is, after all, the view most "good" people have today. We care more for those close to us than for others. To some of us, it just seems like common sense.

From the Greek City-State of Aristotle to the Roman World of Jesus

The basic sense of what it meant to live ethically did not change significantly in the centuries after Aristotle, even though the sociopolitical landscape shifted rather drastically. Already in Aristotle's time the Greek *polis* was losing its place as the center of all social life. Beginning with the conquests of Alexander the Great (Aristotle's own student) and continuing on through the rule of his successors, the eastern Mediterranean became far less localized. Previously independent cities came to be subsumed into larger empires, such as those ruled by Egypt, Syria, and eventually Rome. This shift in governance had a radical effect on what it meant to live in "community." Local aristocrats no longer set the rules and enforced all standards of conduct; new policies and regulations came from impersonal rulers of vast tracts of land who lived in far-off places. The world had become very large. The *polis* was no longer the unique focus of social existence and, as a result, of ethics.

This social transformation was encapsulated in a clever neologism by a philosopher who came in Alexander's wake: the Cynic Diogenes, who, when asked where he was from, replied that he was a "cosmo-politan," a "citizen of the cosmos," that is, of the "world" (Diogenes Laertius, *Lives of Eminent Philosophers*, 1 63)

Despite this shift from local to imperial communities, the classical Greek philosophical traditions of Plato and Aristotle continued to be important in the Roman world into which Jesus and his followers were born some three centuries later. In part, that was because Rome's greatest expertise lay in military prowess and administrative skill: its "high culture" came mainly from the Greeks. In Jesus's day, both trained philosophers and, so far as we can tell, regular ole folk still shared some basic assumptions about how best to live.[14] Practically all Greek and Roman moral philosophers continued to agree that *eudaimonia* was the ultimate goal of human existence. In addition, almost all agreed that maximizing *eudaimonia* required training and practice; it was not a matter of intuition. Some philosophical traditions emphasized virtue more than others, but all agreed that knowing the nature of human existence was key to happiness. For most of these traditions, however, Aristotle's emphasis on the *polis* had disappeared. Many people still did live in cities (though most of the population was rural) and many were committed to the welfare of their municipalities. But the empire no longer had the cohesion of the former Greek city-states, and so living for the good of one's local community had become far less important.

How, then, were individuals to find *eudaimonia*?

Philosophers at the time knew as well as we do that there are obstacles to feeling satisfied with life. All of us have our disadvantages when it comes to education, wealth, social locations, opportunities, personal connections, and on and on. We also have shortcomings written into our character. And circumstances beyond our control often prevent us from doing what we want or getting what we need. Given all that, when the cards are stacked against us, how can we possibly find personal happiness and success—even those of us who have been dealt a relatively good hand?

Prior to the birth of Christianity, several major schools of thought emerged to address this question. Three—the Epicureans, the Stoics, and the (less influential) Cynics—can serve as counterpoints to what we'll eventually find in the teachings of Jesus. These schools offered differing answers to the question of how an individual might find *eudaimonia*. In short, Epicureans argued: Strive for physical wholeness and inner peace, seeking as much simple pleasure and avoiding as much pain as possible. Stoics urged: Strive to live in accordance with the rationality that governs the world, recognizing that nothing outside your control can affect your inner well-being. Cynics advised: Voluntarily abandon everything that can bring pain, frustration, anxiety, or stress if forcefully or accidentally taken from you.

A full discussion of any one of these philosophical schools would take a book, and many have been written on each.[15] Here, I will summarize their distinctive views in broad terms, before devoting the next chapter to their specific perspectives on love, charitable giving, and forgiveness—all of which will serve as context for assessing the alternative teachings of Jesus.

Epicureans: Maximize Pleasure, Minimize Pain

From the days of Epicurus (341–270 BCE), both the philosophical school he founded and the "hedonist" philosophy it promoted have suffered a bad reputation, most of it completely undeserved. Attacking a philosopher who advocates the pursuit of pleasure is like shooting fish in a barrel. The problem is that almost all the opponents of Epicureanism—from its beginning until now—have been shooting into the wrong barrel.

Epicurus was born of Athenian parents on the Greek island of Samos, but like so many budding students of philosophy, he moved to Athens to continue his education and eventually settled there. He became a prolific author, allegedly producing some three hundred volumes of work. Much to our regret, out of that entire oeuvre, only three of Epicurus's letters survive, cited in full some five hundred years later in a work called *The Lives of Eminent Philosophers* by biographer Diogenes Laertius. Fortunately, Diogenes chose three particularly important writings of Epicurus to reproduce, each one summarizing one of his main areas of interest: (1) the natural world—what it consists of, how it came into being, and what will happen to it; (2) astronomic phenomena—an unusually mysterious part of that material world; and (3) ethics—how people ought to live, given the kind of natural world they inhabit.[16]

Many readers today find Epicurus surprisingly prescient in his understanding of the material world. For him, it is indeed all material: there is no "supernatural" element outside the realm of matter. The world and everything in it, including the gods themselves, consist only of material substance and have come to exist purely through time and chance. Matter itself is ultimately reduceable to the tiniest particles that are not themselves made up of anything else. These cannot be divided and therefore are called "atoms," from the Greek word *atomos*, meaning "not able to be cut." Atoms are infinite in number and are falling forever through the void of space. Time as well is infinite, meaning there is an infinite number of combinations of atoms as they collide into one another, joining together in various mixtures, with some of these mixtures themselves intermingling and combining with others.[17] The earth, and all inanimate objects, plants, animals, and humans are simply the current manifestation of these mixtures in this part of an infinite realm where an infinite number of possibilities occur over an infinite amount of space and time.

As a result, all that exists is entirely material, generated by an eternal sequence of material formations, deteriorations, and reformations. The gods, who consist of superior combinations of atoms, differ from us in being perfectly happy and at peace; they are also remote, not interested in or involved with us in the least. We ourselves are like everything else that dies or eventually disintegrates (rocks, rosebushes, dogs, stars). The atoms of our bodies eventually disperse and reunite with other atoms and . . . so it goes, ad infinitum. Our souls are also temporary combinations of atoms that will survive for eternity in different configurations. We die, we dissolve in both body and soul, and our atoms go on their merry way.

One implication of this completely materialist understanding of what it means to be human is that we know what we know only through our physical senses. There are no nonmaterial sources of knowledge, since nothing immaterial exists except empty space, the "void" through which the atoms move, collide, combine, and form everything, including our bodies and minds.

This Epicurean understanding of the world stood very much at odds with the views of most ancient people. Religions had creation stories; humans had nonmaterial souls; and there surely was more to reality than infinite numbers of atoms ramming into each other. Even more offensive to people's sensibilities were the ethical corollaries Epicurus and his followers drew from their views. A materialist world leads to a materialist lifestyle.

According to this view, we think, reason, evaluate, and know what is good and bad only through the experience of our senses, and our sense experience is unambiguous: pleasure is good and pain is bad. It is completely natural to enjoy the one and avoid the other. This empirical reality shows how we ought to live as material beings: we should devote our lives to maximizing our pleasure and minimizing our pain, for as much and as long as we can. This philosophical view is called "hedonism," from the Greek word for pleasure, *hēdonē*.

It is not difficult to understand Epicurus's bad reputation among other ancient thinkers. An ethics rooted in seeking pleasure has been condemned by philosophers for as long as there have been philosophers. It may make for a fun weekend, but it is horribly dangerous and even stupid as a permanent way of living.

This condemnation of Epicurean views, however, is almost always based on a misunderstanding of what Epicurus means by pleasure.

In philosophical discourse as far back as Plato, Socrates, and almost certainly their predecessors, "pleasure" had been a four-letter word. Plato's dialogues, which typically feature Socrates as the main figure, repeatedly portray bodily desires and their satisfaction through physical pleasure as problems. To be sure, pleasure *seems* good. But for Socrates, bodily pleasure is deceptive, in no small part because it is addictive. The more we get, the more we crave. Unless we are disciplined, we can soon think about nothing else, which takes our focus off what really matters in life, that which can provide lasting rather than transient and often self-harming happiness. We today might call this other kind of pleasure the "life of the mind": deep conversations, strolling through the woods in contemplation, coming to understand the world and our place in it, and realizing how shallow and ultimately meaningless it is to focus on nothing but gorging ourselves, getting drunk, and having endless sex. Understanding and pursuing this life of the mind is what philosophers in the tradition of Socrates called *philosophia*, literally the "love of wisdom." It is not that such philosophers thought people should never enjoy themselves. But surely there was more to life than indulging every physical fancy like a wild beast carousing from one brainless indulgence to the next. That was scarcely a way to be human.

Epicureans were often tagged as rank hedonists rather than serious philosophers and mocked for their materialist perspective. But, in fact, their view was simpler to caricature than to understand. In reality, Epicureans emphatically did not condone wild, raucous living. Quite the opposite. To begin with, like virtually all other philosophers of his time, Epicurus believed the goal of a good life was *eudaimonia*. As he says at the beginning of his letter on ethics:

> We should strive to find happiness (*eudaimonia*), because when we have it, we have everything, and when we don't have it, we do all we can in order to get it. (Diogenes Laertius, *Lives*, 10.122.)

To Epicurus, it is obvious that all living creatures—from farm animals, to newborn babies, to mature adults—gravitate toward pleasure and strive to avoid pain. But pleasure and pain are not simply bodily. We experience mental pain as well, and for Epicurus, internal distress is even worse than physical pain. When we are anguished, terrified, or anxious, we are absolutely miserable, worse than when we're hungry or sick. Most physical pain passes after time, but mental pain can last a lifetime. This is key for understanding the kind of pleasure Epicurus thinks we should pursue. As he writes:

> When we say that pleasure is the goal of life, we do not mean licentious pleasures and pure gratification of desire, as we are accused of saying by people who are ignorant, prejudiced, and ill-disposed to us. By pleasure we mean having a body free from pain and a mind that is undisturbed. We are not talking about interminable drinking parties and rowdy evenings, or about sexual liaisons with boys or women, or about expensive meals of fish and other delicacies on a fine table—these are not what provide a pleasant life. Instead, it is sober reasoning, exploring the reasons for what we prefer in life and what we spurn, and ridding ourselves of the views of life that cause the most consternation to our minds. (Diogenes Laertius, *Lives*, 10.131–32)

How does one pursue such pleasure and, at the same time, avoid real pain? By leading a moderate, thoughtful, reflective life in the company of others pursuing the same goals. Epicurus started a community of like-minded people who lived together and shared the important things in life: friendship, reading, reflection, deep conversation, simple food and drink—but nothing excessive, since that could bring a longing for things that don't really matter. His followers started similar groups. These Epicurean communities were relatively isolationist, existing apart from the stresses of the world at large and the major concerns that wear away the souls of those involved in politics, social conflict, and worldly concerns. Cultivating the self meant sharing a life only with those who understood and pursued the truth.

Epicurus connected *eudaimonia* not only to how one lived one's life but even more to how one viewed one's death. The terrors of the afterlife have always been among humanity's worst causes of mental anguish. In Epicurus's day, some people were, as many are now, paralyzed by the idea of nonexistence. Others were and are terrorized by the fear of severe and eternal punishment in the life to come. Epicurus considered such fears baseless. We are made up of atoms that have temporarily combined for the span of our lives; the atoms will continue on after we die, moving through the infinite void to combine in an infinite number of ways forevermore. There is no conscious afterlife. We didn't exist before we were born and we won't exist after we die. We will experience no more terror—or any other emotion—after death than we did before birth. As a result, there is nothing, precisely nothing, to fear.

In his letter on ethics Epicurus articulates this view in rather clever and thoughtful ways:

> Get accustomed to realizing that death is nothing to us, since everything we experience as good or bad comes to us through our senses, but death is the cessation of sensation. . . .
>
> It is pointless to stand in terror of something that lies ahead when we won't feel any terror once it arrives. . . .
>
> Death is nothing to us, since while we exist, we are not dead, and when we are dead, we no longer exist. . . .
>
> Death means nothing . . . either to the living or to those who are dead, since it is not experienced by the one group and the other group doesn't exist.
> (Diogenes Laertius, *Lives*, 10.124–125)

Moreover, once we recognize that life comes to an end at death, that should make living more, rather than less, happy:

> Realizing that death is nothing to us makes our mortal life enjoyable, not because it adds endless time to our lives but because it takes away the longing for living eternally. . . .
>
> For there is nothing terrifying in life for the person who truly recognizes that there is nothing terrifying in not living. (Diogenes Laertius, *Lives*, 10.124)

What then is the point of living? What is the goal of life? How should we live? For Epicurus and his followers, we should do our best to avoid pain. Often, we won't succeed. We will become sick, injured, and (if we're lucky) old. But physical pain as a rule does not last long, and if it is especially severe, it will kill us. If it does, we will feel no more pain and will have no regrets for dying, since we will have no capacity to feel, think, or regret. In the meantime, we should live in peaceful surroundings with others who are equally interested in reflective lives of contemplation and conversation, undisturbed by the affairs of the world.

Everyone, of course, has their own preferences for an ideal life. Speaking for myself, this Epicurean view is unusually appealing.

Stoics: Living in Accordance with Reason and Focusing on What We Can Control

Epicurean thought did not exactly take the ancient world by storm. By far the most widespread moral philosophy at the time of early Christianity was Stoicism, a movement that began with the teachings of a slightly younger contemporary of Epicurus named Zeno (333–261 BCE), who regularly gathered his students in the large "painted portico" (*stoa*) located in the Athenian forum. The portico was a long and spacious building open on one side to the outside and lined with columns to support the roof overhead. Since these philosophers and wannabe philosophers could regularly be seen in the *stoa*, they were called Stoics. Over time their movement spread throughout the

Greek and, later, Roman world to become the dominant philosophical perspective for centuries.[18]

During the early part of the Christian era, a wide range of philosophers embraced and expounded on Stoic views. One mark of Stoicism's broad appeal can be seen from the diverse social standing of its best-known representatives. One of the most famous, Epictetus (55–135 CE), had been a slave. Marcus Aurelius (121–180 CE), on the other hand, was the emperor of Rome. And Seneca (4 BCE–65 CE), the most prolific and best-known philosopher of his day, was one of the most wealthy, famous, and powerful political figures of the first century.

Part of the widespread appeal of Stoicism to thinking people of all kinds derived precisely from its claim that the world makes sense and that, to understand our place in it, we need to see the inherent rationality not just of our lives but of all reality. When we see how the world actually works, we can understand how to fit in with it by shaping our lives in conformity with reality.[19]

On nearly all important matters, Stoic views were diametrically opposed to those of the Epicureans. Stoics did not believe the world consisted only of inert matter (atoms); they maintained there was a decidedly spiritual substance that infused all that is. As a result, Stoics did not think we should or could trust our senses to ascertain the truth: perception could be deceptive. We therefore needed to use logic to understand everything around us. Correspondingly, they did not think that pleasure was the goal of life, but, like Plato, insisted it was a deadly dead end. Nor did they believe pain was to be avoided, for it often cannot be and so is better dealt with realistically. Nor did they believe in separating themselves off from the rest of society to lead contemplative lives of simple pleasures in small communities; on the contrary, they maintained that people had a duty to the world and that life was far better for those who actively participated in it. Most important, they did not think people should pretend they could completely control their circumstances, since we have no say about much of what happens to us. The goal of life is to understand what we actually can control and focus on that. We should not worry about, become distracted by, or be upset about things we cannot avoid.

Despite these differences, Stoics shared with the Epicureans the notion that the ultimate goal in life is to achieve *eudaimonia*. They also agreed with Aristotle that "virtue" is the key to obtaining it. For Stoics, the greatest "excellence" (or virtue) in humans is that which makes us superior to all other living beings apart from the gods: our ability to reason. In fact, it is our rationality that makes us most like the gods. Thus, for us to be truly godlike, we must use our reason to the fullest extent possible. To Stoics, that simply made sense (that is, it was "rational"), and they had a metaphysical reason for emphasizing the point. The divine element that permeates this world and all it contains is reason itself, *logos*, the word from which we get "logic." Reason, or sense, dwells in all of creation.

Since divine *logos* pervades the world, whatever happens in this world is, by nature, logical. And since humans in particular have been endowed with reason, they can—with some guidance, training, and hard work—understand this logic. Anyone who accepts this reality realizes that everything ultimately must make sense. One goal, then, is to figure out *how* the world and all that happens in it is reasonable, how it makes sense, even when it seems to make no sense at all. A bad toothache? Losing a job? An earthquake that levels our community? The death of a child? There is a reason for everything because reason is divine and divinity permeates all existence.

It is a little difficult for many moderns to get their minds around the Stoic idea that "reason" is a divine quality that infuses the world. It is possibly even harder to understand how this divine quality relates to the gods. Do they "have" it in greater quantity than we? Or is Reason itself a distinct divine being of some kind? The problem is exacerbated by Stoic writings, since often an author such as Epictetus will speak of "Reason" and sometimes of "Zeus" (the head of the gods) and sometimes of the "gods"—and in each instance appear to be referring to the same thing. The *logos* that infuses the world can be thought of as the sensibility of the world; it can be "the reason" something happens as it does; it can be "human reason"; and it can be personalized as "Zeus" or the "gods."

Some of the weirdness of this idea may be mitigated for those familiar with the understanding of Christ set forth in the Gospel of John. The term *logos*, in addition to meaning something like "reason" or "sense," can also mean "word." It is by speaking a word that you express what you are thinking. Your word conveys the sense you are trying to make. Your listeners use their reason, their *logos*, to understand your *logos*.

With that in mind, consider the famous lines that begin the fourth Gospel:

> In the beginning was the Word (Logos); and the Word (Logos) was with God; and the Word (Logos) was God. . . . All things came into being through him, and apart from him nothing came into being that came into being. In him was life and the life was the light of humans. (John 1:1–4)

Christ, then, is the divine Logos who was both with God and was God, who created the world and brought life and light ("enlightenment") into it. He is the one who is in the world, has made the world, and has made the world make sense. Knowing him, the Logos, will bring life.

Biblical scholars have long debated whether the author of John was influenced by Stoic views of Logos.[20] John's claim that the Logos became a human is highly distinctive (John 1:14). But for both John and the Stoics the Logos is a divine entity; it is both a God and apart from God / the gods; it is the root of the created order; it is the source of all living beings; it provides light/enlightenment in the world; recognizing it provides the keys to explaining our place in the world and the meaning of our existence.

This Stoics' metaphysical view that the entire world—and therefore everything that happens in it—is infused with "reason" has a direct bearing on Stoic ethics, on how we should live and behave. Since God/Logos/Reason is inherently "good," then what it brings about is necessarily good. Many of us have observed this firsthand: something unpleasant or even awful happens in our lives, but in the long run it works out for the best. There are times when we are actually glad we went through a miserable experience.[21] Stoics took that kind of attitude to an extreme. There is a reason for everything. So why make it worse by stressing about it? And why be anxious or fearful about what might happen *next*? Things happen. We should focus all our mental and moral energies on what we *can* control. They—and nothing else—matter.

One thing you always *can* control is your reaction to what happens, what you choose to complain about and even what to be upset about. You can also control your thoughts, views, and opinions, for example about what you consider to be right and wrong, fair and unfair, good and evil, worth living for and not. Nothing can make you think something is true when you know it is false. No one can prevent you from being honest. No one can force you to do anything you don't want to do.

If you think they can, you misunderstand. The reality is that you yourself are always the one who makes the decision. If your boss tells you he'll fire you unless you fudge the books, you are the one who chooses what to do next. There is no point in explaining, "But I had to do it." No, you didn't. If someone says they will kill you if you don't do what they demand, it's up to you. You have sole control over how you choose to react, and your "moral purpose" or "ability to do what you decide regardless of the consequence" is one thing no one can take away from you.[22]

The former slave Epictetus beats this theme like a drum. Early in the brilliant four-volume account of his lectures, *The Discourses*, he presents a series of dire circumstances and his view of reasonable reactions to them:

> I am condemned to death. Do I have to die moaning and groaning as well? To incarceration. Do I have to complain about it? To exile. Is there anyone stopping me from going with a smile, joyful and content?

He then imagines a series of conversations with a powerful antagonist:

> "Divulge your secrets." I refuse, because that's something that's up to me. "I'll clap you in irons." What are you talking about, man? Me? You'll shackle my leg, but not even Zeus can conquer my will. "I'll throw you in prison." My body. "I'll cut off your head." Well, have you ever heard me suggest that I'm unique in having a non-detachable head? (*Discourses*, 1.1.22–23)

Epictetus sometimes gives actual (or allegedly actual) instances of this complete freedom to do whatever one chooses based on what one thinks is right, such as the response of his older contemporary, Helvidius Priscus, to pressure from the emperor Vespasian:

> When Vespasian told him not to attend a meeting of the Senate, he replied, "You have the power to disqualify me as a senator, but as long as I am one, I'm obliged to attend meetings." "All right then, attend the meeting," says Vespasian, "but don't say anything." "Don't ask me for my opinion and I'll keep quiet." "But I'm bound to ask you." "And I'm bound to say what seems right." "But if you speak, I'll have you killed." "Did I ever tell you that I was immortal? You do your job, and I'll do mine. Yours is to put me to death and mine to die fearlessly. Yours is to send me into exile and mine to leave without grieving." (*Discourses*, 1.2.19)

Stoics thus understood that the way to live—and to live with *eudaimonia*—was to focus on freedom and personal choice, choosing not to be disturbed by things we cannot control, even if everyone around us thinks that hardship, pain, and suffering are what create misery. They don't. Or at least they don't need to. In the end, they are not the things that matter. We need to train ourselves to be "indifferent" to them. And indifference cuts both ways: we should not be upset by what we can't avoid and we should not be desperate to obtain what we don't have. One of Stoicism's key terms is *adiaphora*, literally "things that make no difference," one way or the other.

Among the *adiaphora* are those things most people passionately desire: health, wealth, beauty, pleasure, respect, justice, reputation, even life itself. For the Stoics, if we focus on gaining these things, thinking they will ultimately provide *eudaimonia*, we are bound for frustration and unhappiness. Look around you. How many wealthy, famous, pleasure-seeking people are ever satisfied with what they have? How many are content with their lives? And how many are seeking more, more, more?

The problem is not that you don't have enough of such things. The problem is that you think having them will bring *eudaimonia*. The solution, then, is not to want them. Or, for that matter, not to care if you do have them. And certainly not to care if any of them is taken away from you. Even your health is something beyond your ultimate control. You can obsess about staying healthy and doing all the right things, and a bad diagnosis can still come. It is better to approach even matters of life and death dispassionately. You may choose to live and prefer not to die; but there is nothing frightful about the prospect of death and there may be times when it is more sensible to choose it.

In this the Stoics agreed with the Epicureans. Like their philosophical opponents, many Stoics agreed there is no afterlife. We are here for a time and, for Stoics, there is a reason for us being here. But as the Stoic philosopher Seneca argued, in lines similar to Epicurus, you were certainly not upset about not being alive a thousand years ago; why should you be upset about not being alive a thousand years from now? You didn't exist before you were born and won't after you die. So what's the difference? In Seneca's inimitable Latin phrase: *Non eris nec fuisti*. Literally: "You will not be, nor were you."[23]

In my view there is a lot to commend these Stoic views. Worry, stress, dread, fear: these can eat us alive. So too can pointless passions for more and more and more of anything. Surely being concerned only about what you can yourself control, not riled by circumstances or even disasters, can lead to greater peace of mind—and, as we now know medically, to longer and happier lives.

But there is an obvious downside to this Stoic view when taken to the extreme urged by Epictetus and other philosophers, a downside recognized already in antiquity. If people train themselves to be oblivious or indifferent to accidents, natural disasters, poverty, broken relationships, and untimely deaths, how can they genuinely feel for others who are suffering or comfort others in their pain? You can't comfort someone in despair if you despise their despair. But for Stoics, the path to *eudaimonia* is precisely never to despair. How then does that conviction not lead to seriously callous behavior?

It certainly did lead to callousness in some circumstances, at least according to most modern standards. In the passage above, when Seneca spoke about not caring if you die, he was giving advice to a younger acquaintance, Lucilius, who had lost a good friend. Seneca tells him not to grieve too much. After all, what did it matter that his friend was gone? He was a pleasure to be with when alive, and now the memory of him could be sweet. Why spend excessive time mourning his absence? What do people normally do when they lose something they value, for example, if their favorite tunic is stolen? They go out and buy a new tunic. Instead of grieving over the friend he had lost, Lucilius should simply find another one to take his place (Seneca, Letter 43). Seneca gave similar advice to people who lost family members, including parents who lost children (*Of Consolation to Marcia*). Ouch.

This is why over the years many have asked whether Stoicism is fully human. Where there is no "passion" (longing for something good) there can be no "compassion" (longing for the good of another). Without "pathos" (suffering), there can be no "sympathy" (feeling for someone who has suffered) or "empathy" (experiencing the suffering of another). Is that how we want to live?

Despite this common and powerful objection, there are aspects of the Stoic approach to life that can still be attractive to many people today when practiced with some moderation. So many things happen to us in life that we can't control and that, at the end of the day, don't really matter. Why be so bothered about them? Aren't there more important things in life? Discovering what these are and concentrating on them, rather than worrying about petty setbacks and losses, can help bring calm into our lives and help us understand what we really want to care for, live for, and devote ourselves to, for the good of both ourselves and others.

Cynics: Be Rid of Simply Everything

The third philosophical perspective that was widely known in the world into which Jesus was born did not have the widespread appeal of Stoicism or even Epicureanism, but Cynicism was well known as an option for those on a serious quest for *eudaimonia*.[24] Cynics advanced an extreme view that took the opposition to worldly attachments to its limits. For them, the key to happiness was to avoid mental anguish, and the only way to avoid being crushed by the loss of wealth, possessions, employment, friends, and loved ones was not to have any. Cynics urged people to abandon literally everything that could be taken away by force or accident. If you have nothing to lose then nothing can be taken from you, and you can focus entirely on your inner mental state.

Cynicism cannot rightly be considered a philosophical "school" like the others. Whereas Epicurean and Stoic philosophers developed sophisticated metaphysical theories that explained the nature of reality and provided a logical basis for their ethical views, the Cynics famously cut right to the chase. Their primary and essentially only interest was how to live. On that, their views were nearly the opposite of the Epicureans: not only were bodily comfort and simple pleasure not primary considerations, they weren't in the equation at all. On the contrary, they were part of the problem. On this point, Cynics were like Stoics; in fact, they may appear to be Stoics on steroids. But they actually appeared on the historical scene first. It was Stoics who developed the idea of regulating desire into a more cultivated and palatable form of Cynicism. Rather than insisting people get rid of all externals, Stoics insisted one should not be *concerned* about them. Their Cynic forerunners had a simpler and more coherent view: externals are worse than useless. They are a source of pain, not indifferent so much as dangerous. They should be disposed of preemptively.

Cynics argued there is remarkably little we need to survive and that most of what people have has no bearing on happiness. So get rid of the house. Give up the job. Earn no money. Own only the clothes (or rags) you're wearing. Beg for food. Acquire nothing else. In a sense, this was an easy philosophy, since Cynics generally did not base their ethical views on metaphysical or logical arguments. Since anyone could choose to abandon normal life for abject poverty, there was no need for education or years of mental training. One later Stoic philosopher disparagingly called the Cynic life "a shortcut to virtue."[25]

Cynic philosophy is commonly said to have been founded by Diogenes (404–323 BCE), who came from the city of Sinope on the coast of the Black Sea but eventually, like other well-known Greek intellectuals, moved to Athens.[26] Diogenes was apparently born into a wealthy family and became a learned author, though none of his writings survives intact. He was most famous in antiquity for his peculiar lifestyle. Becoming scornful of the philosophical views of his day, he chose to go his own way. He lived outdoors in a tub, with no possessions but a bag holding a utensil or two and whatever food he'd gotten through begging, harangued those who gathered to hear him speak, and engaged in private bodily functions in very public places. According to one biographer, Diogenes had kept a cup in his bag for water, but when he saw a young boy squatting by a pool and drinking from his hands, he realized he didn't need the cup and threw it away. When he saw a child who had broken his plate using a piece of bread for his lentils, he threw his bowl away as well.

Diogenes's scornful indifference to circumstances, social proprieties, and the opinions of others comes to us in a range of stories. Invited into a rich person's house, he was told not to expectorate inside, so he coughed up some phlegm and spit in his host's face, saying he couldn't find any better place. At another dinner, guests started throwing bones to him as if he were a dog; he responded like a dog and peed on them. At one point he was captured, enslaved, and put up for sale. When a potential buyer asked him what he was able to do, he replied, "Rule over men" (Diogenes Laertius, *Lives of Eminent Philosophers*, 6.32 and 29).

The most famous story of Diogenes's scorn involves his rebuff of the most powerful person of his world, Alexander the Great. Our oldest account indicates that when Alexander came to Corinth, Diogenes's temporary residence, he was waited on by its great politicians and philosophers—but not the famous Cynic. Hoping to meet him, Alexander went with his entourage and found Diogenes in an outer district, basking in the sunlight. He approached and told him he would give him anything he wanted. Diogenes replied, "Well then, stand a little out of my sun" (Diogenes Laertius, *Lives of Eminent Philosophers*, 6.49).

Diogenes's lifestyle and contempt did not ingratiate him with other philosophers of his day (not that he cared). Plato apparently despised him, thinking he had taken the teachings of Socrates—who maintained that pleasure is a deceptive good and people should therefore focus on a life of virtue—to an insane extreme. Plato reputedly said that Diogenes was "Socrates gone mad" (Diogenes Laertius, *Lives of Eminent Philosophers*, 6.54). Later critics said that the followers of Diogenes lived like dogs, *kunes* in Greek, hence the term "Cynic."

Cynics could be found in various major cities of the early Roman Empire. Even though most Stoics considered them wild extremists, others were more sympathetic. Epictetus put a relatively good spin on their approach to life, writing admiringly:

This is the way of the Cynic who has become worthy of Zeus's scepter and diadem, who says, "Look people: you are searching for happiness (*eudaimonia*) and serenity not where they are but where they are not. See, I have been sent to you by God as a model. I have no possessions, house, wife, or children, not even a bed, cloak, or furniture. And see how healthy I am! Put me to the test and see my serenity; hear about my medications and what things have healed me. (*Discourses*, 4.8.30–31)

The Cynic then explains that he has been healed because he "does not desire or seek after anything, not another person, a position, or a way of life." He instead is "equipped all around with self-respect just as other people are equipped with walls, doors, and doorkeepers" (*Discourses*, 4.8.33).

Conclusion

There may well be something noble in the idea of disposing of all trappings of life so that everything you cherish is completely yours and can never be taken from you. But most ancient people ridiculed this solution of radical self-sufficiency. So too today: Who can seriously consider getting rid of their house, clothing, possessions, every penny to their name?

Few seem to have noticed, however, that Jesus promotes a similar view in the Gospels. "Sell *everything* you have and give to the poor," says Jesus (Mark 10:21). "You should have *no concern* about your life, about what you eat or drink, or about your body, what you wear" (Matthew 5:25). Jesus praises his disciples for abandoning not just their jobs and homes, but their wives, siblings, parents, and children (Luke 18:29). Jesus, of course, was not interested in Cynic or Stoic self-sufficiency, but in the Kingdom of God. Still, his injunctions for how to live are remarkably similar.

Most followers of Jesus today would say he didn't literally mean it, or at least didn't mean it for *them*. Did Diogenes? It is, after all, how he chose to live. And isn't it also how Jesus chose to live? He apparently left home with no possessions but the clothes on his back and urged his followers to do the same. It is no wonder that recent New Testament scholars have sometimes argued that Jesus is best understood as a kind of Jewish Cynic philosopher, urging his followers to escape the trappings of this material world to focus exclusively on the spiritual realm.[27]

In fact, however, Jesus's concerns were quite different from those of Greek and Roman moral philosophers, whether Epicurean, Stoic, or Cynic. In their different ways, the pagan thinkers were all intent on what most people today are also mainly concerned about, even Christian people: How can I flourish? How can I lead a good and meaningful life, content and satisfied with who, what, and where I am? How do I find *eudaimonia*? Jesus, however, did not promote an ethics designed to secure his followers' earthly happiness. As we will see, he urged them to focus instead on the welfare of those in need, insisting people live not for their own comfort but for the good of others. At first glance, this may appear to be a kind of pure altruism. But it is not just that. Living like this, Jesus argued, was the way to inherit the Kingdom of God. Somewhat ironically, it was an altruistically oriented form of deferred gratification.

Before getting to the teachings of Jesus himself, however, we need to continue our exploration of Greek and Roman moral philosophy, especially as it pertained to issues of particular concern to us here: love of others as demonstrated especially through acts of material giving and gracious acts of forgiveness.

Chapter Three

LOVE, CHARITY, AND FORGIVENESS IN THE GREEK AND ROMAN WORLDS

As I became seriously involved in debate in high school, I developed a passion for constructing arguments, adducing evidence, and making a case. Later, when that passion combined with my born-again experience, I naturally gravitated to the "proofs" that should convince just about any thinking person—or so we told ourselves—of the existence of God, the resurrection of Jesus, the inerrancy of the Bible, and other "fundamentals" of the faith. At that point I discovered a keen interest in Christian apologetics, the defense of Christian truth-claims based on rational argument.

I eventually became enamored with the "moral argument" for the existence of God. I first found it in C. S. Lewis's classic *Mere Christianity*, which for many of us at the time was virtually scripture. The argument began with an intriguing premise: all humans have a moral system and, by and large, it is the same everywhere, with some regional differences and the proviso that people don't stick to it all the time. But everyone has a conscience; everyone has a sense of right and wrong; everyone knows deep inside what they should and should not do. What's more, basic moral principles are constant across the human race: rules about killing, stealing, loving parents and children, and so on. How can that be explained? Clearly billions of people over so many millennia could not share a similar moral common sense unless it had been given to them. God had instilled it in each of us. Nothing else could explain the consistency.

It is interesting how an argument we find blindingly obvious at one point in our lives seems so blindingly flawed at another. Today, when someone explains this argument to me (almost always someone trying to convert me), I wonder if they might benefit from a course on cultural anthropology. Is humans' moral sense the same across cultures and time? And does a basic shared sense of appropriate behavior require a transcendent divine source? There are indeed Christian philosophers today who still make the argument.[1] But I have to admit that whenever I see or hear it, I can't help but ask: "Really?"

There do indeed appear to be basic ethical principles shared by most human societies: it is good to treat (some) people well, it is often wrong to take a human life, parents should provide for their children, and the like. But these characteristic attitudes are easily explained on evolutionary grounds. They all contribute to the survival of the species and so have been broadly transmitted in our shared genetic code.[2] But apart from the basics of what it means to be human (as opposed to being a slug or a gardenia), what is particularly striking is the wide range of *contradictory* moral principles and practices among our fellow "sapiens," some of which don't seem so "wise" to us at all. Think, for example, of societies that regard pederasty as the noblest form of love; that urge blood vengeance; that engage in child sacrifice. Or, to bring matters closer to home, societies that do not merely find it unobjectionable but biblically justified to enslave men, women, boys, and girls for cheap labor.

Ethical codes have always been enormously wide-ranging, from person to person, time to time, society to society. They come to us from our genetic makeup, but also from our upbringing, culture, and personal experience. In this chapter, I want to consider social context and the pressure it exerts on individual action. This will help explain how the ethical perspectives that eventually arose in Christian cultures varied in at least one key way from those otherwise dominant in the pre-Christian West. A radical shift occurred in the understanding of how to treat others, especially when the "other" was an outsider or a stranger.

The Greek and Roman Ideology of Dominance

Like most cultures in the history of humanity, the Greek and Roman worlds embraced particular ideas about human relations and interactions. Ideologies—beliefs and ideals shared by nearly everyone in a social group—provide the quiet underpinnings for how group members go about their lives, understand what is right and wrong, and interact with one another. I call these underpinnings "quiet" because they entail a group's "common sense," their unquestioned understandings of life that are rarely even noticed. Most of my undergraduate students, for example, simply assume that capitalism is the only sensible economic system and democracy the only reasonable form of government. Over the course of their education, they may come to question these ideologies, but the reality is that most Americans never question them at all. They are just obvious. But are they obvious in China? Would they have been obvious in medieval Europe or ancient Rome?

Throughout all of antiquity and still in many places today, interpersonal relations were governed by a perspective we might call an "ideology of dominance." For nearly all ancient people on record—from the Babylonians to the Egyptians to the Greeks to the Romans—it simply made sense that those who were powerful should dominate the weak. That's why they were powerful. By divine or natural right mighty empires or cities were entitled to overwhelm weaker ones, killing and enslaving their inhabitants if they chose. This had life-shattering consequences for the conquered, but that did not make it *morally* problematic. So too, masters were expected to dominate slaves, who were property like livestock, there to do the work. Fathers were to dominate their families, wielding the power of life and death over their children. Men were to dominate women, not just socially and economically, but sexually, as they saw fit. In those worlds, who decides what is right? Those who can.

This ideology of domination is ubiquitous in ancient writings. It is not argued for; it is simply assumed in literature as far back as we have it, whether ethical treatises, medical writings, political discourse, epic poetry, personal correspondence, name your genre.

One of its more forthright and chilling expressions is found in the work of the great chronicler of the Peloponnesian War, the Greek historian Thucydides. The war was an extended conflict spanning 431–404 BCE between the Greek city-states seeking control of the Peloponnese, the peninsula that makes up the southern part of Greece. Athens headed one group of cities, Sparta the other.[3] Before the war began, the city of Corinth appealed to Sparta to launch a first strike against Athens, which, in its opinion, needed to be beaten down before it could go on the offensive. Representatives of Athens refused to relinquish their military and political ambitions, maintaining they were simply doing what had always been done: "It was not we who set the example, for it has always been the law that the weaker should be subject to the stronger" (*Peloponnesian War*, 1.76).[4]

Such a view underlies the entire narrative. Later in the war, in 416 BCE, the Athenians were set to attack the island of Melos, a Spartan colony. Their plan was to slaughter all the adult males and enslave everyone else. Before the assault, the Athenians sent representatives to offer the Melians a choice: surrender or face the hellacious consequences. The Melians tried to sway their aggressors: they had remained neutral in the war and did not deserve to be assaulted. The response of the Athenian embassy was harsh and to the point: "You know as well as we do that right, as the world goes, is only in question between equals in power, while the strong do what they can and the weak suffer what they must" (*Peloponnesian War*, 5.89). The Melians understood the logic but refused to surrender, and the slaughter began.

We are obviously dealing with an extreme case here, but the underlying ideology of "might makes right"—that is, the morality of domination—was indeed common sense, on every level of society. Those who suffered as a result certainly did not appreciate the reality, and we occasionally hear their protests. But they object to their suffering, not the ideology that leads to it. We have plenty of stories of those who are weak exploiting those even weaker, along with tales of the exploited becoming exploiters themselves once they acquire the power. It is one thing to object to being on the losing end of an ideology and another to object to the ideology itself.[5]

In such a world, what would be the role of altruism?

I do not mean this as a rhetorical question. The Greek and Roman worlds were not exclusively cultures of pure brute force. When it came to daily life, they were much like cultures today: people were born into caring families, had friendships, fell in love, worked for a living, enjoyed social occasions that let them eat, drink, and be merry, and had a sense of right and wrong. My question is: Given both the acceptance of dominance and the centrality of love, in what contexts and in what ways, then, would we find altruistic behaviors?

When considering this question, it is important to remember we are not talking about monoliths. The cultures of ancient Greece and Rome spanned vast spaces and many centuries. Over seven hundred years passed between our first Greek literary source, Homer, and the Roman Empire at the time of Jesus. By that time, the empire reached from Spain to Syria, and local variations in culture were significant. But there were also striking commonalities across time and place, especially when it came to the topics of our particular concern: how love, charitable giving, and forgiveness were understood and practiced. We will consider these in turn.

Love in the Greek and Roman Worlds

Every human society understands, endorses, and practices love in one way or another. But love is a complicated phenomenon, even if we restrict our consideration to a very narrow time and place. Just in English, "love" can mean a whole range of things. You can love your spouse, your grandmother, a book, your boss, a fine Bordeaux, and your neighborhood; you can love God; you can make love, show love, and be in love. So what does love mean? Even if there is a common element tying all these things together, they are very different notions: love can mean admiration, desire, appreciation, concern, attraction, care, obsession, passion, and yet other things. You don't love your chili the way you love your child.

So too in other cultures. As in English, ancient Greek and Latin used a variety of terms for love and, to the perennial confusion of modern readers of ancient books in translation, these terms are sometimes translated the same way (simply as "love," for example) and sometimes in different ways. Sometimes the same word is translated in different ways in different contexts. Not infrequently, that affects how an English reader will understand a passage. Unless everyone masters the ancient languages, that will always be the case. The bigger problem is that even experts argue about the nuances of each term and how to translate it.

When I was doing graduate work in New Testament studies in the early 1980s, we were taught that the previous generation of biblical scholars had blundered in its understanding of the Greek words for love. That kind of generational one-upmanship is very common in scholarship: there is a natural propensity to dismiss the academic giants of earlier periods as unsophisticated by the standards of our own refined brilliance. Teachers in that earlier generation commonly said there were three Greek words for love: *eros*, *philia*, and *agapē*. These terms were described as meaning, respectively, passionate love, friendly love, and active love. We, their successors, were taught that, in fact, the terms could be used synonymously.[6] We ourselves would never have been caught dead saying there were three Greek words for love.

The issue mattered for us New Testament scholar wannabes because two of the words, *agapē* and *philia*, create famous problems of interpretation, for example, in the final chapter of the Gospel of John (John 21:15–17). After his resurrection, Jesus appears to his disciples and speaks to Peter, who a few chapters earlier had denied him three times. "Peter, do you love me?" Jesus asks, using the verb *agapaō*. Peter replies, "Yes Lord, you know that I love you." But instead of using the same verb (based on *agapē*) Peter uses *phileō* (based on *philia*). Interpreters in the previous generation had taken that to mean that when Jesus asks Peter if he really, deeply, truly loved him enough to do anything for him, Peter responds, "Yes, I do like you." And that explained why Jesus asks Peter a second time if he truly loves him (*agapaō*), with Peter again replying that he likes him (*phileō*). So, Jesus asks a third time, but he now comes down to Peter's level by using the term *phileō*, and Peter responds, using the same verb, indicating he really loves him as much as could be asked. Jesus is satisfied and stops asking.

We the self-assuredly more sophisticated exegetes, however, saw the flaw of this interpretation. The two words for love were actually *synonyms* and so the distinction other interpreters were making was not well-informed. The point is not that Peter had to be cudgeled into confessing his love. The point is that the three admissions of love were to make up for his three denials.

No matter how one interprets these verbs, it is a difficult passage and my goal is not to resolve the problem here but to consider the vocabulary choices that create it. To begin with, one reason it is very strange for anyone—whether a New Testament scholar or not—to say that there are *three* Greek words for love is that there are others as well, including one that occurs fairly often in Greek literature: *stergō*. Possibly one could argue this word is not included among "the three" because it never occurs in the New Testament, but neither does the word *eros*, yet it is always included. Maybe theological scholars just have a penchant for the number three . . .

In any event, it is certainly true these various Greek terms for love are sometimes used interchangeably. But normally not. In most ancient Greek writing, they do signify different things, and sometimes they are explicitly set in contrast with one another in writings outside the New Testament.[7] The verb *stergō* most commonly refers to affection you can find in a family, for example that of parents for children and siblings for one another. *Eros*—from which, obviously, our word "erotic" derives—almost always refers to a passionate kind of love, for example, sexual desire. *Philia* (think: Phil-adelphia, the city of "brotherly love") typically refers to a kind of affection you have toward someone with whom you have good chemistry or comradery; it can be used to describe familial relations too, but more often refers to really liking someone as a friend. *Agapē*, as it turns out, is never used as a noun in pagan Greek writings; its verb form (*agapaō*) means something like to cherish or value. The word first shows up as a noun in the Greek translation of the Old Testament, but even there it is used only a few times. It appears all over the New Testament and other early Christian writings, however—*not* in reference to love as an emotion of passion, attraction, or admiration, but as loving action taken in the best interests of another. *Agapē*, in other words, is a term for altruistic behavior.

Throughout ancient Greek writings generally, far and away the most common words for "love" are *eros* (passionate love) and *philia* (friendly love). While the difference between the two is quite clear, going back as far as Plato and Aristotle, both words can also refer to altruistic feelings and behaviors toward loved ones.[8] That is especially surprising with *eros*, since one normally does not think of passionate desire as a particularly altruistic emotion. Quite the contrary, people seized by erotic passion are often highly *irrational*, acting according to bodily desire rather than reason. This was a problem for ancient philosophers from at least the time of Socrates and Plato, who commonly juxtaposed body and spirit, the animal drives that satisfy the desires of the flesh and the human activities that improve the mind and soul. That makes it all the more interesting that Plato produced an extensive and glowing account of *eros* in his famous dialogue, *The Symposium*, where he explores its highly positive ethical and philosophical possibilities, positioning *eros* as the pinnacle of all human experiences.

Eros in Plato's Symposium

The narrative settings of Plato's dialogues sometimes seem whimsical, but a closer reading almost always shows something more profound at play. A drinking party may not seem a particularly apt context for serious philosophical reflection, but that is what a "symposium" is (literally: a "drinking together"), and it is where Plato sets his most profound reflections on love (*eros*). *The Symposium* narrates a social gathering in 416 BCE, some years before the dialogue itself was written, when a group of intellectual, social elites come together to celebrate the theatrical victory of one of its members at the annual Athenian festival in honor of Dionysus, the god of wine, festivity, and theater. The playwright is named Agathon, which means "good" in Greek, even though—in typical Platonic style—he is presented as rather vapid, prone to facile rhetoric instead of serious thought. Like the others named at the gathering, Agathon was a historical figure, even if the account is fictional.

With the exception of Socrates, all the participants are hungover from the celebrations of the night before and so decide to drink with moderation at this evening's event, rather than getting plastered. (We learn over the course of the dialogue that Socrates can drink anyone under the table without feeling or acting tipsy.) Thus, the setting is festive, the wine is (moderately) flowing, and the company decides to reflect on a rather dizzying subject: the virtues of Eros, the god of passionate love. One of them notes that all other gods have songs of praise dedicated to them—but, oddly, not the god of passion. To make up the deficit, the group decides they will each compose a speech that best celebrates the god and the actions he inspires.

The dialogue mainly consists of their five speeches, followed by a long deliberation from Socrates and ending with the late appearance of another companion, who provides yet a different perspective. Each speech lauds the great virtues and glories of passionate love. Each speaker considers *eros* not only a particularly thrilling aspect of human existence but also one of its most noble. Each of their perspectives, as one might expect given the patriarchal setting of ancient Athens, is that of an elite, refined, adult male. For modern readers, this makes it all the more jarring that every one of them assumes—and at times insists—that the most gratifying and desirable object of male passion is not a woman but a boy. Among other things, *The Symposium* is a paean to pederasty.

I earlier argued that moral "common sense" can differ radically from one culture to another. Here is a particularly puzzling case in point. In ancient Athens, as in other Greek city-states at the time, love affairs between elite adult men and adolescent boys were not merely tolerated but celebrated, assumed not just to be perfectly normal but beneficial.[9] The practice was governed by social mores (though not laws) about what was appropriate and what was not, and acceptable activities differed somewhat from one city to the next. But the basic idea was relatively constant: an elite adult male sexually attracted to an adolescent boy would make overtures and, if fortunate, convince him to engage in an intimate relationship. The roles of the two were strictly defined: the adult was the "lover" (*erastēs*) and the adolescent the "beloved" (*erōmenos*).

In the ideal situation, the relationship was perceived to bring benefits to both. The beloved, who now spent considerable time with the older man, learned the ways of society and acquired the wisdom and practical experience he needed for later life as a member of the cultured elite. In exchange, the infatuated adult received sexual favors—not intercourse, widely considered (at least in elite circles) inappropriate between males, but typically intercrural sex to gratify the lover but not arouse the youth. The relationship was meant to be exclusive and would normally not continue once the adolescent had developed into full maturity.

And the wives in all this? They were not part of the equation, although the man typically had a spouse and children at home. (We do not know of a similar practice among women and girls, in no small measure because they were expected to be sexually chaste outside of marriage.)[10]

The speakers celebrating *eros* in *The Symposium* all assume that adolescent boys were far more sexually desirable than women. They understand sex with their wives as necessary for the production of offspring, but they maintain (or simply assume) that real *eros* comes only in relatively short-term relations with handsome, intelligent, and virtuous adolescent boys. Each speech thus celebrates the glories of pederastic *eros* by explaining why passionate love is "good," including in ways that are altruistic: of benefit to the partner, not just the self.

Roughly speaking, the speeches become sequentially more sophisticated in their expositions of the virtues of *eros*. Phaedrus begins by endorsing a simple view he considers rather profound: *eros* produces virtue that can benefit the *polis*, especially in times of war. That is because the adult lover is so smitten with his beloved, so intense on earning his favor and avoiding his scorn, he would never do anything cowardly or craven. His passion motivates him to perform acts of bravery on the battlefield. *Eros*, therefore, contributes to the welfare of the state.

Pausanias then gives a more nuanced speech, arguing there are two kinds of *eros*. One is vulgar, concerned only for bodily pleasure. For that, women can serve as the object of desire just as well as boys. The other kind is heavenly and honorable, the passion for an adolescent whose education and virtue can be enhanced by the lover, thereby improving his soul. Unlike vulgar passion, this more refined *eros* provides significant benefits for both parties: one helps society by passing along his wisdom and experience, the other receives the intellectual and moral training that will promote not only his own well-being but also that of the *polis*.

Of the remaining three speeches, the one by Aristophanes is by far the most interesting and entertaining. In real life, Aristophanes (446–386 BCE) was the most famous comic playwright of classical Athens who, in one of his surviving plays, *The Clouds* (423 BCE), lampoons Socrates as a detached pseudo-intellectual whose recondite but wild speculation about physical reality has been misleading the youth of Athens. These in fact were among the charges actually leveled against Socrates at his trial twenty-four years later. Plato, who disliked theater and poetry generally and was writing *The Symposium* long after the conviction and execution of Socrates, does not directly mock Aristophanes in his account. He does, however, portray his defense of erotic passion as very comic indeed, insightful but also a bit buffoonish.

In his speech Aristophanes maintains there are different kinds of gendered passions: male/female, male/male, and female/female. (This is one of the few direct discussions of lesbianism to come down to us from antiquity.) That is because gods originally created not just two kinds of human—male and female—but also a third, the androgyne, literally a "male-female." In this imaginative tale of origins, Aristophanes explains that humans were not created as two-legged, two-armed, one-faced creatures. They were round beings with four legs, four arms, and two faces looking in opposite directions. What we now know as backs and sides were originally the exterior portions, all around. These humanoids moved not by walking but by cartwheeling—quite easy to do with eight limbs sticking straight out.

The humans, Aristophanes explains, were powerful and haughty, and in their foolishness they decided to attack the heavens to displace the gods. Zeus decided not to slay them with a thunderbolt, but to rob them of their facility of transport by slicing them in half, down the middle. Now the one being was two and each had to walk on two legs. If these debilitated creatures continued to threaten the gods, Zeus could slice them again to make them hop around rather helplessly on just one leg.

To allow the creatures to function in their newly transformed state, Zeus arranged for their faces to be swiveled; the eyes that had originally been looking out over what we think of as the back were shifted to face the front, so a person could see where they were going. The genitals, formerly on the outside, likewise needed to be shifted to the stomach side.

And so, people who were originally one being now had become two. Naturally the two halves were—and still are—desperate to reunite with each other. *Eros*, according to Aristophanes, is the desire for your other half. Sometimes your other half is male, sometimes female. That is why some people have such powerful longings for either same-sex or other-sex partners.

Once you find your other half, you want nothing more than to be physically reunited with them. When a man comes upon a youth he finds not just likable and admirable but sexually desirable, it is because he is seeking one like himself with whom to connect; the youth in turn wants all that the older man can provide. Proof that this is a good thing for the couple and society as a whole, Aristophanes says, is provided by the social reality of the *polis*: only those youths who have been involved in relationships with older men proceed to public careers and further the purposes of the city. When they reach that stage as adults, they too have no real interest in women, but marry only because of custom and the need for children to promote the welfare of future society.

Aristophanes sums up his view: "I am speaking about everyone, men and women alike, and I say there is just one way for the human race to flourish [literally 'to have *eudaimonia*']: we must bring love [*eros*] to its perfect conclusion, and each of us must win the favor of his own young man, so that he can recover his original nature" (*Symposium*, 193c).[11]

Following the other two encomia, Socrates delivers an alternative view in the longest speech of the evening, as one would expect from the perennial hero of Plato's dialogues. As one would also expect, the Socrates who regularly disparages the body and bodily pleasure in favor of nourishing the soul and cultivating its excellences takes an entirely different view from his companions of the importance of *eros*. He too sees it as a potential good—in fact, one of the great goods—but not because he favors indulging in physical desires. On the contrary, for Socrates the passion one feels for a youth is a good that can lead to higher, much better goods, such as an understanding of what "good" is in and of itself, and a grasp of the nature of ultimate reality.

Just as Plato does not take credit for his own views throughout his dialogues, but puts them on the lips of Socrates, so too in this dialogue Socrates does not take credit for his insights. He instead indicates he learned them from a woman philosopher named Diotima, who educated him in the nature of *eudaimonia* and the importance of *eros*.

How can a man's *eros* lead to the ultimate good? It happens through a series of realizations as the deeply reflective lover moves from one level of consciousness to the next. It all begins down here in the very physical world of bodies, relationships, and desires. In particular, it is rooted in the almost universal desire to escape death, to be immortal.

Diotima had pointed out to Socrates that everyone desires (has *eros* for) good things and always for the same reason: because we think having them will bring happiness (*eudaimonia*). But none of us wants the good we experience to be temporary. The only way to have perpetual good, however, is to be immortal. We clearly are not immortal, and so (subconsciously) we try to obtain immortality by passing ourselves on to future generations. Most people do that through the common, vulgar kind of *eros*: having heterosexual intercourse to make babies. In a sense, we physically "live on" through our descendants.

But humans of the greatest virtue do more than that. They strive to pass their virtuous traits on to future generations. That does not happen by begetting biological children, who may or may not possess their parental virtues, but rather through pederastic relations. A man passionate for an adolescent boy has the opportunity to mold his character with understanding and virtue, thereby passing his own wisdom to generations to come. Intergenerational wisdom is thus facilitated by *eros*, a passionate desire aroused by the beauty of the youth. But even more important is the beauty of his soul, which can be shaped into a source of goodness and truth.

For Diotima this soulish attraction is just the beginning of the lover's ascent through *eros*. Once a man realizes that the powerful, physical beauty of the boy can lead to a yet higher form of virtue and goodness, he sees that it is not the individual young person he longs for but the greater beauty itself, which can be found in other persons as well. This does not, however, lead him into wild polyamorous sexual abandon. On the contrary, sex is simply an entry point into the recognition of what is far superior: beauty itself, found in many other people. The man realizes it is a trivial matter to be obsessed with one person, when the souls of so many are either filled with or can be turned to beauty. The man then falls in love with beauty itself, not with just one individual who has it.

That advance leads to yet another, as he realizes that the life of society as a whole can promote the beauty of virtue and goodness. And so, he starts to contemplate the beauty of customs, traditions, and laws that can protect and promote the cultivation of the soul. From there he realizes that other branches of knowledge and culture contribute even more significantly to beautifying our souls, and so he falls in love with those as well—a much deeper, meaningful love, a passion for all that improves the soul, to the point where he realizes that sex with a boy is a paltry and trivial matter. It was useful as an entrée to the glories of beauty, but beauty is more than an attribute some people or objects have: it is a thing in and of itself, a kind of essence or idea that infuses all kinds of persons, relationships, and material objects.[12] Once this person begins to contemplate beauty in and of itself, he has reached the pinnacle of understanding the good. Mere physical pleasure pales in comparison.

This sequence of enlightenment thus involves an ascent of the soul as it moves upward from recognizing the physical beauty of a boy to seeing his true beauty rooted in his soul, rising from there to see such beauty in other people and things, ascending further to observe it embodied in social structures that promote virtue, and rising yet further to see that there is, far above this coarse material world we inhabit, a realm in which the essence of beauty itself dwells. This essence is not transient. It is immortal. It does not grow old. It contains nothing ugly or unpleasant and is not part of something else. It is an entity unto itself, in and of itself beauty. We can partially detect it at times in our banal lives here below, since it can be manifest in such things as works of art, virtue, and gorgeous adolescent boys. The goal of life is to move beyond these glimpses of beauty to see it in its full splendor and to meditate on it. That is how we can obtain the true good.

In a sense this ascent of the soul is an individual quest. Its goal is to discover what is truly good and to mold oneself to it, and through doing so to find ultimate satisfaction in life, true *eudaimonia*. Since the process entails ultimately becoming "good," it obviously also has good effects on others—friends, family, society at large. But neither Diotima, Socrates, nor Plato reflects on the altruistic benefits of the journey. The stated goal of the ascent is self-improvement and personal happiness, not actions beneficial to others.[13]

That point will be worth bearing in mind when we later explore the alternative vision of goodness that appears within the Christian tradition, an alternative that will appeal to some readers as more virtuous and noble, and to others as rather bleak and obligatory in comparison.

Philia in Aristotle's Nicomachean Ethics

Plato's student Aristotle was the most influential moral philosopher of antiquity and, arguably, of all time. Even though ethics had long been a topic of philosophical discourse, no one had devoted an entire work to the topic before him, culminating in his ten-volume *Nicomachean Ethics*, a work that continues to occupy philosophers and students today.[14] As we saw in chapter 2, Aristotle begins his discussion by considering the ultimate goal of life: obtaining *eudaimonia* through developing the human virtues. Much of the work provides a systematic discussion of three key virtues in turn: courage, justice, and temperance. But there are also, strikingly, two entire books (8 and 9) devoted to *philia*, commonly translated in this context as "friendship."

Greek writers often set *philia* in contrast to *eros* as denoting the kind of love between friends and relatives based on kindness and comradery. It involves enjoying someone for who they are and how they live. Aristotle provides a characteristically deep and nuanced discussion, insightful still for anyone interested in the nature of friendship. Here, I will simply summarize some of the key points that can serve as foils for later Christian views on love.

For Aristotle, *philia* can exist within hierarchical relationships: for example, a father and son, a husband and wife, a ruler and his subjects. *Philia* differs in each of these instances, of course: you love your spouse differently from how you love your child or king. But there is an important commonality as well: the love is unequal because of the differentials of power.

Aristotle's main interest, however, lies in nonhierarchical relationships in friendships between relative equals. These come in three basic kinds. Some friendships are based on utility: that is, when a "friend" can provide advantages. For Aristotle, that is not pure friendship. If you befriend the fellow next door because he is a handyman who can prove useful when you need some home repairs, that is not the same as liking him for who he really is. Other friendships are based on pleasure: you like the other person because she is witty, agreeable, and entertaining. It is not that you're deeply interested in understanding who she really is—her aspirations in life, what hardships she goes through, or how you can help her. She's just fun to be around.

Modern readers may find it odd that Aristotle maintains that these two inferior kinds of friendship are typically found in different age groups. Friendships based on utility, he avers, are especially common among old folk, in part because they're past the point of enjoying much pleasure in life. Young people, on the other hand, gravitate toward friendships based on pleasure, since for them enjoyment is what matters most. For Aristotle, both kinds of friendship are ephemeral, since they are contingent on egoistic desires, on what you can get from another. He writes, for example: "Those who are friends on account of utility dissolve the friendship at the same time as the advantage ceases, for they were friends not to each other but to the profit involved" (8.4.2).[15] These kinds of friendship are also less than optimal because they are ultimately undiscerning: they can arise between two people who both have bad characters, between one who is good and one who is bad, or between two people who aren't either particularly good or bad.

The best kinds of friendship come between two people who are "good" or "excellent," that is, virtuous. Those who embody virtue naturally seek out others like them to enjoy a reciprocal exchange of goodness. This alone leads to a truly altruistic friendship: "a friend wishes for the good things for the friend for his friend's sake" (8.7.6). A friendship like this necessarily requires the feelings to be mutual; it cannot, therefore, be found in other kinds of appreciation or fondness. Nor is it like enjoying an inanimate object for its "excellence." You can't be "friends" with your boat. But you also can't be friends with someone who does not return the feeling and act on it. Since perfect friendship requires reciprocity, it can exist only because and while the two people are fundamentally equals. If one is or becomes more or less virtuous, wealthy, or socially important, parity can no longer exist. That would mean the end of the perfect friendship.

One might suspect this would necessarily lead to an ironic situation where a true friend could never want the best for the other. If two friends, for example, are in the same basic economic class, then surely neither of them would wish the other to receive a large inheritance and become incredibly rich. That would put them on different levels and end their friendship. But Aristotle does not accept this view. The two would indeed cease to be friends, but that does not mean that while they *are* friends, they do not want the best for the other. They each want what is good for the other, "for that friend's own sake" (8.7.6). True friendship, in other words, involves altruism, a selfless concern for the other.

That makes friendship fully mutual and proactive: "Friendship seems to consist more in loving than in being loved" (8.8.3). In fact, each of the friends "is eager to benefit each other, for this belongs to virtue and to friendship; and since they compete with a view to this, there are no accusations or fights: no one is annoyed by someone who loves and benefits him, but if he is refined, he retaliates by doing some good to his friend" (8.13.2). One gives for the sake of the other, not for what one gets out of it. In a sense, this is treating the other as the self. And so, Aristotle affirms the aphorism that friends share "one soul" (9.8.2).

Aristotle may never have pronounced the biblical dictum "Love your neighbor as yourself" (Leviticus 19:18), but he did believe you should "Love your friend as yourself." The difference is as important as the similarity. Aristotle is speaking about relationships between best friends, not between one person and any random other. Moreover, he acknowledges that no one can have many such friendships; they are necessarily rare given the deep intimacy involved.

Even in Aristotle's most extreme statements of altruistic *philia*, however, he does not imagine—let alone embrace—complete, selfless altruism. Egoism, to some extent, is always in the picture. Aristotle notes that *philia* will sometimes lead a person to die for his friend, or even for his beloved country... but in no small measure that is because doing so means "securing for himself what is noble" (9.8.9). So too in more quotidian situations: a friend is sometimes willing to suffer a significant financial loss by giving money to his companion. That is certainly altruistic, in that the other gets the money. But the giver benefits as well, since "he gains what is noble'" and "assigns to himself, therefore, the greater good" (9.8.9).

The reward of "nobility" is a major consideration for much of Aristotle's ethics of friendship. "It is nobler to do good to friends than strangers." That is why "the good man will need those who may be done some good" (9.9.2). Generosity is important, but less for the sake of the other than for the nobility of the self.

As we will see, this is a decided contrast with the views of Jesus. For Jesus, anyone can love their friends. It is loving those in need that reveals one's true character. This perspective makes it all the more striking that in our modern, Christian world, most people would probably still side with Aristotle rather than Jesus on this question, even though they've never heard of something called the *Nicomachean Ethics*. They may pay lip service to the Sermon on the Mount and its insistence on focusing on those in need. But, in reality, they follow the path of Aristotle, putting their energies into cultivating good friendships. To us that seems like common sense. But that does not mean it was the sense shared by Jesus.

Love after Plato and Aristotle

Discussions of love are scattered throughout later Greek and Roman moral discourse, as one would expect, but the dominant voices up to Jesus's day continued to be those of Plato and Aristotle. Plato's specific celebration of *eros* never became mainstream, but Aristotle's exposition of *philia* proved influential and continues to be favorably treated among moral philosophers.

It should be clear that the different words for love and their nuances do not necessarily entail a *choice*: it is perfectly possible to have either *eros* and *philia* for another, or to have both, or neither. Modern readers may find it odd that no Greek philosopher, including Plato and Aristotle, devoted any mental energy to considering the kind of love embodied in the later term *agapē*—love that actively focuses on the other, apart from any emotional attachment and whether or not they are a friend or lover.[16] But it was coined only later by the translators of the Jewish Scriptures into Greek and taken over and exalted to unusual heights by the Greek-speaking authors of the New Testament, their communities, and their successors. Even so, as we have seen, both *eros* and *philia* could and did have altruistic possibilities, and these were widely understood as intrinsically desirable outcomes.

Altruism, of course, comes in multiple forms: we can visit a friend who is sick, mourn with one who is bereaved, volunteer, help someone find a job, fix a neighbor's car (or chariot), or do any one of a thousand things that can show affection and concern. Among these myriad options, two of the most powerful acts of altruism involve sharing material resources with those in need, an especially concrete act, and restoring a broken relationship, a particularly intimate one. Both charity and forgiveness were widely known and discussed in Greek and Roman antiquity prior to the Christian movement. But what they actually entailed were very different in these contexts.

Love and Charity in the Greek and Roman Worlds

For the majority of people today, wealth is not seen as a moral problem. Relatively few people have it; those who don't have it want it; and those who do have it want to keep it, often taking extraordinary measures to do so. Rarely do the wealthy think they should become poor, and rarely do the poor have qualms about acquiring wealth.

None of this, of course, is new. Even so, just as you "always have the poor with you," so also you always have the opponents of serious affluence with you. In our world, the ethical issue usually involves equities of distribution. Is it really right for billionaires to continue accumulating wealth when hundreds of millions live and die in poverty? Is it right to own a luxury yacht, a private jet, and multiple mansions when (as actually happens) some twenty-five thousand people die of starvation each and every day?

Enormous inequities of distribution also plagued the ancient world, but they were almost never considered a moral problem. As difficult as it is to imagine, we have no records of moral outrage (at least in our written sources, which were, it should be noted, produced almost entirely by or for the elite) over the fabulously rich getting richer while the poor became poorer: no calls for redistributions of wealth, no governmental interventions to feed the starving masses, no private charities to disperse funds to those in desperate need.[17]

There was, however, a moral problem with wealth, expressed repeatedly in ancient writings of nearly every genre: philosophical essays, drama, private letters, satire, imaginary literature, take your pick. Wealth could be very bad indeed. Oddly enough, though, the harm came to those who had it. Wealth could have a negative effect on a person's character. It might make them greedy, miserly, mean-spirited, self-centered, and generally less than virtuous. That would be bad, not just for their influence or effect on others but even more for their own well-being. Since it was impossible to find *eudaimonia* apart from virtue, the wealthy—for the sake of their own happiness (poor souls)—should be generous with their wealth.

That certainly did not, however, mean giving large sums to the poor and destitute. That would be insane, or at least irresponsible. When those with any abundance shared their wealth, it was to be done judiciously, not recklessly, with family members or friends who needed it. If on occasion those with abundance provided funds to others not related to them biologically or socially, it was only to be people of "their sort," that is, acquaintances in their same socioeconomic class, or to devoted underlings (clients) who could be counted on to provide other kinds of favors in return. The idea of giving generously to strangers in dire straits was not just frowned upon, it was often discouraged. As a rule, when the wealthy did provide material support to those of the lower classes—and the vast majority of people were in the lower classes—it was not out of sympathy. It was to prevent riots.

To understand ancient attitudes toward wealth, we need some idea of the demographics of the Greek and Roman worlds. A nuanced discussion is not possible here, given the massive stretches of territory and centuries; for our purposes some relatively well-documented generalizations can suffice. At nearly all times and places, the population of antiquity was predominantly rural. In the period of the New Testament, probably 80 to 90 percent of the Roman Empire lived outside the cities, even though nearly all our literary records come from urban elites. These sometimes do describe rural life, but necessarily from the perspective of outside observers, even if they did own country estates. As a result, the vast bulk of our sources' interests lay with urban life, where virtually all wealth was located. Most of this wealth did come from agricultural estates, generated by the masses working the fields and engaging in support operations. Urban landowners who accumulated wealth off the backs of poor laborers were known everywhere to be far more concerned with their profits than the welfare of those who provided them. Some things never change.[18]

Life in rural areas of the Greek and Roman worlds was normally a hand-to-mouth existence. Most people lived off what they could grow on small family plots and engaged in a barter economy with others nearby. So too, those laboring on agricultural estates were simply allowed to keep some of what was produced for themselves. It is impossible to quantify the levels of rural destitution at any time and place, but it almost certainly was always high.[19]

We are better placed to estimate the levels of economic stratification in well-attested urban areas such as Athens and Rome. These can help us make educated guesses about other, less well-documented cities. In a world such as ours, where about half the population is middle class, it is hard to imagine economies with very little middle class at all. It is not that everyone in the Greek and Roman worlds was either filthy rich or desperately poor, as many oversimplified descriptions have often suggested. But the discrepancies of wealth were nonetheless stark, and relatively few people were living comfortably. The best analyses have concluded that only about 2 to 3 percent of the population enjoyed abundant wealth, while another 5 to 8 percent had more than they needed to survive; these would mainly have been merchants, traders, and artisans. Probably about 10 to 20 percent were not in danger of immediate want. But some 55 to 60 percent of the urban population lived very much on the edge, just at or below subsistence level, and 10 to 20 percent significantly below it.[20] That is to say, 65 to 80 percent of urban dwellers were dangerously poor or completely destitute.

When we study ancient history we typically read the writings of the 1 percent and scarcely think about the impoverished masses they rarely mention. Even ancient moralists didn't think much about them or, when they did, they did not think much *of* them. Several philosophers writing at the time of early Christianity—including the Roman Seneca (4 BCE–65 CE) and the Greek Plutarch (46–119 CE)—wrote treatises on wealth and its problems, and in every case the problems they decry do not involve destitution among the masses, but the potential character flaws that threaten the very rich.[21]

Charitable Giving

Seneca would know all about these threats to character. As the tutor and then court advisor of the emperor Nero, he was one of the richest people in the Roman world.[22] From that position of authority he spoke at length about the dangers of wealth and condemned those who succumbed to greed and high living (Epistle, 108.2). At one point—apparently straight-faced—he argues that "having wealth was more torture than seeking it" (115.16). His logic is that it is very hard indeed to be virtuous with the temptations of gold lying all around. And so he urges readers who thought riches desirable to consult a tycoon to see how miserable it can be (115.17).

For a committed Stoic like Seneca, the problem was not actually having money, but having the wrong *attitude* toward money. In his view, money could not be inherently good; if it were, those who had it in abundance would be abundantly good. But obviously lots of wealthy folk are scoundrels, so wealth is not a virtue. Still, Seneca advises against giving money to those in need unless they are "deserving": they wouldn't make good use of the money, so what would be the point of giving it to them (*On the Happy Life*, 24.1)? Seneca does concede that someone of his stature might occasionally toss a copper to a beggar or give them a piece of bread. But such casual gestures do not confer giving away a real "benefit," since they are petty and insignificant (*On Benefits*, 4.29.2). As a rule, one should never be liberal to those who are "unsightly and unworthy." He does allow one exception: it can be useful for someone who is virtuous to buy votes for an upcoming election from the disreputable, so long as they come from good families (*On the Happy Life*, 24.3).

Seneca does regale the virtues of generous giving to the right people: principally family and friends, but even to household slaves if they have a good head on their shoulders.[23] For him, this kind of personal giving is a true virtue, and in fact reveals one of the great moral benefits of having wealth in the first place. Those who are poor have nothing to give to their friends and family. Only the rich, therefore, have the means to acquire the virtue of generosity. On the other hand, they alone must pass over a high hurdle of vice. No one who is poor can be obsessed with their money and so cannot have their character corrupted by it. It is unfortunate they lack the opportunity to move past the vice to acquire the virtue, but this is the real moral problem of poverty for Seneca, not that they will starve.

Reflections on the problems of wealth did not originate in Seneca's day. They had been around since the beginning of moral philosophy in classical Athens. Xenophon, a contemporary of Plato, also wrote a book called *The Symposium* and also framed it as a conversation among friends of Socrates. In this instance, though, the discussion does not center on the virtues of *eros* but on the potential evils of riches and how to deal with them. In the back-and-forth, a character named Charmides sets forth a view embraced by Cynics: the best way to avoid the perils of wealth is to get rid of it. All of it.

Charmides, we learn, had once been very rich, but his wealth led to a life of misery: he was always afraid of being robbed, blackmailed, or called upon by the government to fund municipal projects. It was a nightmare. Then he lost it all. Went bankrupt. Now, he avers, he is as happy as can be. He sleeps like a baby, fears no threats, and receives no civic demands. People leave him to do whatever he wants. He is perfectly content.

The friends of Charmides think he has gone too far. They insist the problem is not having wealth, but wanting more and spending more than you have no matter how much that is. In their view, the secret is to live frugally, even if you're rich, to refrain from coveting more and more, to be honest and pursue virtue. As with Seneca later, they think money can be useful, and losing it all—or even giving it away—would be very bad. The problem is addiction, not affluence.

This was far and away the solution preferred by most ancient moral philosophers and, almost certainly, the wealthy themselves, at least those who had any qualms about the matter.

If wealth and disparities of wealth were not intrinsically problematic, one may well wonder whether there was ever any incentive in the ancient world to give resources away. We have already seen some of the private reasons for doing so: it could improve one's self-image, enhance one's reputation, and, of course, make possible tangible benefits in return, down the line. There was also the widespread institution of patronage, in which wealthy and well-placed individuals had clients to attend them, do them favors, and generally be available at their beck and call in return for social and especially financial support. Since the institution was status-driven, the wealthy generally had no interest in accepting lower-class, disreputable, or failed clients. But one of the ways a member of the relatively small "middle" class could keep above the threshold of need was through serving a rich patron willing to give resources in exchange for nonmaterial benefits.

Other reasons for largesse have been enumerated by French scholar of antiquity Paul Veyne in his classic study of giving in antiquity, *Bread and Circuses*: "Careerism, paternalism, kingly style, corruption, conspicuous consumption, local patriotism, desire to emulate, concern to uphold one's rank, obedience to public opinion, fear of hostile demonstrations, generosity, belief in ideals."[24] It is quite a list, but it is telling that every incentive on it involves the interests (good or bad) of the person giving the funds, not the needs of those receiving them. That is true even of "generosity," since, as we have seen, targets were almost always other socially connected people, and the goal of generosity was to obtain honor.

Many scholars, including Veyne, go out of their way to stress that even if the giving was for the sake of the giver, others did benefit—and sometimes the benefits trickled down to the lower classes.[25] Public giving was expected and even demanded of rich members of a community for the benefit of all, a practice termed "euergetism," which literally means something like "doing good" (for the community).[26] Municipal projects in antiquity were not funded by taxes on the general public but by private individuals, especially those who were given, or were required to take, a public office. It is a little difficult for us to imagine having to *pay* to serve the city as a mayor or treasurer, but that was indeed the case. These posts went to the wealthy, whose duty, in part, was to provide their own funds to support the work that needed to be done. Sometimes the expense was exorbitant, and in numerous instances the obligations led to bankruptcy. But the "honors" were difficult to decline.

Even for those not in office, the reciprocal character of euergetism motivated the wealthy to fund public buildings and entertainments such as races, theatrical contests, and gladiatorial fights. All such public expenditures came with clear benefits for the donors themselves. In a world that celebrated domination, public honor provided an obvious route to popularity and superiority, and there could be serious competition to produce the largest building or the most lavish games. Such wealth-sacrificing routes to honor continue to our day, of course: most alumni who donate fantastic amounts to a university don't want to provide scholarships for English majors; they want their name displayed for all to see on a new building, the library, or, even better, a new football stadium. At my university, $15 million will get you a practice field.

It is true, as Veyne and others have argued, that ancient euergetism could sometimes benefit others in the community besides the wealthy: the poor, for example, could have access to the public fountains of fresh water and the public buildings. On the other hand, the money would not be used to provide them with affordable housing. So too poor citizens could come to the gladiator shows for an afternoon of entertainment, even if it did mean returning afterward to their poverty. And they could participate at civic religious festivals that involved animal sacrifices along with the banqueting that followed, providing a rare opportunity to eat meat. But that would not help them find a meal the next day. Despite the optimism of many scholars who want to insist that "it wasn't all bad," the occasional public benefits of euergetism were paltry in comparison with the need.[27] And we must remember that even these benefits came only to *citizens* (not to slaves and others) and only to those who lived in cities, in a world where 80 to 90 percent of the population were rural dwellers.

It is often claimed that the problems of poverty were mitigated by grain doles provided to the poor in major cities. But there are problems with imagining the doles made a huge dent in the ubiquitous poverty. For one thing, they were found only in a few of the cities of the empire (chiefly Rome). For another, they were again only for citizens, that is, free adult males. Moreover, they were not even available to all free adult males, but only certain ones, at most times a slice of the citizenry. In addition, the grain was not free, but discounted. And finally, the grain available for discount to a free adult male was enough, as a rule, to feed two people, not, say, a family of five.[28] As William Harris, professor of ancient history at Columbia University, puts it, the attempt to relieve hunger "was a marginal phenomenon in relation to the mass of Roman provincial destitution."[29]

It is also important to remember that these grain doles were never conceived of out of compassionate feelings toward those who were hungry. Ancient sources are unequivocal: governmental assistance, when it did happen, was driven by the very pragmatic concerns of the wealthy. In times of scarcity, riots did happen. We have accounts of senators and even emperors running for their lives from hungry crowds.[30] Yet still, as Harris writes, among the political and social elite of Rome, "poverty as such was never considered a 'problem'" and "no counter-measures significantly diminished the impact of Roman destitution prior to the advent of mass Christianity."[31]

This last point will be worth bearing in mind. It was only with Christianity that poverty and hunger broadly came to be seen as problems that required solutions.[32] Once the Christian church came to dominate the Roman world, the teachings of Jesus as carried on by his followers significantly changed the moral discourse and the practices that emerged from it. This new way of moral reasoning didn't solve poverty: "The poor you always have with you." But as we will see, it did redirect moral thinking and motivate both private individuals and, eventually, governments to care for the impoverished "other." Moreover, it eventually led both to social programs to help in the endeavor and to governmental assistance. These developments reflect a transformation of the moral conscience of the West that generated entirely new institutions focused on helping those in need.[33]

Forgiveness in the Greek and Roman Worlds

Providing financial assistance for those in need is obviously not the only way to love others. Even with no funds to spare, one can share a meal with a stranger, sit with one who is grieving, volunteer at a homeless shelter, or even just lend someone a hand. One of the most powerful expressions of love comes with no price tag at all, when we forgive someone who has done us harm and feels badly about it. Just as charity is a distinctively concrete expression of love, forgiveness is a particularly meaningful interpersonal expression, even when the conflict involves a complete stranger. As the word itself indicates, "for-give-ness" involves a gift—and in its purest sense, a gift is never required or obligatory. It is freely given.

In the discussion that follows, I will be promoting a bold thesis: "forgiveness" as a free gift was not part of moral discourse or practice in the Greek and Roman worlds. It was introduced into the Western world by Jesus.[34] To explain what I mean and justify my claim will require a good deal of explaining.

Like so many other English terms—including "love" and "charity"—"forgiveness" has come to be used in a variety of ways today, meaning different things to different people, especially in religious contexts. Some people reserve the term for "unconditional forgiveness," that is, forgoing anger, resentment, or retribution with no stipulations whatsoever against someone who has caused offense, even if the person does not ask for forgiveness or even want it. Many others use the term to designate forgoing further anger or retribution after some kind of penalty has been paid—as when people say that God "forgives" people because Jesus died for their sins. In that usage, "forgiveness" is graciously given, but not free of cost (Jesus paid the penalty). I will be using the term in a different way. To begin I need to explain the major categorical difference between a "word" and a "concept."

We have already seen that a single *word* can convey a variety of different (if related) *concepts*. The words "love" and "charity" can mean a range of things in different contexts. You don't love a child the same way you love a boss, let alone a house or a book. What a word means requires knowing which *concept* it conveys. I am not overly concerned with how the word "forgiveness" is used by other people (including ancient authors), because my focus is not on the word itself but on a particular concept I want to address. I say this in order to preempt someone from objecting, "No, that's not what forgiveness is!" I'm not saying how the word has to be used. I'm indicating what *I* mean by it in this context.

The concept of forgiveness I will be using has been developed by contemporary philosophers of ethics such as Charles Griswold, Martha Nussbaum, and the late David Konstan.[35] It involves a specific way of restoring an interpersonal relationship broken by a hurtful act. This restoration involves a sequence of events, each of which must transpire for the concept to apply. There can be minor variations in what the sequence entails, but in every case, it begins with one person willfully doing or saying something that hurts another, causing a kind of breach in their relationship. That is a requirement: the breach is caused by someone who has acted intentionally, knowing full well that the other person will be hurt. "Forgiveness," in the way I'm using it, then requires the following steps:

- *Recognition.* The offending party admits to themselves they knew their action would bring the victim pain, loss, or hurt . . . but they did it anyway.
- *Regret.* They wish they had not done it.
- *Remorse.* They also feel badly for the pain they have inflicted on the other.
- *Reformation.* They decide to change how they behave and not do such a thing again.
- *Repentance.* They communicate with the offended party, admitting they have done wrong and conveying their regret, remorse, and determination to change.
- *Request.* They ask the person to forgive them.
- *Resolution.* The victim does forgive them—that is, they forgo their resentment and/or anger and agree not to punish or penalize the offender in any way.

They will not do anything hurtful in return or require any further payment or penalty, whether material or emotional.
- *Reconciliation.* The two people are now restored to the relationship they had before. This does not necessarily mean they "forgive and forget." They will probably not forget, possibly ever, but once more they are on good terms.

The main point I want to stress is that "forgiveness" in this sense is freely given out of love. There can, of course, be egoistic motives as well. The forgiver may benefit from the restored relationship, for example, and that may be one of the driving factors for choosing to forgive. Even in this case, though, part of the decision to forgive, if not most of it, must be driven by altruism.

Another point I need to reiterate: this concept is decidedly not "unconditional forgiveness." There *are* conditions. The offending party has to experience regret and remorse and repent. But that's all they have to do.

This concept of forgiveness is not to be confused with "atonement," although the terms are often muddled up, even among theologians and other thinkers. "Atonement" literally refers to a restored relationship in which two individuals (or groups) who were at odds become "at-one" ("at-one-ment") because a price has been paid, a penalty assessed, or a punishment meted out. By its very nature, atonement is not freely given. It is a kind of retributive justice.

One way to imagine the difference is to liken it to a financial arrangement (an admittedly imperfect analogy since, like all analogies, it is not precise). Suppose I have loaned you $1,000 and given you a year to pay me back. The year passes and you tell me you don't have the money. There are several ways we could deal with the situation. I could simply give you more time to pay. Or I could restructure the loan and agree to let you off for $300. I could have you work it off, say, by employing you around the house for fifty hours. You could arrange for someone else to pay for you—you call your brother, he pays the debt, and then we're good. Or I could make you pay in some other way: take your car, take you to court, or send in Vinny and the boys.

All of these could in theory lead us to be back on good terms (except the Vinny option). But none of them is forgiveness as I am using it. Forgiveness is when you come to me, admit you can't pay, express real regret and remorse, apologize, and ask me to forgive the loan. And I do so. There is no repayment, restructuring, penalty, or punishment.

Something similar can happen with a moral debt. Any of us who has ever been burdened with regret and remorse for an awful thing we have done and then received a free gift of forgiveness knows firsthand how incredibly liberating it is, what an act of true grace.

When the concepts of forgiveness and atonement are understood in this way, they are mutually exclusive. Forgiveness is not possible if there is atonement and where there is atonement there is no forgiveness. In the Christian context, to say that Christ died for your sins so God would "forgive" you is a confusion of categories. God can forgive. Or he can accept an atonement. But logically, he cannot do both at once.

As I stated earlier, the concept of forgiveness as understood by contemporary ethical philosophers could not be found in the Greek and Roman worlds. It arrived through the teachings of Jesus. This is a radical claim, but I am not the first to make it. It was most famously asserted by the great philosopher and political theorist Hannah Arendt, decidedly not a Christian apologist, who maintained: "The discoverer of the role of forgiveness in the realm of human affairs was Jesus of Nazareth."[36] Her view has been disputed, but I think she was right. Jesus taught forgiveness, not atonement; for Jesus, that applied both to sins against God and hurtful actions toward others.

The irony, as I will later show, is that almost immediately after Jesus's death, his followers reverted to traditional Greek and Roman views, abandoning his teachings on forgiveness and insisting on the importance of atonement, claiming that Jesus's entire mission, in fact, was to die for the sins of others in order to restore their relationship with God. God, in this view, does not freely forgive. His justice needs to be satisfied, a penalty has to be paid, and Jesus paid it.

Before explaining the evidence for these views in chapters to come, I need to discuss the wider Greek and Roman context within which Jesus and his followers lived.

It is not really possible to know why one culture or another has not developed words for certain phenomena or embraced certain concepts. But often one can make a plausible guess. In light of what we have discussed about the ideology of dominance in Greek and Roman antiquity, it would make sense that forgiveness in the sense I am using would not have arisen there. In a world where the powerful are right to lord it over the weak, any damage done to an inferior would not require forgiveness. If, on the other hand, a powerful person were offended by someone weaker, they would have little or no incentive to forgive. The more natural response would be to exact a payment. That is what we find throughout our ancient sources.

In some instances, an offended party might pardon the transgressor, but not in the sense of forgiveness I've been discussing. The ancient Greek word typically translated as "forgiveness" is *sungnōmē*, which literally means "to know with." That is, it involves a "meeting of the minds." As David Konstan, professor of classics at Boston University, convincingly argued, this term, from Aristotle onward, refers to situations in which an offender is pardoned only because they have convinced their victim they either had no real choice or acted in ignorance.[37]

Suppose you are a wealthy city official whose wife was attacked on the street and robbed of her jewelry. You learn the culprit's identity and have your slaves track him down and bring him to you. You threaten him with serious bodily harm. But if he pleads his case and convinces you he didn't realize the woman he robbed was your wife—it was a case of mistaken identity—you might let him off the hook. Alternatively, if he convinces you that someone else compelled him to do it—say, they threatened to kill his daughter unless he committed the deed—you might accept he had no real choice and let him go. In either case, you would agree there were mitigating circumstances; your power and honor were not willfully put under attack.

Thus, with *sungnōmē*, the punishment is rescinded because of a good excuse, not because the offender regrets having willfully and knowingly done the harm.

On other occasions in antiquity a powerful person might show mercy simply because an offender begged for it. This sometimes happened in times of war, when kings and generals would respond to pleas of mercy by being openly and gratuitously magnanimous, furthering their reputation for superior virtue. But yielding to supplications is not the same as providing forgiveness in the terms I've expressed. As Konstan has pointed out, supplications are not normally expressions of regret and remorse. Captured leaders of an opposing army might indeed regret going to war in the first place. But they rarely would feel remorse for the casualties they have caused. They would be terrified at the prospect of being tortured to death and plead with all their might to be shown mercy by the virtuous and magnanimous conquering general.

Thus the concept of forgiveness as I'm using it is quite different from both *sungnōmē* and mercy shown to supplicants. All this will change with the teachings of Jesus, who insisted his followers forgive one another freely without retribution or repayment, and claimed this is how God himself acts toward those who had transgressed his law and repent. As with charity, this understanding of forgiveness, both human and divine, was intimately connected with Jesus's broader understanding of love.

Conclusion: Then and Now

The term "pagan" has taken on derogatory connotations in modern times, often being used to denigrate someone as an unethical lout ("my next-door neighbor is a real pagan"). Historians of antiquity, however, continue to use it as a neutral term to refer to anyone who was neither a Jew nor a Christian. Many people today do think of the average Roman pagan as an unethical lout, but that's unfair to our cultural ancestors. In most ways, average Romans were just as moral (or immoral) as Westerners today: they loved their children, spouses, and friends; did good things for the people they knew; believed in honesty, justice, and integrity; and worked to make their lives and the lives of their loved ones better.

As we've seen, one of the major differences between now and then involves the target of their altruism. In very rough terms, we might think of Greek and Roman altruism as "tribal," in that it was almost always directed toward those who were genetically or socially related.[38] Part of the reason for that—though not the only one—involves the basic conditions of antiquity. In our day, we can help those who are suffering outside our personal spheres because we know about them, read about them, and sometimes visit where they live. We have the technology to send relief to earthquake victims in Pakistan or starving children in Somalia. Ancient citizens of, say, Ephesus or Antioch would never have engaged in these kinds of relief efforts. They didn't have the institutional framework for disaster relief or the technological ability to intervene for those living far away. More than that, rarely would they have even heard of disasters in remote places. No one will support hurricane victims in Haiti if they've never heard of Haiti.

Another difference between now and then involves the ideologies governing social relations. Most people in the West today at least pay lip service to the ideas of human equality, that all people have the same basic rights, and that the strong should not oppress or exploit the weak. In practice, of course, it rarely works that way, but at least it is a widely held ideal and many people strive for it. Not so for most people in Greek and Roman antiquity. More common was the recognition that "the strong do what they can and the weak suffer what they must."[39]

There certainly were peacemakers in antiquity and there must have been large numbers of people, especially the oppressed, who did not much appreciate the common worldview. Even so, dominance was the dominant perspective. Even among philosophical thinkers there was almost no resistance to the idea: no moral objections to the slaughter of innocent populations in times of war, no protests against the exploitation of rural populations to fund the luxuries of the urban elites, no urgent demands for the redistribution of wealth from the very rich 1 to 5 percent of the population to the 64 to 80 percent who were either living on the very brink or completely desolate. The wealthy and powerful were as a rule loving to their families, friends, and others of "their sort." But love had its boundaries. It was not expected to translate into charitable giving to the poor or penalty-free forgiveness to those who offended a person's honor.

This will change with Christianity, first in the ideology it promoted in its public rhetoric, then often in private behavior and, eventually, in public institutions. I will not be saying that Christianity has made everyone an altruist. Just a brief look at the headlines shows otherwise, with exquisite clarity. People will be people, whatever their religious commitments, and the difficult balancing act between egoism and altruism will always be among us.

Not surprisingly, the egoists appear still to be winning, and given modern human potential for doing good, their (our) culpability is far greater. For the past century or so, for the first time since life appeared on earth, we have the scientific and technological wherewithal to solve many of the most horrible forms of suffering. There is almost precisely no reason we could not feed the world's population if we wanted to. We simply lack the political will, and political will is ultimately driven by personal preference.

Even so, as I've said and will try to show, we have made progress from our ancient forebears: a much smaller portion of the world's population, for example, is starving now than then, and most of us deeply lament the suffering of innocent strangers and wish more were being done to stop it, even if we ourselves are not particularly committed to being part of the solution. Moreover, unlike in antiquity, a sizable number of good and hardworking people are committed to ridding the world of hunger, homelessness, illiteracy, injustice, oppression, and violence. An even larger portion of the Western population is involved in smaller ways, giving money to disaster relief efforts and celebrating those who give part or all of their lives to engaging in them. On both personal and institutional levels, we are different from our cultural ancestors of the pre-Christian world.

Christianity made the difference. I'll start to explain how and why by considering the teachings of Jesus in his own first-century Roman and Jewish context, and then showing how his teachings came to affect the whole of Western civilization.

Chapter Four

THE JEWISH ROOTS OF JESUS'S ETHICS

Jesus's early followers understood him in an astonishing variety of ways. Even in the New Testament, Luke's views differ in important ways from from Mark's. John is quite different from them both. Paul has his own perspectives, and the view set forth in Revelation is highly unusual. After the New Testament the variety becomes yet more pronounced, with some Christian teachers insisting Christ was not actually divine, or not human, or that he was literally the God of the Old Testament, or that he was sent by some other God altogether.[1]

In modern times as well, scholars of the historical Jesus hold widely ranging views, arguing that he was a kind of Jewish Cynic philosopher, military zealot, rabbinic mystic, countercultural guru, proto-Marxist or proto-feminist reformer, and so on. With that said, there is one aspect of Jesus that practically all modern scholars agree on. Whatever else you might say about him, Jesus was a Jew. To understand his life, mission, and teachings, you have to situate him in his own first-century Jewish context.

That realization swept through New Testament scholarship in the mid-twentieth century in the wake of the Holocaust, as scholars began to recognize how distorted understandings of ancient Judaism lay at the root and heart of modern anti-Semitism.[2] Historians began to delve more deeply into Judaism in Jesus's time and to reject old stereotypes based on superficial readings of Jewish texts from the period and Christianized understandings of what Judaism must have been like. This led to a major reevaluation of early Jewish traditions and practices.

Unfortunately, many people outside the realm of scholarship continue to hear, believe, and repeat perspectives that academics abandoned decades ago. Many of my undergraduate students continue to hold views of Judaism that I myself learned in my early years (which, alas, really were many decades ago)—that Judaism is a highly legalistic religion based on thousands of laws in the Old Testament that are both complex and impossible to keep; that the only way to obtain salvation in Judaism is to earn God's favor by meticulously doing all that he demands and that anyone who fails in the effort will be damned to hell with no hope of reprieve; that no one can possibly keep the myriad picayune laws of Moses and so everyone is bound for eternal torment. That is why they need Jesus, who died on the cross to deliver Jewish sinners from the desperate situation God had imposed on them by giving laws they couldn't keep and then sending them to hell for breaking them.

As it turns out, nothing about this understanding of Judaism is correct. That is worth knowing not only for understanding ancient Jews on their own terms but also for making sense of the teachings of Jesus, a thoroughly Jewish teacher who had an ancient Jewish (as opposed to contemporary Christian) view of the law.

To describe all the intricacies of ancient Jewish religion would take volumes. For our purposes in understanding the ethical teachings of Jesus, I will begin simply by explaining several perspectives shared among virtually all Jews at the time.

The Jewish Law

The Law of Moses is found in the four books of Exodus, Leviticus, Numbers, and Deuteronomy, which along with Genesis make up the Pentateuch, the "five books" that begin the Hebrew Bible and that are sometimes called the "Torah" (the Hebrew word for "law"). The Torah had always been a central component of Judaism, but not as an incomprehensible set of laws that could not be kept, an unbearable burden on those who wished to be faithful but knew it was impossible. On the contrary, throughout the history of Judaism—and certainly in Jesus's day—the vast majority of Jews considered the Torah a great joy to keep, the most amazing gift God could give his people. It was not seen as a burden, and it was never considered to be the way to earn salvation.

According to Scripture, God gave his people the Torah only *after* they had been saved. They had been God's "chosen ones" from the time of their remote ancestors, and he proved his loyalty and commitment to them by bringing them out of slavery in a foreign land, as recorded in the book of Exodus. After that, God gave them his law through Moses, but not as a way to be saved. They had already been saved. The Torah was a set of instructions to guide them as God's chosen ones.

Even today, most people who believe in God want to know how he wants to be worshipped and how he wants us to live. Wouldn't it be great if God would simply tell us? That's what the Torah does. Even though the word "Torah" is usually translated fairly woodenly as "law," it means something more like "guidance" or "instruction." Nearly the entire Torah focuses on two issues: how God's chosen ones are to worship him and how they are to live their communal lives together.[3] That is to say, the God of the universe explains what every religious person desperately wants to know. How good can it get?

The Law begins with the Ten Commandments (Exodus 20), which can be grouped into two parts: laws about worshipping God ("You shall have no other gods before me"; "Do not make idols") and laws about how to live in community ("You shall not murder"; "You shall not bear false witness"). Is there anything particularly burdensome about these laws? Of course not. The same goes for the rest of the Torah, where more issues are addressed, both cultic (how to worship) and ethical (how to behave).[4]

Cultic laws include instructions on festivals to observe, sacrifices to perform (and for what reasons), foods to avoid, etc. Ethical laws involve explicit directions about activities to avoid (sorcery; sex with animals) and to do (pay a fine if your ox misbehaves; show respect to the elderly). Many of the laws about community interactions involve case studies: if your ox gores your neighbor, this is the fine you must pay; if you accidentally strike a pregnant woman and she miscarries, this is the penalty.

These laws were never meant as a way to earn salvation. Israelites understood they were given as a gracious guide for how to live, and they accepted this guidance and often did their best to follow it out of love and devotion. When they failed, there were provisions for how to dispel God's displeasure, for example through repentance or certain sacrifices. No one was going to be perfect; that was one reason there was a sacrificial system in the first place. Jews prior to Jesus never imagined they would need a messiah to die for their sins: they had atoning sacrifices and God was forgiving. We have no record of Jews expecting a future, suffering messiah, as I will explain more fully in chapter 5.

Understanding the law this way is key to making sense of the ethical teachings of Jesus. Like all Jews of his day, he would have subscribed to the teachings of the Torah, as well as to the ethical guidance found in other books of Scripture. The Hebrew prophets, for example, consistently declare that God's people have fallen short of his commands—Isaiah, Jeremiah, Ezekiel, Hosea, Amos, take your pick: God's own people have forsaken his ways and he will therefore punish them. Or he has punished them. Or he is punishing them. These prophets repeatedly urge people to return to God's ways and do what he demands to keep from suffering an utter crisis of destruction or exile.

Many Christians today assume the Hebrew prophets are principally focused on foretelling the coming of Jesus. But anyone who simply reads the books from beginning to end will see that is decidedly not the case. Invariably, the prophet indicates when he is writing, what situation he is addressing, and what he wants his readers and hearers to do in order to avoid the catastrophes soon to hit, sent from God because they have not obeyed him. Some prophets such as Hosea focus on cultic issues: the people of God have abandoned him to worship other gods. Others focus on more ethical issues connected with exploiting the weak, robbing the poor, or refusing to help those in need. In our minds, these might seem like quite separate things—how to worship and how to behave—but in the Jewish Bible they are an amalgam of two key aspects of what it means to be faithful.

With respect to how Israelites have failed to behave toward one another, two of the earliest prophets, Isaiah and Amos, have a lot to say. As four examples out of a multitude of passages:

> *Your princes are rebels*
> *And companions of thieves,*
> *Everyone loves a bribe*
> *And runs after gifts.*
> *They do not defend the orphan,*
> *And the widow's cause does not come before them (Isaiah 1:23)*

> *The* **LORD** *enters into judgment with the elders and princes of his people. . . .*
> *What do you mean by crushing my people,*
> *by grinding the face of the poor? says the Lord* **GOD** *of hosts (Isaiah 3:14–15)*

> *Thus says the* **LORD**:
> *For three transgressions of Israel,*
> *and for four, I will not revoke the punishment;*
> *because they sell the righteous for silver,*
> *and the needy for a pair of sandals—*
> *they who trample the head of the poor into the dust of the earth,*
> *and push the afflicted out of the way (Amos 2:6–7)*

> *I know how many are your transgression,*
> *And how great are your sins—*
> *You who afflict the righteous, who take a bribe,*
> *And push aside the needy in the gate (Amos 5:12)*

Throughout these prophets we find a recurring emphasis on God's concern for the poor, the outcast, and the vulnerable. He expects his people to be actively concerned as well, helping rather than exploiting those in need.

Jesus, Scripture, and Other Jewish Teachers

Living centuries later, Jesus shared the Hebrew prophets' assumptions about what it meant to live as God wants—above all, to care for others and especially those in need, rather than focusing on one's own life and desires. The "Golden Rule" is one of Jesus's best-known sayings: "Do unto others as you would have them do to you." Or as he expresses it in the Sermon on the Mount: "Everything that you want others to do for you, do also for them; for this is the law and the prophets" (Matthew 7:12). This "rule," then, summarizes all of Scripture.

Jesus was not the first to articulate this rule: it can be found in a range of even more ancient cultures, from classical Greece to ancient China. Often it was expressed in the negative: do not do to someone else what you do not want them to do to you (Herodotus, *History*, 3.142; Confucius, *Analects*, 15.23).[5] Among Jewish teachers in Jesus's day, it was articulated most famously by Rabbi Hillel in a rather amusing anecdote. A gentile approached the great teacher and asked him to teach him the Torah while standing on one foot. Hillel did so, lifting one of his legs and saying: "That which is hateful to you, do not do to your fellow. That is the whole Torah: all the rest is commentary" (Babylonian Talmud, *Shabbat*, 31).[6]

Many of Jesus's other teachings also can be found in Jewish tradition before his day. Interesting examples come from someone else named Jesus, living two centuries earlier. This other Jesus calls himself "the son of Eleazar son of Sirach." His book, *The Wisdom of Jesus Son of Sirach* (Ben Sira), or *Sirach* for short, is one of the deuterocanonical writings that Roman Catholics and Greek Orthodox accept as part of the Old Testament, but Protestants relegate to the Apocrypha. Jesus son of Sirach wrote in Hebrew, but his book was mainly preserved in a Greek translation made by his grandson.

Some of the many ethical teachings of Jesus son of Sirach are intriguingly similar to those of Jesus of Nazareth. Consider the following:

> **Jesus son of Sirach:** "Do not reject a suppliant in distress, or turn your face away from the poor; Do not avert your eye from the needy and give no

one reason to curse you" (Sirach 4:4–5, NRSV). **Jesus of Nazareth:** "Give to all that ask of you; and do not turn away the one who wants to borrow from you" (Matthew 5:42).

Jesus son of Sirach: "Stretch out your hand to the poor, so that your blessing may be complete" (Sirach 7:32); **Jesus of Nazareth:** "Blessed are you who are poor, for yours is the Kingdom of Heaven" (Luke 6:20).

Jesus son of Sirach: "The Lord overthrows the thrones of the rulers, and enthrones the lowly in their place" (Sirach 10:14); **Jesus of Nazareth:** "The first will be last and the last first" (Matthew 20:16).

Jesus son of Sirach: "The greater you are, the more you must humble yourself, so you will find favor in the sight of the Lord" (Sirach 3:18); **Jesus of Nazareth:** "Everyone who humbles themselves will be exalted and the exalted will be humbled" (Luke 14:11).

Jesus son of Sirach: "Someone becomes rich through diligence and self denial . . . and he says 'I have found rest, and now I shall feast on my goods!' He does not know how long it will be until he leaves them to others and dies" (Sirach 11:18–19); **Jesus of Nazareth** [speaking about the "rich fool" who builds bigger and better barns for all his produce and says]: "'Soul, you have ample good laid up for many years; relax, eat, drink, be merry' but God says to him 'You fool! This very night your life is being demanded of you'" (Luke 12:16–21).

Jesus son of Sirach: "Do not delay to return back to the Lord and do not postpone it from day to day; for suddenly the wrath of the Lord will come upon you and at the time of punishment you will perish" (Sirach, 5:6–7); **Jesus of Nazareth:** "The time is fulfilled, and the kingdom of God has come near; repent, and believe in the good news" (Mark 1:15); "At that time there will be great suffering, such as has not been from the beginning of the world until now, no, and never will be. . . . Truly I tell you, this generation will not pass away until all these things have taken place" (Matthew 24:21, 34).

Clearly these teachings are not identical, and many of Ben Sira's teachings are not found in the Gospels or Jesus's teachings in *Sirach*. My point is that the two had very similar emphases, along with distinctive twists of their own, as had other Jewish teachers at the time.[7] Comparable teachings sometimes pop up in the works of Greek and Roman moral philosophers as well, but many of the key interests of Jesus and other Jewish teachers, such as a focus on the poor and needy, are almost entirely lacking in pagan circles.

If many of Jesus's ethical teachings were not revolutionary in his own Jewish context, why have I been saying they, in particular, transformed the conscience of the Western world? Why not say that Jewish teachings did? For two reasons. One is that, as I will try to explain, some of Jesus's distinctive emphases were not shared by most of his Jewish compatriots, and yet remain important to Christians still today. The other is that it was Christianity, not Judaism, that took over the Roman world. By the fifth century, the majority of the Roman world was Christian. The emperors were Christian. The ethical teachers were Christian. Most people were thinking in Christian ways. And these widely accepted Christian teachings—many of which stood at odds with Greek and Roman moral philosophy—were rooted specifically in the sayings of Jesus.

A Defining Feature of Jesus's Teachings

There is one other important feature of Jesus's historical and cultural context we need to consider before turning to a more detailed consideration of his ethical instruction. There were numerous Jewish teachers, ideologies, and ways of understanding Scripture in his day. Here we do not need to delve into the distinctions between, say, Pharisees, Sadducees, Essenes, and others.[8] But we should consider one particular religious perspective that significantly influenced Jesus's ethical teachings, a view that emerged within Judaism some two hundred years before Jesus's public ministry, after most of the Hebrew Bible had been written. It is a perspective that radically shaped the thinking of many Jews of Jesus's day, including both Pharisees and Essenes, but also John the Baptist immediately before Jesus, Jesus's own disciples, the earliest converts to the faith after his death, and the apostle Paul a bit later. Scholars have labeled this perspective "apocalypticism."

Around the time of a Jewish uprising called the Maccabean Revolt in the 160s BCE, some Jewish thinkers developed an explanation for national and individual suffering that differed significantly from the teaching of the Hebrew prophets. These thinkers came to realize that Jews in Israel were not experiencing extreme hardship because they refused to keep the Torah, but precisely because they were keeping it. This suffering could not, therefore, come from God; it must be caused by powers opposed to God and those he had chosen.

By this time the nation of Judah had experienced a series of military and political disasters, going back centuries to the Babylonians, whose troops destroyed Jerusalem and the holy temple in 586 BCE, to the Persians who conquered the Babylonians and took over the rule of the Promised Land in 539 BCE, to the Greeks under Alexander the Great, who conquered the Persian empire and imposed his will on what was now called Judea in 330 BCE, to the Egyptians who took over the land after the death of Alexander in 323 BCE, and to the Syrians who wrested away control of the land in 200 BCE. Some decades later, the Syrian king decided to bring cultural unity to his vast realm by compelling its inhabitants to adopt Greek culture, which had originally been brought to the Eastern Mediterranean by Alexander. For Jews, this attempt at enforced acculturation had serious ramifications. Their own distinct customs were not simply traditional; they were enjoined by the sacred Torah itself. A clash arose when Syrian officials proscribed features of Torah observance, such as circumcision and kosher food laws, on pain of death.

It was difficult for some Jewish scholars at the time to imagine that the ensuing tortures and martyrdoms had been inflicted directly by God as punishment, since they resulted from *obedience* to the law rather than disobedience. This led them to believe there must be other superhuman, cosmic powers standing in opposition to God and his people. These powers could not very well attack God directly; but they could attack the people who sought to obey him. Scholars today label this perspective "apocalypticism," from the Greek word *apocalypsis*, which means a "revealing" or an "unveiling." Those

Jews who held to it believed God's relationship to the world was not as Israelites had always thought. God had now "revealed" to them heavenly truths that could make sense of their dreadful human realities.

The apocalyptic view entailed a dualistic understanding of reality, a conflict between the forces of good and evil. The almighty God had a less mighty but nonetheless formidable counterpart, eventually construed as the Devil. The Devil cannot be found in the Hebrew Bible. A figure named "the satan" does appear in several passages, most famously in Job 1–2. The name "Satan" means "adversary," but he is not God's adversary. He is the one who plays "devil's advocate" at God's council meetings and is then dispatched to bring suffering on the righteous man Job at God's bidding. With the rise of apocalyptic thinking, this Satan figure came to be configured as the Devil: an evil supernatural being, possibly a fallen angel, who wreaks havoc on earth in opposition to God. He came to be known by a variety of designations: Satan, Beelzebub, Beliar, the Prince of the Power of the Air. In this view, the Devil is not working by himself. Just as God has angelic beings doing his bidding, the Devil has his demons, principalities, and powers that cause suffering and wreak havoc among the righteous and bring power and dominion to the wicked.

Different Jewish apocalypticists had different understandings of how these forces of evil came into existence, but all agreed they were not eternal and would not hold sway forever. On the contrary, for unknown and mysterious reasons, God had relinquished control of this world to these alien powers, allotting a set amount of time for them to do their worst. Here at the end of the age, things were spiraling out of control. But the reign of terror was nearly over. Soon God would intervene in human history to overpower the forces of evil, either destroying them or sending them to eternal torment.

This coming judgment was reserved not only for superhuman beings making life miserable for the people of God but also for everyone who had sided with them. In this dualistic construction of good and evil, everything and everyone was on one side or the other. There was no neutral territory. When the end came, those who had remained faithful to God would be rewarded. In the beginning, God had made this world a paradise, a Garden of Eden for humans to inhabit forever; but they strayed and were cast out. God's plans, however, cannot be thwarted. His faithful ones were destined to enjoy the paradise he had made for them. The Kingdom of God would be here on earth.

But what of all the others, the masses of humanity who rejected the true God and preferred to serve evil? These people might prosper now, but when God's day of judgment arrived, they would be taken out of power and brutally annihilated. And that applied not only to those who happened to be living at the time. At the time of judgment there would be a resurrection of the dead. Everyone who had ever lived would be raised back to life, the righteous to be rewarded in the eternal kingdom of God, the wicked to be shown the error of their ways and subjected to a painful annihilation, to last for all time.[9]

Jewish thinkers had various ways of understanding how all this would happen. In the prophecies of Daniel—the final book of the Hebrew Bible to be composed, around 167 BCE—the protagonist Daniel foresees a sequence of evil kingdoms, portrayed as savage wild beasts emerging from the sea, one worse than the other, creating horrible suffering among God's people (Daniel 7).[10] Then he sees a humanlike figure descending from heaven to destroy the wicked forces and establish God's new kingdom. Daniel calls this cosmic judge "one like a son of man." In later Jewish apocalyptic texts, he is called a variety of things, including "the Son of Man"—a term Jesus himself used (for example, Mark 8:38).

Jesus taught that the Son of Man was coming from heaven in judgment to bring God's kingdom. People needed to turn back to God and commit themselves to following his ways. This message is found in the first words Jesus is recorded as saying: "The time has been fulfilled, the Kingdom of God is near! Repent and believe this good news" (Mark 1:15). It is easy to skip over these words without reflecting on them, but they embody a profoundly apocalyptic message. "The time has been fulfilled"—that is, there is a certain amount of time that has been allotted to this age, and it is up. "The Kingdom of God is near"—that is, the long-awaited utopian kingdom ruled by God through his chosen one is almost here. "Repent and believe the good news"—that is, turn back to God and devote yourself fully to him, trusting that the end of your suffering is imminent.

Throughout his teachings, Jesus declared this kingdom was "near" and "coming soon." In Mark's Gospel he tells his disciples, "Truly I tell you, some of you standing here will not taste death before they see the Kingdom of God having come in power" (Mark 9:1). In other words, it will happen in their lifetime. Or as he says later: "Truly I tell you, this generation will not pass away before all these things take place" (Mark 13:30). The end was not thousands of years away, or centuries, or even decades. No one knows exactly when it will come, but it is very near: "And so I say to you what I say to everyone: 'Watch for it'" (Mark 13:36).

As we will see, this view significantly affected Jesus's ethical teachings about how to live here at the very end of time. But when the end did not arrive, his followers began to alter his teachings in significant ways.

Finding the Historical Jesus

Knowing what Jesus actually said and did is not an easy task: we simply don't have the kinds of sources historians need for high levels of certainty. It is one thing to write an account of the life of Billy Graham: we have thousands of eyewitness reports, myriad newspaper and journal articles, his own writings, film clips, recorded radio programs, living relatives and friends and associates to consult, and on and on. With the life of Jesus, we have none of the above. It is difficult to describe the life and teachings of an itinerant preacher from a remote region of the Roman Empire two thousand years ago. On the upside, we know far more about Jesus than just about anyone else from his part of the world at the time (or most any other time in antiquity). But the gaps in our knowledge are significant, and even the information that fills the gaps is regrettably sparse, sometimes contradictory, and not always reliable.

To know about *any* figure of the past, of course, we need sources of information, and for the distant past, those sources are almost entirely written. Scholars do not rely on what "everyone says" about a historical figure, whether Abraham Lincoln or Abraham the father of the Jews. When "everyone says" something it is because they heard it from someone else, who heard it from someone else, who heard it from someone else (or, of course, who read what was written by someone else). Where did these someone elses get their information, say, about Jesus? Maybe your Sunday school teacher told you what he had learned in a Bible study. Where did the leader of the Bible study hear it? Maybe from the pastor. Where did the pastor hear it? Possibly her teachers in seminary. Where did her teachers hear it? Likely from books they read. Where did the authors of those books hear it? And so it goes . . .

Ultimately, for knowing about Jesus, we need ancient sources. But we have no written records about him from his actual lifetime. Our oldest accounts are based on what later authors heard or possibly read.

Historians interested in knowing about Jesus examine every possible source, evaluating their accounts critically to determine if what they say is probably accurate. The process of doing so is, in principle, not much different from how historians deal with sources for any other figure from the past, whether they lived a hundred or three thousand years ago. In every case historians prefer having numerous sources rather than just one or two; they hope some of these sources date to a time relatively close to the events they narrate; they determine whether any of the sources come from eyewitnesses or at least from writers who based their accounts on eyewitness testimony; they look for sources that are independent of one another, rather than simply repeating what was found in another; and they hope that some of these independent sources corroborate one another.

Historians pay special attention to contradictions between sources, alternative perspectives they present, and general plausibility. If a source reports that the Greek army marched from the capital of Persia to Athens in two days, or that Julius Caesar regularly vacationed in the Himalayas, or that the emperor Constantine said three Hail Marys before going into battle, they simply wouldn't believe it. Incredible claims are . . . not credible. Historians also pay careful attention to the biases of their sources; if an account is written to praise its protagonist for his superhuman accomplishments, whether the first-century pagan Emperor Vespasian or the eighteenth-century Jewish mystic Baal Shem Tov—both of whom are recorded doing incredible miracles based on eyewitness reports—critical scholars take careful note of what those accounts say, while understanding they were probably written in part to further the interests of their authors.[11]

With that said, what do we have by way of source material for Jesus? When it comes to Jesus's ethical teachings, nearly all scholars agree that our principal sources of information are the four Gospels of the New Testament: Matthew, Mark, Luke, and John.[12] Most people don't realize how unusually well-situated we are in this respect: about whom else from first-century Israel do we have four different accounts of his life and teaching? No one. So that part is very good indeed. The problem is that these accounts, by virtual consensus among critical historians, were written forty to sixty-five years after Jesus's death, by people who did not claim to be and almost certainly were not eyewitnesses, who lived in different parts of the world from Jesus and spoke (and wrote in) a different language, and who in many passages (but not all) are dependent on one another and yet frequently contradict each other elsewhere.

Moreover, each of these authors puts forth his own perspective on what Jesus did and said. None of them was a disinterested observer simply stating facts that were known; all were followers of Jesus who saw him as the Savior of the world and Lord of all. They each wrote their account to proclaim the "good news" (the literal word for "Gospel") so that others would be confirmed in their faith. By their very nature, in other words, our only surviving sources are unapologetically biased in their views.

That's bad news for historians who simply want to know what happened. The good news is that in numerous places we have multiple independent sources that confirm one another, and are fully consistent with other historical records, and that present information that does not appear to have been shaped by their authors' own biases.

Given the nature of our sources, there always have been and always will be many contentious issues among scholars who engage in the endeavor of determining what Jesus actually said and did, some of them major and lots of them minor. Major differences include the very basic questions of what Jesus was trying to achieve and why he was executed. Minor differences of opinion emerge all over the place, even among scholars who have the same basic overall perspective: Did Jesus actually do this or that thing? If so, what can we know about it? Did he actually teach this or that thing? If so, how did he word it?

Despite the problems and the controversies, there is very wide agreement on some key points: Jesus was a Jew from a rural area of Galilee in northern Israel. He was raised in a Jewish culture and learned at least some of the Jewish Scriptures and eventually became a teacher of the Jewish law. As an adult, he associated with the apocalyptic movement of John the Baptist and became one of his followers for a time. He eventually broke off and began his own public ministry in the Galilee region, preaching about the coming kingdom of God. He called twelve of his followers to be an inner circle. The last week of his life, he and his disciples journeyed south to Jerusalem to celebrate the annual Passover festival. While there, he caused a disturbance in the Temple and offended Jewish authorities. They arranged to have him arrested and then turned him over to the Roman governor, Pontius Pilate. Pilate put him on trial and immediately condemned him to crucifixion for insurrection against the state, charging him with calling himself the king of the Jews.

One other crucial point on which everyone agrees is that Jesus—whatever else he did and said—delivered extensive ethical instruction to his followers. It is still quite common today, even outside the world of scholarship, for people to say that Jesus was one of the great moral teachers of all time. Most people, however, have not considered the historical context within which Jesus delivered his moral instructions. Moreover, few people recognize—or at least allow themselves to believe—how extreme and divisive Jesus's ethical teachings were. That is usually because modern readers naturally assume that Jesus urged ethical behavior for the same reasons people do today. That is a major mistake.

Today, most people who spend time considering why they and others should be ethical have very practical goals in mind. It is commonly argued that we cannot live long and happy lives if we behave in ways hurtful to ourselves and others, and that society as a whole will not function well or for long if people regularly behave badly or contrary to social norms. That is to say, the incentive for moral behavior is usually personal welfare and the good of society for the long haul.

Not Jesus. For one thing, Jesus was not focused on personal happiness in this life. As I will explain, his ethics ran counter to the quest for a happy and comfortable life. Nor did he urge ethical behavior to promote the welfare of society for the long haul. He didn't think there was going to *be* a long haul.

Like other apocalypticists, Jesus expected the end of the age to come very soon. People needed to repent in preparation for the imminent day of judgment. They needed to live as God demands because only then would they survive the coming onslaught and enter into God's eternal, utopian kingdom. Jesus's ethics were a Kingdom ethics.

Recognizing this apocalyptic context vitally affects how we understand Jesus's teachings. For one thing, Jesus's demand for change was urgent: there was not much time left, and those who lived contrary to the will of God faced imminent destruction. Moreover, returning to God involved extreme demands. Over the centuries many, possibly most, people who have heard Jesus's teachings have thought he just could not mean them. But he did mean them, precisely because he thought there was almost no time left and the crisis of the moment required both urgent and radical action. As we will see in the next chapter, Jesus taught his disciples to abandon their homes, spouses, children, families, jobs, and everything else to be his followers. They were to sell all they had and give to the poor, with no concern to save up for a rainy day or even to have spending money for the current one. The end was imminent, and to enter the kingdom required a radical commitment.

In a sense, Jesus's ethical teachings were designed to implement the ideals of the future kingdom already in the present. Those who followed God's demands could begin to see what this utopian future would be like, a world of peace and no suffering. Jesus's followers could not actually inaugurate the kingdom: it would be brought by God in a cosmic upheaval on the day of judgment. But they could begin to experience the kingdom in a small way now as they devoted themselves to lives of love and fellowship. The kingdom of God was like a small mustard seed, which is the smallest of all seeds, but once planted grows and becomes an enormous bush. The kingdom started with Jesus's tiny band of followers, but it began to grow and spread; in the end, it would consume the world (Mark 4:31–32).

The parable of the mustard seed was a symbolic story of a natural phenomenon that holds a deeper spiritual truth. But it was also a kind of prophetic foreshadowing. Jesus and his followers had begun to embody the realities of the future kingdom in the here and now. In the kingdom there would be no hunger, so they were to feed the hungry now; no one would be without clothing or shelter, so his followers were to provide essentials to the impoverished around them; there would be no sickness, so his followers were to heal the sick; no one would be lonely, so his followers were to visit those in prison; there would be no demonic powers, so they were to cast out demons; there would be no war, so his followers were to practice peacemaking; there would be no injustice, so they were to help the oppressed and the outcast; there would be no animosity and hatred, so his followers were to love their enemies.

Those who chose to implement the ideals of the kingdom in this brief time before it arrived would be welcomed into it on the day of judgment. Those who refused—who continued their self-centered lives, adopting the Roman ideology of dominance and rejecting Jesus's urgent message to repent—would be left outside the kingdom with "weeping and gnashing of teeth," before being sent off to annihilation (see Matthew 8:11–12; 13:42).

Even though it appears that Jesus had little, if any, contact with non-Jews in his lifetime, he clearly understood that his ethical instructions were not only for his own people.[13] Jews were to treat non-Jews as they treated their compatriots, and gentiles who followed the ethical principles set forth in the Jewish Scriptures would thrive in the coming kingdom. That was because, for Jesus, when God intervened to overthrow the wicked rulers of this age, salvation would come to the whole *world*, not just to Israel. And so his message applied to those outside. Love crossed all borders. Jesus said gentiles would "come from East and West" to dine with the patriarchs of Israel in the coming kingdom, while many of the "sons of the kingdom" (that is, Jews) would be cast into the outer darkness (Matthew 8:11–12). So too, multitudes from among "all the nations of the earth" would be brought into God's glorious kingdom, to the chagrin of those who would be left out because they chose not to live for others (Matthew 25:31–46).

Jesus's Alternative Ideology

Some of Jesus's ethical principles would have resonated with pagans around the Roman world. Nearly everyone everywhere agreed it was wrong to murder, steal someone else's spouse, burn down their house, be governed by greed or passions, be ruthless, cruel, untrustworthy, and so on. But Jesus's ethics were also different in important ways. Not only were they rooted in the Hebrew biblical tradition and deeply informed by a Jewish apocalyptic worldview, they also were based on a very different understanding of what it meant to be human.

Jesus opposed the ideology of dominance otherwise accepted as common sense throughout the Greek and Roman worlds. His counter-ideology was anti-dominance, an ideology of service. Following Jesus meant not asserting power over others, not compelling them to do your will. Being a disciple meant living in service and submission, giving up power, possessions, and self-will.

This view was so contrary to ancient ideology and almost universal common sense that still today, two thousand years later, people have difficulty getting their minds around it, let alone endorsing it—especially in this period of national aggression and the assertion of personal rights, where the rich get richer, the poor poorer, the strong stronger, the weak weaker. It is the rich and strong who rule us, make our laws, control our media, and enforce their will. It was that way in Jesus's day as well, of course, and it has been that way in virtually all cultures and societies over the course of human history. Jesus, though, had a different view. Some of his followers today still accept his view, but as an empirical reality, most do not, even his most vocal supporters. Nearly everyone has come "to be served" not "to serve" (see Mark 10:45).

Jesus, however, repeatedly insisted that to be his follower required becoming as powerless and insignificant as a child (Mark 10:15); serving others instead of being served by them (Mark 10:45); becoming a slave to others (Mark 10:43–44); and taking up the cross and giving one's entire life for others (Mark 10:34–35). These injunctions are often treated, when they are not simply ignored, as prompts to be nice. They are rarely taken seriously, as actual instructions for how to live.

But Jesus was quite explicit. When two of his disciples, James and John, requested special places of power and glory in the coming kingdom, Jesus rebuked them and told the entire band of disciples to reject the ideology of this world that stressed the value of personal and social superiority: "You know that those who are supposed to rule the gentiles lord it over them and their great ones exercise authority over them. It is not to be this way among you, but whoever wishes to be great among you is to become your servant, and whoever wishes to be first among you is to be the slave of all" (Mark 10:42–44). This is one of many paradoxes taught by Jesus. To become great requires giving up greatness; to become most important requires giving up importance. It is not the masters but the slaves who are superior.

That is why Jesus says that "the last will be first and the first last" (Matthew 20:16). This wasn't a clever witticism for us to remember when stuck in the slowest line at checkout. He meant it. The lowly, poor, and outcast will be rewarded in God's coming kingdom; the powerful, rich, and influential will be humbled. This was an eschatological reality. The way to succeed before God was to fail in the eyes of the world. That is why no one should be called "teacher," "father," or "master." For "the one who is great among you will be your servant; and whoever exalts themselves will be humbled and whoever humbles themselves will be exalted" (Matthew 23:8–12). In this passage, Jesus is speaking specifically to religious leaders and condemning their sense of spiritual and moral superiority. Here is another thing that never changes.

What does Jesus think ministers in his name *should* do? When he sends his disciples to carry his ministry afield, he tells them explicitly to help those in need and take no money for it: "When you go, preach that the kingdom of God is near. Heal the sick, raise the dead, cleanse the lepers, cast out demons. You received without paying; give without being paid" (Matthew 10:7–8). Almost no one today would take that as a literal description of what Jesus wants of his ministers. It is completely impracticable. I don't disagree. But it is a mistake to think that Jesus meant to be practicable. Notice how the injunction begins: "The kingdom is near." Jesus's call for radical action was rooted in his apocalyptic sense that the world was soon to come to a crashing halt. The moment called for extreme measures. In all four Gospels, Jesus himself follows these measures emphatically and tells his followers to do so as well. They are to be enslaved in service to others.[14]

Altruism and Egoism in the Ethics of Jesus

In the next chapter we will see how this ethics of service played out in Jesus's specific teachings on love, charity, and forgiveness. Even this broad sketch of Jesus's ethics, though, shows how radically they differed from those of the Greek and Roman moral philosophers we discussed earlier. For centuries—if not millennia—the dominant ideology of domination dominated because everyone assumed it was natural. That's how ideologies work. They seem like common sense. But Jesus had a different sense. For him, it seemed obvious that people should serve others, not dominate them. In the end, this ideological conflict had world-altering consequences.

Even so, it would be a mistake to think that ethics in the Greek and Roman worlds were completely egoistic—always all about the self—and that Jesus's ethics were entirely altruistic. Neither is true. As we have seen, there was a good deal of altruism in the moral views pronounced by pagan philosophers and practiced by ancient peoples. Rarely was it extreme in the way Jesus insisted, and rarely did it involve others beyond family and close social relations, but it was nevertheless an important component of what it meant to live as a good person.

It is likewise difficult to see Jesus's ethics as entirely altruistic, especially if we consider that thorny issue of motivation. As we have seen, it is hard to think of any human activity as "purely" altruistic. That certainly applies to the life promoted by Jesus. Recall the incentive Jesus regularly gives for feeding the poor, clothing the naked, and caring for the sick. Those who do so will "inherit the kingdom of God." If the reason to live for others is to acquire eternal benefits for oneself, then these altruistic actions are necessarily motivated, at least in part, by an egoistic desire for reward. To be sure, since the rewards have been deferred to the life to come, they differ significantly from those propounded throughout the Greek and Roman worlds, where life in *this* world was principally what mattered. Since for most Greeks and Romans this one precious life is all there is, it is to be enjoyed to the utmost and lived to its fullest, in pursuit of *eudaimonia*.

Jesus and his followers took a different line. The "good life" entailed self-abnegation, a life of sacrifice now as a path to glory in the age to come. Readers may blanch at this idea. There surely must be something deeper to "love thy neighbor" than deferred gratification . . . right? Didn't Jesus want people to serve God and live for others with no concern for personal welfare? It is an understandable objection, but if true, why does Jesus so often incentivize this sort of sacrifice by appealing to the life to come? "Sell all you have and give to the poor, and you will receive treasure in heaven" (Mark 10:21). Why not leave the rewards out of it? Why not just say it's the right thing to do?

We can debate motivations and incentives, but what is clear is that Jesus's ethical injunctions focused not on improving a benefactor's character and personal well-being in life, but on assisting those in need. This realignment of what it means to be a good person radically affected Western civilization. When millions of people began to internalize Jesus's teachings—even just in part—and to implement them in their lives, it led to a transformation that was not only personal and internal but social and political. Eventually, the idea we should care for the hungry and the homeless, the outcast and the defenseless, became a dominant common sense.

Chapter Five

LOVE, CHARITY, AND FORGIVENESS IN THE TEACHINGS OF JESUS

If you are looking for a great conversation stopper at a cocktail party, tell someone you are a professional biblical scholar. They will almost always look puzzled, say, "Oh, how interesting," and wander off to talk with someone else. On occasion, though, your fellow imbiber will be pleasantly surprised and eager to dig in. Rarely does the digging go deep (it's hardly the right setting), and almost invariably, in my experience, it leads to a standard refrain, expressed with confidence, contrasting the Old Testament God of wrath with the New Testament God of love.

I'm never quite sure where to go with that one. Sometimes I simply ask, "Have you ever read the book of Revelation?"

The reality is that love is central to the Old Testament and wrath to the New. In the Old Testament, God loves the people of Israel, saves them from slavery in Egypt, teaches them how to relate kindly to one another, guides and assists them in their wanderings and struggles, and gifts them the Promised Land. One of the principal commandments given in the law of Moses, still recited daily by observant Jews, is to "Love the Lord your God with all your heart, with all your soul, and with all your might" (Deuteronomy 6:5). Another is "You shall love your neighbor as yourself" (Leviticus 19:18). Many people think these love commands come from Jesus. No. He was quoting Jewish scripture.

Wrath also figures prominently in the Hebrew Bible, invariably as God's righteous response to disobedience. He commands his people to worship him and him alone, and he instructs them to treat each other well and take care of those in need. When they choose to do otherwise, he responds by punishing them in hopes they will return to his good graces. Sometimes the punishment is purely retributive, but usually it is rehabilitative. God loves his people and wants the best for them. This is the message of nearly the entire Jewish Bible, from Genesis to Malachi.

The same can be said of the New Testament: Who would deny love is a central theme? God loves the world and sends Christ to die for its sins. Jesus lives a life of love, eventually sacrificing himself for others. He commands his followers to care for one another and to go much further, to love strangers and even enemies. After his death his followers form cohesive communities focused on mutual self-care and love of others.

At the same time, the New Testament contains a significant amount of divine wrath. Jesus preaches that those who have turned from God will face the full force of his anger: they will be cast into the outer darkness where there is weeping and gnashing of teeth and then thrown into fire to be annihilated. Paul too speaks about the "coming destruction," as do most of the other writers of the New Testament. The Apocalypse of John (also known as the book of Revelation) has much to say about the "wrath of God and of the Lamb," that is, Christ (6:16–17), and describes it in a variety of gory ways. Never does the book mention God's love for anyone or anything.

Thus both testaments are deeply rooted in love and wrath. Why then, in a Christian culture, is it common to contrast the Old Testament God of wrath and the New Testament God of love? My guess is that it is an unconscious but deeply ingrained bias against Jews and their Scriptures. In this view, Jesus teaches a gospel of love to save us from the Old Testament (that is, Jewish) God of wrath.

Even New Testament scholars shared this bias for a long time, and in many cases continued doing so even after the problem became more widely acknowledged in the field. For generations, college students and seminarians were taught that contrary to the harsh tones of Hebrew Scripture, the New Testament was focused on "love," the guiding principle for all ethical behavior. That, however, is simply not true. As we will see in the next chapter, after Jesus's death his followers embraced numerous ethical principles, some of which are surprisingly unrelated to the commandment to "love your neighbor as yourself."

As it turns out, the pendulum of scholarly opinion has swung in recent decades, not just somewhat away from the idea that love is the be-all and end-all of New Testament ethics but, in some circles, to the complete—and admittedly unexpected—opposite extreme. Some major New Testament specialists have argued that love is not a major theme *at all* in early Christian moral thinking. These are not just marginal scholars intent on making outlandish claims for attention. They include an erudite and learned New Testament interpreter who does not devote a single section to the concept of love in his 508-page book on New Testament ethics. Instead, he spends three pages arguing that love is not an important topic for discussing early Christian morality. In large part, he avers, that is because the term "love" has become "debased" in the modern world to the point that it has lost its meaning. It is even used, he notes, to refer to intimate relationships outside of monogamous heterosexual marriages. How, he asks, can such a profane term be useful for understanding the New Testament?[1]

I find it remarkable that anyone can discuss the ethics of the New Testament without plunging deeply into the importance of love, and I consider this rationale for excluding it disturbing. Empirically speaking, the word "love" is a key term in the New Testament: the verb *agapaō* is used 144 times, the noun *agapē* 117. Yet more important than the word is the concept, which can be expressed without using the word itself. If I say that a husband is so committed to his wife that he is willing to die for her, I am talking about the depth of his love, whether or not I use the actual word. The *concept* of love is ubiquitous in the New Testament.

In this chapter, I will be focusing only on the teachings of Jesus in their historical context; I'll devote the chapter that follows to a discussion of ethics in the New Testament as a whole. My contention is that love stands at the very center of Jesus's ethical instruction. My discussion is heavily influenced by the fact that Jesus inherited his ethical ideas from the Hebrew Bible and the Jewish traditions that developed after it. Jesus's apocalyptic views in particular played a significant role in his understanding of the importance of love here at the end of time. Moreover, this love for others was to be manifest materially through charitable giving and interpersonally through penalty-free forgiveness.

Love in the Teachings of Jesus

Greek moral philosophy principally focused on passionate love, *eros*, and friendly love, *philia*, topics Jesus does not address. *Eros* never occurs on Jesus's lips—or anywhere else in the New Testament. And in the early Gospels of Matthew, Mark, and Luke, which provide our most reliable reports of Jesus's teachings, Jesus never uses *philia* to refer to the positive emotion of affectionate or friendly love.[2] Jesus's teachings on love consistently use the noun *agapē* and its verb *agapaō*. As I noted earlier, this noun is never used in secular Greek before the New Testament, and when the verb is used it means something like "to cherish" or "to be fond of." The words do occur in the Greek translation of the Old Testament, but in the noun form only rarely even there. In the Gospels both words denote altruistic behavior and an active concern for the well-being of another.

As I discussed in the last chapter, Jesus's understanding of altruism is best understood in the broader context of his proclamation of the imminent day of judgment. To prepare for this impending crisis, people needed to "repent," a term that in Greek (*metanoeō*) literally means "to change one's mind or purpose." Those behaving badly needed to realize the error of their ways and live differently.

Not every Jew had the same idea of what that might mean, in practical terms. Many people today think of ancient Judaism as a kind of monolith, with all Jews basically sharing the same beliefs, holding the same perspectives, and engaging in the same religious practices. I am frequently asked what "the" Jewish view was of the messiah, or the afterlife, or abortion, as if there were a single view. That is much like asking, "What is the *American* view of the death penalty?" Or immigration? Or gun control? Well, which Americans do you have in mind?

In Jesus's day, Judaism was enormously complex. Even with our relatively abundant sources of information it is difficult for us to know just how variegated it was. Still, I can summarize some of the better-known forms of Judaism in order to set Jesus in his historical context and show how he aligned with some Jewish teachers, but stood at odds with others.

Here are four of the basic options. All of them accepted the basic Jewish perspectives I laid out in chapter 4, but emphasized different aspects of Judaism as of primary importance. These four emphases are not necessarily mutually exclusive: many Jews held some or even all of these views at once.[3]

The Law

Almost all Jews in Jesus's day revered the law of Moses, understanding that God gave it to his people to show them how to worship and live together in community. This was God's greatest gift and he meant for it to be followed. Doing so brought joy and happiness.

The problem is that much of the law is vague, often lacking detailed instruction about how it was to apply to diverging circumstances. One of the Ten Commandments, for example, says to observe the Sabbath as a holy day. That obviously means that a person is not to work on the Sabbath. But the Torah does not provide much detail about what counts as work. Is it work to harvest your fields? Almost certainly. But what if a hungry farmer goes into his field on the Sabbath just to pick something to eat? Is that work? There could be reasonable disagreements about it. What if a farmer walks through his fields and accidentally knocks off some of the grain? Is that work? Here again, some Jewish teachers might say no, of course not, others might say yes indeed: you may not mean to be harvesting, but you are. If that's the case, then walking through a field of ripe grain on the Sabbath would be a bad idea and should be forbidden. What if the plants haven't produced any fruit yet? Is it okay to walk through the field then? The questions keep coming.

By Jesus's day, some Jewish teachers had developed a set of detailed subsidiary laws that, if followed, would ensure that the mysteriously vague or general laws of the Torah were being strictly observed. Sometimes this has been called "building a fence around the Law": if you don't want to violate God's Law, these additional laws surrounding it make sure you do not get anywhere close. If you do not walk through an apple orchard on Sabbath, you won't accidentally knock off any of the fruit.

This multiplying of laws into a refined system of dos and don'ts may seem a nitpicky way of going about being religious, but it makes a good deal of sense. It is, after all, rooted in the desire shared by many religious people to do exactly what God wants. The more completely you do so, the better.

In Jesus's day, the sect of the Pharisees was particularly intent on providing these kinds of detailed interpretations of the law. The group eventually acquired a reputation among outsiders, especially early Christians, for legalistic hypocrisy, but that is not a helpful way to look at them. Pharisees were concerned with obeying God and took steps to make sure they did so. Later, rabbis who produced the holy texts of the Mishnah and the Talmud—which became the basis for much of Judaism down to our day—traced their lineage back to the Pharisees.

Pharisees are portrayed as Jesus's arch enemies in the Gospels and have traditionally been considered by Christian readers to be the "bad guys" of ancient Judaism. Jesus is most scathing in his attacks on Pharisees in the Gospel of Matthew (e.g., in chapter 23). Rarely do readers notice, however, that in Matthew Jesus also insists his followers keep the Pharisaic rules (Matthew 23:2). The problem, according to Matthew, is that (some? most? all?) Pharisees don't practice what they preach (e.g., Matthew 23:23–28).

It can be debated whether Matthew's view that the followers of Jesus should generally try to observe the Pharisees' practices were those of the historical Jesus, but it is clear that Jesus did not share the Pharisees' ultimate concerns. On the contrary, he appears to have thought that focusing on the scrupulous observance of minute details of the law can lead to missing its ultimate point: loving others. The historical Jesus maintained that following Jewish law meant taking care of the needs of others, even if that required breaking subsidiary laws. That is the principal reason for most of his conflicts with the Pharisees in the Gospels: Jesus thought it was indeed acceptable to eat grain in a field on Sabbath or heal one who was sick, so long as it was for the sake of human need. The Gospels indicate the Pharisees thought otherwise. Whether they (all? most? some?) actually did so is difficult to say.

The Temple

Every religious Jew believed it was important to follow the law of God, but some maintained the law was ultimately concerned less with quotidian behavior than with the proper worship of God. That meant observing the sacred rituals set forth in the Torah, especially with regard to the liturgical practices connected with the temple in Jerusalem and the sacrifices performed there.

Unlike Greek and Roman religions in which a god could have sacred shrines in numerous places and sacrifices could be performed in a variety of ways in accordance with local customs, mainline Judaism understood there was to be only one temple for God. Only there could sacrifices be performed, only in the ways God instructed, and only by priests God designated. For those who focused on this aspect of Judaism, living for God meant engaging in these cultic practices.

The original temple in Jerusalem was built by King Solomon in the tenth century BCE, but was destroyed by the Babylonians in 586 BCE and then rebuilt about fifty years later. In Jesus's day the temple had been expanded and turned into a truly magnificent structure, with surrounding walls some ten stories high, glorious architecture, and a central sanctuary in which God himself was thought to dwell in a room called the Holy of Holies, that is, the most holy place. God, of course, was everywhere, but his physical presence was in this room, and no one was allowed to enter except once a year, on the Day of Atonement, when the Jewish high priest would go behind the thick curtain that separated the room from the rest of the temple, into the presence of God, to begin a sequence of sacrifices that would atone for his own sins and the sins of the people.

Within the temple, outside the Holy of Holies, sacrifices were made regularly in accordance with instructions found in the Torah, especially in the book of Leviticus. These were to be made only by priests, the direct male descendants of Aaron, the brother of Moses, with the assistance of Levites, other descendants of Levi, one of the twelve sons of Jacob, who were not from the line of Aaron. There were numerous kinds of sacrifices to honor God, to thank him, and to atone for sins.[4]

The view that the temple-centered worship of God was the most important aspect of religious life was most commonly associated with the group of Jews called the Sadducees, who appear to have been principally aristocratic Jews residing in Jerusalem. In the days of Jesus, they were the power players in the city, making up the majority of the local ruling council, the Sanhedrin, the leader of which was the high priest himself. In the Gospels, the Sadducees do not play a major role in Jesus's ministry before his final week; he was in Galilee and they were in Jerusalem. They do make their appearance, though, when he comes to the city with his disciples to celebrate Passover. It is they, not the Pharisees, who decide to have him arrested and turned over to Pontius Pilate for punishment. As I'll later argue, the Sadducean leadership was especially incensed that an unknown preacher from Galilee opposed all they stood for, the temple and its sacrificial practices.

Ritual Purity

Whereas the Pharisees and Sadducees play prominent roles in the Gospels, a third Jewish group called the Essenes is never mentioned at all. Ironically, we know more about them than the others because of our noncanonical sources. The Essenes are mentioned in the writings of the Jewish historian Josephus, the Jewish philosopher Philo of Alexandria, and the Roman polymath Pliny the Elder, but we know most about them because a large number of their own writings were discovered in the mid-twentieth century.

The Essenes stood in direct opposition to both the Pharisees and the Sadducees. They did not appreciate the oral laws of the Pharisees, which they saw as attempts to bypass the law's literal intent. The Essenes thought Pharisees were lacking in rigor. And they particularly did not look favorably on the Sadducees, who, in their judgment, endorsed corrupt practices of worship. In their view, the priestly leaders in the Jerusalem temple had led the people of Israel astray, in large part because the high priest did not descend from the correct, divinely appointed genealogical line as dictated by Scripture.

Rather than emphasizing what they saw as the technicalities of the Pharisees or the corrupt worship practices of the Sadducees, the Essenes focused on maintaining their own ritual purity. Some of them started monastic-like communities where they could practice their devotion to God apart from the contaminating influences of other Jews.[5]

Our principal source of information about the Essenes comes to us in the Dead Sea Scrolls, which were discovered in 1947 and appear to have been produced by a group of Essenes from a community near the wadi Qumran, about twenty-five miles east of Jerusalem, near the northwest edge of the Dead Sea.[6] The scrolls were apparently hidden by members of the community in surrounding caves at the time of the uprising against Rome that led to the destruction of Jerusalem in 70 CE. It is usually thought the community had hoped to retrieve its precious writings after the war ended, but was instead destroyed by the Roman armies.

There are numerous kinds of writings among these scrolls, including copies of the Hebrew Bible a thousand years older than any we had before, biblical commentaries, guidelines to be followed by community members in their lives together, and apocalyptic predictions of what was yet to come. It is clear from the scrolls that these Essenes expected an imminent day of judgment that would involve a prolonged military conflict with God's enemies (the Romans) from which they would emerge victorious, to be ruled, at last, by God through his human representatives. To prepare for this coming end of the age, members of the community were to observe strict practices of purity, maintaining their holiness so as to be ready for the final battle and the new period to be ushered in for God's faithful ones. In short, what ultimately mattered for the Essenes were not the oral laws of the Pharisees or the cultic practices of the Sadducees, but their own purity in anticipation of the coming great event that would bring in a new age.[7]

The Land

Other Jews at the time of Jesus had still another understanding of what it meant to be faithful to God and committed to his will: regaining the Promised Land from their foreign oppressors. Some of these Jews may well have been committed to the principles of one of the other groups we have mentioned, but they were not principally focused on keeping the law down to every last detail, engaging in cultic activities in the temple, or maintaining their ritual purity in isolation from the corrupting influences of society. God had promised the land of Israel to his people; he had later given it to them; others now had taken it away. It was time to take it back.

Jews with these aspirations did not form a single group with a set purpose, policy, and mission. Older scholarship sometimes did speak of them as a coherent entity, calling them "the Zealots," and there was indeed a group of that name discussed by the Jewish historian Josephus. But it did not appear until some decades after Jesus's day, at the time of the Jewish uprising against Rome in 66–70 CE. The basic ideals of this later group, however, were held by a swath of zealous Jews in earlier times. The Romans controlled the land of Israel and required Jews living there to pay taxes to support its rule. Some Jews found this untenable and contrary to the will of God. The land was theirs by divine right, and God planned to restore it to them. Just as he had driven out the Canaanites from the Promised Land in the days of conquest under Joshua, he intended to do so again. There would need to be a military uprising against the Romans.

Some of those who held this view anticipated that God would raise up a mighty warrior to lead the Jewish troops into battle against their enemies.

This would be a descendant of Israel's greatest king, David. In Scripture, God had promised David he would always have a descendant on the throne ruling Israel (2 Samuel 7:11–14). As we have seen, a Davidic dynasty did last four centuries, up until the Babylonian destruction of Jerusalem in the sixth century BCE. After that a sequence of foreign powers took control of the land: the Persians, the Greeks, the Egyptians, the Syrians—and now the Romans. But God was set to renew his promise and bring liberation through a new warrior king.

Kings appointed to the throne of Israel were ceremonially anointed with precious oil to show that God had favored them above all others. The word for "anointed" in Hebrew is *meshiach*, that is, "messiah." When there was no longer a king after the Babylonian destruction, some Jews came to anticipate that God would fulfill his Scriptural promise of an "eternal" Davidic kingship. A descendent of David—a messiah—would arise, one who would engage the enemy, renew Israel as a sovereign state, and rule over it as king.

Jesus was no zealot. He never raised an army and almost certainly had no intention of doing so. He did proclaim God's Kingdom was coming, and he may well have thought that he himself would be its ruler. That, at any rate, is why Pontius Pilate ordered his execution: Jesus called himself the "king of the Jews." But Jesus was no sword-wielding messiah. He was expressly opposed to taking up arms.[8]

It is not that Jesus was opposed to violence per se. A good deal of his message focused on the violent destruction soon to come. But like other apocalypticists of his day, Jesus did not think the kingdom would come through human military intervention. God himself would intervene, sending a cosmic judge from heaven, one called the Son of Man, to slaughter his enemies. This victorious judge would then appoint Jesus as the ruler of God's new kingdom, the "king of the Jews."[9]

When authorities in Jerusalem learned Jesus was declaring himself the future Jewish king, they had him arrested and sent to the Roman governor, Pontius Pilate, for trial. Pilate had no interest in the niceties of Jewish apocalyptic theology. Jesus's belief in a coming cosmic judge would have seemed visionary nonsense. But calling himself king was obviously a political matter.

As the current ruler of Judea, Pilate nipped the problem in the bud. Jesus's trial was probably very short. He was taken off and summarily nailed to a cross.

Jesus the Jew

Jesus identified with none of these various sects of Judaism. He regularly engaged in verbal duals with Pharisees over their priorities and interpretations, rejected the Sadducean emphasis on the temple and sacrifices, had no interest in strictly maintaining purity in isolation from others like the Essenes, and refused the path of organized violence. This may make Jesus seem like an outlier in his era, but the reality is that very few Jews belonged to any of these groups. The largest of them, according to Josephus, were the Pharisees, with just six thousand members. The world population of Jews at the time was something like 4 million. Most Jews didn't belong to *any* party, any more than most Americans belong to the Rotary Club or the Chamber of Commerce.

Even so, the views of these groups were broadly held by individual Jews. Other Jews no doubt had yet other views. Many Jews didn't have much of any view at all. Multitudes, often mentioned en masse in our sources, were not overly concerned in one way or another about being actively religious, just as many self-identifying Christians today would have a hard time proving it in a court of law.

And there certainly were many Jews with views similar to those of Jesus, for example, Hillel and Ben Sira. Most of them may not have been particularly outspoken about it or gathered disciples to spread their views, and none of them in the end started a religion that would take over the world. But other Jews certainly believed that God's ultimate desire for his people, and for all people, was to engage in active love with one another. That too was the teaching of Jesus, as repeatedly seen throughout our Gospel records.

Jesus and the Love Commandments

Jesus's first recorded injunction is to "repent" (Mark 1:15)—that is, to return to God by committing to obey his will as expressed in the Torah. The key question, then, involves what God ultimately wants. Jesus addresses the issue in our earliest Gospels of Matthew, Mark, and Luke, nowhere more clearly than in an account found in all three.

Mark gives the oldest version of the story. A Jewish scholar approaches Jesus and asks: "What is the primary commandment of them all?" Jesus's response would have resonated with most Jews: the most important commandment is the Shema found in Deuteronomy 6:4–6, "Hear O Israel, our Lord God is one Lord, and you shall love the Lord your God with all your heart, and all your soul, and all your mind, and all your strength." Unsolicited, Jesus then adds: "This is the second: 'You shall love your neighbor as yourself.'" This too is an important passage of Torah, a direct quotation of Leviticus 19:18. Jesus concludes by saying, "There is no commandment greater than these" (Mark 12:28–31). From the way Mark phrases Jesus's answer, one might assume he considers these two commandments equally important, or possibly even equivalent in meaning (to love God means to love your neighbor and vice versa). It is also possible that by listing them as "first" and "second," he may be prioritizing one over the other.[10]

Matthew's version of the story states Jesus's conclusion in even stronger terms: "On these two commandments hang all the Law and the Prophets" (Matthew 22:40). In other words, these two commandments are not only the most important ones, together they summarize all of Scripture. We should recall that the Ten Commandments themselves can be divided into two sets of injunctions: those centered on the worship of God (e.g., "You shall have no other gods before me") and those focused on life in the community (e.g., "You shall not steal"). Jesus's summary of the law via the two commandments he cites follows this pattern, but it is now expressed in terms of love. Love (and, by implication, worship) God with everything you have (heart, soul, mind, strength) and love your neighbor (attending to your communal life).

Despite its apparent simplicity, however, the second commandment contains some perplexing ambiguities, such as: Who exactly is my neighbor? Is it just the guy next door?

The answer is relatively clear in the original context of Leviticus 19:18: the "neighbor" refers to any fellow Israelite. The very same verse rephrases the term "neighbor" as "anyone of your own people." The command, in other words, does not require Israelites to love anyone outside their own community. In the narrative that follows—starting in the next book, Numbers, and then even more memorably in the book of Joshua—God in effect orders the Israelites *not* to love those outside the community. They are to slaughter the Moabites, the Midianites, the Canaanites, and others occupying "their" land (see, e.g., Numbers 31; Joshua 6). In Leviticus, the "neighbors" that Israelites are commanded to love may well be strangers, but they are Israelite strangers.

A second ambiguity in the love command is even more perplexing, though possibly not as often considered. How exactly can you be *commanded* to love someone? For that matter, how can you be commanded to love God? You may be commanded to do something (say, pray to God) or not to do something (make idols), but how can you be commanded to have an emotion? You can't decide to feel well disposed toward someone or to enjoy something. Emotions come over you, like it or not. What good would it be to order you to admire your teacher, adore the girl next door, or like broccoli? Are you required to feel something you don't?[11]

The love commandments make sense only when we consider the particular concept of love they promote. In the Old Testament, the word "love" can refer to an unusually fond attachment between friends (as with David and Jonathan; 1 Samuel 18–20) or to familial care (loving your children; e.g., Proverbs 4:3), to erotic passion (as in the Song of Songs), or to actions toward others that promote their interests rather than your own.[12] This last concept does not necessarily involve passion, attraction, or fondness, though it certainly can. What's more important is that it is visible in the way you treat others, which can, of course, be commanded. This must be the meaning of the term in Leviticus 19:18.

The love that is commanded, therefore, is a way of behaving. Loving your neighbor as yourself means treating them the way you treat yourself. You feed yourself, clothe yourself, provide yourself shelter, keep yourself out of danger, take care of yourself when you are sick, and so on. If you do those things for yourself, you should do them for a neighbor whenever they too need food, clothing, shelter, assistance, or nursing. These acts may be driven by emotions, but they don't need to be. You can certainly show love for yourself in these ways without feeling particularly pleased with yourself. Even when you do not like who you are, you usually still give yourself the food, clothing, and shelter you need. You should do the same for your neighbor who is in need, whether you like them or not.

This love command, then, is instruction to behave altruistically, not just toward family, friends, and other like-minded acquaintances, as in the Greek and Roman worlds, but toward *everyone* who shared the same ethnicity and religion. In the days of Leviticus, the nation of Israel would have been a relatively small and closed society. Centuries later, in the Roman period, the command to love fellow Jews was a bigger ask, since Jews were dispersed throughout the empire. Jesus, as we will see, expanded the definition of the love commandment even further.

I should note that this altruistic definition of love does not apply to the *first* commandment, the one requiring you to "love God" with all your being. Altruism involves engaging in activities that help someone else even at a cost to one's self. But that presupposes the other person needs some kind of help. That cannot apply to God in the Israelite or Christian tradition. The Lord of the universe does not "need" anything—no food, no clothing, no shelter. He certainly may *want* things, such as worship. But worshipping God is not providing what he needs; it is giving what he demands and deserves. And so loving God must mean something slightly different from loving your neighbor. Both commands require a focus on the other instead of the self. But for God, love means being fully committed to him and his demands; for your neighbor, it means being fully committed to them and their needs.

Jesus saw these two commandments as the heart and soul of the Torah. When he urged people to "repent," he meant they should turn their lives around and commit themselves to the worshipful and obedient love of God and to the concern for and altruistic love of their neighbors.

On one level, that may seem dead easy. How simple can it get? Love. On another level, it is well nigh impossible.

How can you actually love your neighbor as yourself if *everyone* is your neighbor? Even if your neighbor is just everyone in your country or just in your local community? Everywhere we turn, people are starving and homeless, while most of us have a roof over our heads, more than we need to eat, and a car in the garage; many of us have an extra bedroom or more, a second car, closets full of clothes, the wherewithal to eat out on occasion, and so on. What would it mean to love your needy "neighbor" as yourself? You could, surely, do more than you're doing now. But that would not be enough. There is no way you could afford to provide all these things to everyone in your community, let alone the world. The seemingly simple love command, when taken seriously, is clearly impossible. Just imagining following it literally is depressing.

Even so, it is once again a mistake to assume Jesus could not have meant it literally, or to console ourselves by imagining we are actually doing what he demands since we do our share. Loving your starving neighbor as yourself is not about doing your *part*; you don't partially keep yourself alive.

In Mark's Gospel, after Jesus answers the scholar's question about which is the greatest commandment, his interlocutor agrees with him: these two commandments are "much more than all burnt offerings and sacrifices" (Mark 12:33). In other words, giving oneself wholly to God and treating others as well as oneself are what God wants, not sacrifices performed in the temple. You can debate whether this shows that Jesus and his unnamed dialogue partner are actually *opposed* to temple sacrifices. Nothing in this particular text suggests they are. But it is clear that for them the cultic practices in the temple—even though commanded in the Torah—are not what ultimately matter before God. What matters is how people live in relation to one another.

From a historical perspective, it makes sense that someone from Jesus's background would consider ethical interactions far more important than anything that went on in the temple. Jesus was raised in a small village in Galilee some hundred miles north of Jerusalem. Almost no one from there would be able to participate in temple worship in Jerusalem, possibly ever. Most poor rural folk could not afford to make a two-week trip to the temple and back. Surely people in a town such as Nazareth—not to mention the millions of Jews living elsewhere in the world—knew about temple practices in far-off Jerusalem, but these had very limited relevance to their lives. Behaving toward one another in ways God commanded, on the other hand, would be a daily affair. Which was more important: Doing what God wants, day in and day out, or visiting the temple once in your life, if ever?

Jesus's Teachings on Love

Jesus's teachings on love are central to all the Gospels. It is a dominant theme, for example, of the best-known sermon Jesus delivers, arguably the most famous speech of all time: the Sermon on the Mount (Matthew 5–7).[13] Much of the Sermon is a paean to love without ever using the word. Jesus begins by explaining that the "blessed" are the humble, the merciful, the ones who strive to do what is right. He urges his followers to do good deeds for others, not to get angry with others or even resist an attacker; to befriend their accusers; give to everyone who asks and give even more than requested, love their enemies; pray for their persecutors, and . . . and that is just chapter 5.

The virtues of meekness, forgoing retribution, and refusing to assert oneself cannot be found in the repertoire of moral philosophers of the Greek and Roman worlds, with their ideology of dominance (contrast Matthew 5:5, 22, 39). Instead of hating enemies and punishing or even killing them, Jesus says to pray for them. He asks: "If you love those who love you, what reward do you get? Don't even tax collectors do this?"(Matthew 5:46). His followers are to bless their persecutors, love people they don't know or even like, and offer no resistance to those who do them harm (5:43–47). Happiness and fulfillment are not rooted in life here on earth. They will come in the kingdom of God. It is those who love others even at an extreme cost to themselves who will receive heavenly benefits. Those who are hated, reviled, and persecuted can rest assured: "Your reward is great" (5:11).

The Golden Rule has long been recognized as a brilliant and succinct summary of Jesus's ethical teachings. It occurs toward the end of the Sermon: "Everything you want others to do for you, do for them. For this is the Law and the prophets" (Matthew 7:12). Here is another injunction to engage in altruistic love without using the words "love" or "altruism" themselves. How do you want to be treated by others? That's how you should treat them.

It is quite clear from the sermon who these "others" are. They are not just your family and friends, people next door who share your religion, or even compatriots. They include people who beat you (5:29) and strangers who beg from you (5:42). Jesus says it expressly: even though others tell you to "hate your enemy, I say to you, love your enemies and pray for those who persecute you, so that you may be sons of your Father who is in heaven" (5:44–45). Obviously, here again, Jesus does not mean that his followers are to conjure up warm, fuzzy feelings about those who want to harm them. They are to treat them well.

Nowhere does Jesus teach this lesson more clearly than in the parable of the Good Samaritan (Luke 10:25–37). Even though it is found only in the Gospel of Luke, there are good reasons for thinking the story goes back to Jesus himself.[14] It occurs in the context of Luke's distinctive version of "the two great commandments" that we have already examined in Mark and Matthew.[15] In this recounting, the person who approaches Jesus is an expert in the law of Moses who asks him what he needs to do in order to inherit eternal life.[16] Jesus, Jewish teacher that he is, asks him what the law itself says, and the man cites the two commandments to love God completely (Deuteronomy 6:5) and to love your neighbor as yourself (Leviticus 19:18). Jesus is pleased to hear the response and indicates that yes indeed, those who do these things will have eternal life.

But in this Gospel the conversation does not stop there. The man wants to "justify" himself—that is, to defend himself by showing he is already doing what is right, possibly in the face of a suspicion he is not. So, he continues by asking Jesus, "Well, who is my neighbor?"—clearly hoping Jesus will give him an easy answer. If his "neighbor," for example, is the fellow next door, he is safe. But, as anyone who knows Jesus's teachings will expect, the answer will not be easy or straightforward. Instead, Jesus tells a story, one of the most familiar tales of the New Testament (Luke 10:29–34).

A man walking from Jerusalem to Jericho is attacked by robbers, who strip and beat him, leaving him half dead by the side of the road. A priest comes along and sees the fellow, but ignores him and passes on the other side. Next a Levite comes and does the same. But then a Samaritan arrives and feels pity for the man. He treats his wounds, loads him on his beast, takes him to an inn, spends the night caring for him there, and the next day pays the innkeeper to keep an eye on him until he returns.

It is a simple tale, but told to make a powerful point. Jesus asks the lawyer which of the three was a "neighbor" to the man who had been beaten. The lawyer naturally replies it was "the one who showed mercy on him" (10:37). Jesus instructs the man to behave like that. In other words, that is what it means to "love your neighbor as yourself."

The point of the tale is remarkably clear, but also has nuances easy to overlook. The man who is beaten on the road leading away from Jerusalem is almost certainly a Jew who has been to the holy city for the same reason most Jews traveled there: to worship in the temple. Since the robbers (presumably also Jewish) beat him to within an inch of his life and leave him "half-dead" (10:30), he is probably unconscious. That is significant because of what happens next, when two fellow Jews pass by, but refuse to help. First is a priest also coming from Jerusalem. Remember: priests were the sacred officials who performed sacrifices in the temple in accordance with the laws of Moses. The second is a Levite, that is, an official helper of priests in the temple. These are not simply two Jewish fellows out for a stroll. They are highly placed religious officials whose lives center around the worship of God in the temple. The fact that they, of all people, have no pity for the injured man and avoid even coming near him shows their religiosity is not focused on helping those in need. The story may be a castigation of those who are publicly religious and focused on sacrificial practices of worshipping God, yet do not live the way God demands.

But there is more to it than that. In order to officiate at the temple and perform the sacrifices there, priests and Levites were required to keep themselves ritually clean. Impurity was not a sin, but it prevented a person from standing in the presence of God. One of the sources of ritual impurity was a corpse. Anyone who touched a corpse was not allowed to enter the temple for seven days (see Numbers 19:11–13). It may well be that Jesus chose a priest and a Levite for his story not simply because they could be assumed to be highly religious, but also because they were more focused on maintaining their ritual purity than helping someone in desperate need. They don't know the man is alive—he is "half-dead"—and so, rather than risk contamination, they pass him by.

Then comes the Samaritan, who goes out of his way to help the man in desperate need, a beautiful illustration of what it means to love your enemy, in a story where priest and Levite refuse even to love their Israelite "neighbor."

Samaria was located in the central part of what is now Israel, between Galilee in the north (Jesus's home area) and Judea in the south (with Jerusalem as its capital). For centuries, Jews had considered Samaritans false worshippers of the God of Israel. Samaritans claimed their own temple on Mount Gerizim was the true sanctuary of God, rather than the temple in Jerusalem, and they had their own version of the Torah.[17] The religious differences between Samaritans and Jews were reflected in long-standing mutual animosities, as attested both in the writings of the Jewish historian Josephus and the Gospels of the New Testament. In just the preceding chapter of Luke, Jesus had passed through Samaria and sent followers to find lodging in one of its villages. But the villagers refused to let him spend the night. Here was a case of an "enemy," a Jew heading to Jerusalem, wanting hospitality, and it simply wasn't going to happen (Luke 9:51–56).

Jesus's famous parable shows a different way. It is a Samaritan who exemplifies the law of loving one's Jewish neighbor.[18] The neighbor is *anyone* in need, even an archenemy. This is a universalized ethic, not focusing on assisting loved ones but hated ones. You won't find a story like that in ancient Greek or Roman moral philosophy.

In some ways, an even clearer expression of Jesus's understanding of love is the famous parable of the Sheep and the Goats found in Matthew 25:31–46. The story comes at the conclusion of Matthew's two-chapter "apocalyptic discourse," where Jesus explains what is to happen at the judgment soon to come. At that time, the cosmic judge of the earth, the Son of Man, will be seated on his throne, in the presence of his angels, with "all the nations" before him, divided into two groups, the "sheep" on his right and the "goats" on the left. The judge first turns to the sheep and welcomes them into God's kingdom, explaining how they have earned their eternal reward: when he was hungry, they fed him; when he was thirsty, they gave him something to drink; when he was a foreigner, they welcomed him; naked, they clothed him; sick, they visited him; in prison, they came to see him. The sheep are astounded. They don't understand what he means: they don't recall doing any of these things for him. But the Son of Man tells them that whenever they did such things for "the least of my brothers and sisters," the lowliest among them, they were doing them for him. With some surprise, the sheep enter the kingdom of eternal life. They have earned this honor by taking care of others in need.

The judge then turns to the "goats" and castigates them for not taking care of him when he was hungry, thirsty, a foreigner, naked, sick, or in prison. They too are astonished: they've never seen him in need, let alone refused to help. But he tells them that since they did not do these things for others, they also refused to help him. They too, then, are getting what they deserve. They are sent off to annihilation, an eternal death.

This parable almost certainly originated with Jesus himself. It is highly unlikely that later Christian storytellers would have invented the tale and put it on Jesus's lips. Think about it: How did the earliest Christians believe people would be saved from the wrath of God to enter paradise? It was by faith in Christ, who died for the sins of the world. But not in this story. Here, belief in Jesus has no bearing on the question. The sheep are not saved by accepting the message of the Christian gospel. They are saved because they helped those in need. Neither the sheep nor the goats appear even to know who this Son of Man is. But even if they have never seen or recognized him, they have seen the hungry, thirsty, foreign, naked, sick, and imprisoned. If they were concerned for these people and helped them in their time of need, they were doing the will of God and will thereby earn an eternal reward. Since this is *not* the view of Jesus's later followers, they would not likely have come up with the story. It is what Jesus himself actually taught.[19]

It is important to notice that the sheep and the goats represent "all the nations" of earth. They are not only Jews and they are not identified as followers of Jesus. Jesus insisted that the God of Israel had commanded his chosen ones to "love their neighbor as themselves." People of all nationalities and religions can do that. Those who do so will be rewarded with the kingdom. Those who do not have no excuse.

The word "love" does not occur in this passage, but it is all about love. This kind of love is not passion, desire, fondness, endearment, attraction, or an emotion of any kind. It is love that is active, that treats others well and provides for their needs. This, for Jesus, is what God demands, not just of Jews but of all people, whether they know the God of the Jews or not. Loving actions are more important than religious belief, ritual, outward piety, reading of Scripture, attendance at worship, or anything else. However his later followers may have changed his message after his death, he himself proclaimed that altruistic behavior—active love toward those in need—would bring eternal life.

Jesus's Teachings on Charity

Jesus's views on wealth and charity will come as no surprise given his focus on service to others and active love for those in need.[20] Unlike the Greek and Roman moral philosophers of his day, Jesus was not concerned about the corrupting influence of wealth on personal character or the difficult quest for *eudaimonia* among the rich. The problem instead was the poor.

Once again, this is a perspective deeply rooted in the Jewish tradition Jesus inherited. We have seen that the Hebrew Bible often portrays the God of Israel as the God of the poor, and stresses that his people should share his concerns. Those with resources were to provide for those without. In prophetic books such as Isaiah and Amos, God castigates those who tread on the needy, who feast while others starve, and who live in luxury while others struggle to survive (e.g., Isaiah 3:14–15; Amos 2:6–7). Conversely, as stated in the book of Proverbs, those who follow God's commands will be rewarded: "Whoever is kind to the poor lends to the LORD, and will be repaid in full" (Proverbs 19:17). Helping the poor is, in a sense, making a loan to God himself. The impoverished may not be able to repay, but the Almighty certainly will.[21] Closer to Jesus's time are, once again, the teachings of Jesus son of Sirach:

> Be patient with someone in humble circumstances,
> And do not keep him waiting for your alms.
> Help the poor for the commandment's sake
> And in their need do not send them away empty handed. (Sirach, 29:8–9)

Also prior to Jesus is the intriguing book of Tobit, which is famously concerned for the welfare of the poor:

> Give alms from your possessions and do not let your eye begrudge the gift when you make it. Do not turn your face away from anyone who is poor, and the face of God will not be turned away from you. If you have many possessions, make your gift from them in proportion; if few, do not be afraid to give according to the little you have. So you will be laying up a good treasure for yourself against the day of necessity. For almsgiving delivers from death and keeps you from going into the Darkness. (Tobit 4:7–10)

> Prayer and fasting is good, but better than both is almsgiving with righteousness. . . . It is better to give alms than to lay up gold. For almsgiving saves from death and purges away every sin. (Tobit 13:8–9)

Jesus inherited such concerns and pushed them to an eschatological extreme. It is sometimes hard to appreciate just how radical Jesus's views of charitable giving were. We might expect him to urge his followers to be generous, possibly to sacrifice 10 percent or more of their income (the standard "tithe"). That would certainly win most people's ethical stamp of approval. But it would not win Jesus's. He was living at the very end of the age, and it was no time for half measures. His requirements may seem impracticable—even impossible—but again, there is scant reason to suppose an impoverished, itinerant Jewish preacher from a rural backwater of the empire who truly believed that the day of judgment was imminent would share our principles of practicability. Jesus's teachings about wealth are prophetic ethics on apocalyptic steroids.

Consider the Sermon on the Mount:

> Do not acquire treasures for yourself on earth, where moth and rust consume and where thieves break in and steal; but acquire treasures for yourself in heaven, where neither rust nor moth consume and where thieves neither break in nor steal. For where your treasure is, there your heart is also. (Matthew 6:19–21)

Far too often readers modify this saying (in their heads) by adding an adverb to it: "Do not acquire treasures for yourself *only* on earth." But that's not what it says. It says don't acquire treasures on earth. Instead—not "in addition"—acquire them in heaven, that is, in the coming Kingdom of God.

So too several verses later:

> No one can serve two masters; for either she will hate the one and love the other or she will cling to one and despise the other. You cannot serve God and mammon. (Matthew 6:24)

Here as well, many readers think Jesus is speaking about priorities, saying that privileging money over God is bad. In this understanding, Jesus teaches that you should put God first and possessions second. But that is not what he says. He says you can't serve two masters *at all*. Even if God is 80 percent of your focus, you still have a competing master. To serve one master 100 percent means you cannot have any other, period.

And so, as Jesus indicates in another saying often taken as a whimsical exaggeration, when a merchant finds "a pearl of great price," he sells all his possessions to obtain it (Matthew 13:45–46). All of them. He doesn't argue for a more reasonable deal. God's kingdom is worth, and requires, everything.

Jesus's views of wealth are most famously found in the parable of the Rich Man and Lazarus (Luke 16:19–31),[22] another account commonly misinterpreted by readers not comfortable with its actual implications. The story is about a fabulously wealthy man who is clothed in the finest raiment and eats sumptuous meals. A beggar named Lazarus lies outside his estate, starving, desperate for the scraps from his table, covered with festering sores that are licked by stray dogs. Lazarus dies and is taken up to paradise, the "bosom of Abraham"; the rich man dies and is sent down to torment in fire. When the rich man looks up and sees Lazarus, he calls out to Abraham, asking him to send Lazarus down to dip his finger in water and touch his tongue for a tiny bit of relief. But Abraham reminds him that he enjoyed all manner of good things during his lifetime, while Lazarus was miserable. Now, after death, their roles have been reversed. There is nothing Abraham or Lazarus can do about it: the great chasm between them and the rich man cannot be crossed. Their fates are fixed.[23]

Once again, it is easy to assume that Jesus's words mean something they probably don't. Most people think the rich man is condemned for being greedy, whereas Lazarus was righteous even though he was impoverished. The story, however, doesn't say anything about sin or greed or righteousness. It only speaks of wealth and poverty. We don't learn anything about Lazarus's beliefs or piety and hear nothing of the rich man's worship habits or social commitments. Their respective fates are not because they believed different things, practiced their faith in different ways, or treated others differently. To assume the rich man is punished for not sharing is a big assumption. In the text itself, the rich man is punished for having an excess of good things on earth and the poor one rewarded for not having any. On those terms—having excess in a world of poverty—which of us can escape judgment?

This may seem like an odd and possibly unfair perspective, but it coincides with Luke's views elsewhere. Both Matthew and Luke record Jesus's Beatitudes, sayings that indicate how and why someone is "blessed." But the two evangelists word the sayings differently. Matthew's version begins with the familiar "Blessed are the poor in spirit" (Matthew 5:3). Luke, however, has a slight difference in wording that entails an enormous difference in meaning. Here Jesus says: "Blessed are you poor" (Luke 6:20). In this Gospel, Jesus is not praising those who are humble or downcast or whatever else "poor in spirit" might mean, but those who live in poverty. So too when Matthew's Jesus pronounces: "Blessed are you who hunger and thirst for righteousness" (Matthew 5:6), Luke's declares: "Blessed are you who hunger and thirst" (Luke 6:21). Why would someone be blessed because they are starving? Because they are the ones who will enter the Kingdom of God.

Moreover, unlike Matthew, Luke provides a corresponding set of "Woes" to accompany his Blessings. "Woe to you who are rich, because you have received your comfort." "Woe to you who are full now, because you will go hungry" (Luke 6:24–25). Yes, the well-off may have it good now, but when the end comes, they are the ones who will suffer. If that's the case, what should those with resources do to be saved from torment at the time of judgment?

Jesus's message is again both extremely simple and seemingly impossible. They are to give it all away.

Nowhere is this lesson taught more directly and powerfully than in the story of Jesus and the Rich Man, found in all three of our Synoptic Gospels.[24] In Mark, the earliest account, a man approaches Jesus and asks, "Good teacher, what do I need to do to inherit eternal life?" (Mark 10:17).[25] To no surprise, given what we have seen, Jesus tells him to do the will of God as expressed in the Torah, reminding him of the commandments: Do not murder, do not commit adultery, do not steal, etc. Jesus is obviously not giving a comprehensive list, but it is interesting that the commands he mentions involve human interactions, that is, "ethics." There is nothing here about what to believe, how to worship, what rituals to follow.

When I teach this passage, I am always struck that students rarely see the startling implications of Jesus's reply. He explicitly indicates that eternal life comes to those who keep the commandments of Scripture. It does not come from believing in him. It does not come from his (future) death and resurrection. It comes from keeping the law.

To help my students see the problem, I pose a thought experiment. What if this same man, twenty years later, came up to the apostle Paul and asked him the same question: What do I need to do to inherit eternal life? Would Paul say: "Keep the commandments"? "Follow the Torah"? Of course not. Paul explicitly states on repeated occasions that keeping the Jewish law cannot bring salvation (for example, Roman 3:28; Galatians 2:16). Paul would instead say, emphatically, "Believe in the death and resurrection of Jesus."

How do we account for this difference? Many people simply assume there is no real difference. How could there be? Paul and Jesus must have had the same views, right? But there's an enormous difference. If Paul is right that no one can be saved by simply keeping the law but only by believing in Jesus's death and resurrection, how can Jesus be right that a person can be saved by following the law? A common response is that Jesus could not very well tell the man to believe in his death before he died. Fair enough. But if Jesus really meant what he said—that a person could be saved by keeping the commandments (and the ones he cites are certainly not difficult to follow)—why would he *have* to die? Why couldn't people just go on doing what Jesus says? Follow the ten commandments! That is an issue we will return to in a later chapter.

To get back to the story, even the man himself is not satisfied with Jesus's answer. He replies that he *has* kept these commandments, presumably thinking this is surely not enough, or possibly hoping to learn how to earn an even greater reward in the coming Kingdom. Jesus then gives him the full lowdown: "You are lacking one thing. Go, sell everything you have and give to the poor, and you will have treasure in heaven. And come, follow me." This is too much. The man just cannot do it. He tries to obey God and he wants eternal life. But he is also tied to this life. His face falls and he walks away in grief, "for he had many possessions" (v. 22).

For Jesus, you can't have both wealth now and rewards to come. No one can serve two masters. Anyone who wants treasures in heaven must give up the treasures of the earth.[26] The story continues with a conversation between Jesus and his incredulous disciples. He begins by telling them how difficult it is for a rich person to inherit the kingdom (v. 23). They have trouble understanding: they, like most others, simply assume that those with material comforts are especially favored by God. After all, he is the giver of all good things. If rich folk are not favored, who is? Jesus responds by doubling down on his claim with a famous and incredibly lucid metaphor: "It is easier for a camel to go through the eye of a needle than for a rich person to enter the kingdom of God" (v. 25).

The disciples can't believe he means it, and many readers today still don't. People who hear me discuss the passage often tell me that Jesus didn't really mean a *camel*. That would be impossible. (They appear not to notice that two verses later, Jesus himself actually says it is impossible.) And so they have an alternative explanation. Most often, they tell me that Jesus is referring to the "Camel's Needle," a gate in the walls of Jerusalem that was so low camels had to get on their knees to crawl through. Doing so was hard, but not impossible. Despite its popularity, this interpretation is simply not right. The "Camel's Needle" gate was put into the walls of Jerusalem in the Middle Ages, almost certainly in reference to Jesus's metaphor.

Others will say that Jesus did not say "camel" but a similar-sounding

Aramaic word, "rope." That too does not work. The word they have in mind specifically refers to a "hawser"—a very thick, heavy rope used for mooring a ship—which of course can't go through the eye of a needle any more than a camel can. In any event, Mark was written in *Greek* and the Greek word means "camel," and does not sound like the Greek word for "hawser." It is far better just to accept the passage for what it says, especially in light of the fact that Jesus often conveys his message by using stunning and humorous metaphors that are "impossible" when taken literally—such as the injunction not to worry about the "speck" in someone else's eye when you have a "log" stuck in yours (Matthew 7:3–4).

Jesus concludes by emphasizing that rich people really never can enter the kingdom: "It is impossible." But then he appears to open the door to exceptions. Even though it is impossible for people, it is not impossible with God. "For everything is possible with God" (v. 27). Every wealthy Christian for the past two thousand years has lapped up these words. There's still hope for me, right? There is no way I'm going to give away all my money—or even huge chunks of it. But God can save me anyway, if he wants to. Everything is possible! He can even save the rich! And hey, I'm a decent guy. Isn't that great?

Unfortunately, that's not what Jesus means. He is not saying God might still save those who are filthy rich. He's saying that even though no one has the internal resolve necessary to give away all their material resources, God can stir their heart to make it possible. He can provide the strength needed to divest everything for the sake of the kingdom. He can make the impossible possible.

In the Gospel story itself, the disciples realize Jesus really means it—people have to give up everything. Peter immediately seeks some assurance that he and the others are safe: "We ourselves have left everything to follow you" (10:28). Jesus affirms they have done the right thing: "There is no one who has left home or brothers or sisters or mother or father or children or fields on account of me and the Gospel who will not receive a hundred times as many in this world—homes, brothers, sisters, mothers, children, and fields—along with persecutions—and in the age to come eternal life" (10:29).

On the surface, this seems an altogether pleasing prospect. Who wouldn't want more than they have left behind as they join a new family of the faithful, plus eternal life on top of that? But Jesus's statement is also deeply troubling. Normally, readers think these twelve men have made a noble sacrifice to follow Jesus: They gave up everything! What dedication! But consider the implications. If these men abandoned their families—their homes, wives, and children—what would have happened to *them*, the ones left behind?

Anyone in that world would know full well. As head of the household, the father was almost always the sole breadwinner. If he abandoned his wife and children, there would be no money or provisions. How were they to live? Possibly other relatives could help, if they were themselves lucky enough to live above a pure subsistence level. But these disciples were manual laborers from impoverished rural areas. Surely their wives, children, and other dependents (including possibly aging parents) could survive without them only by scrounging for calories and/or doing things for money that are very unpleasant to think about. It may be fine for the disciples. They will have people taking care of them in exchange for their preaching. But their families?

Jesus's seemingly heartless demand for adult men to abandon their dependents may have been rooted in his belief that the final day of judgment was coming very soon. The families would need to survive on their own for just a short while. Then they too would find an eternal reward. But what if the end were nowhere in sight? And the days of the breadwinner's absence stretched into weeks, then months, then possibly years? Maybe Jesus expected that others who became his followers would give all their wealth to the abandoned families of the apostles. But if these too gave it all away, what about their own families?

Jesus in Contrast with His World

Whatever Jesus had in mind about those who were abandoned, he clearly thought his followers were to take on voluntary poverty. This was not to free them from the corrupting influences of filthy lucre, as in Greek and Roman moral philosophy. Think of the difference between Jesus's views on possessions and the indifferent attitude expressed by the Roman Stoic Epictetus.

Like other Stoics, Epictetus argued a person should focus only on things they could control, such as their own decisions about what to desire and what to avoid. This would result in a carefree attitude toward possessions—take 'em or leave 'em. And so Epictetus speaks to a pretend dialogue partner about his worldly goods:

> If you want the things I have in the countryside, go ahead, take them. Take my servants, take what I'm in charge of, take my measly little body. But you will not be able to make me desire something I don't, nor will you change what I want to avoid.

He is happy to lose everything, since it is not what matters to him. How different that is from Jesus's view. Epictetus has no interest in giving resources to the poor, no concern for the needs of others. He focuses on achieving a state of personal tranquilty, untouched by adversity—true *eudaimonia*.

The yet-more-radical Cynics insisted on giving everything away, and that may sound more like the teachings of Jesus. As I earlier noted, toward the end of the twentieth century some New Testament scholars contended that Jesus is best understood as a kind of Jewish Cynic philosopher.[27] The similarities are indeed intriguing, but again, the differences are substantial. Cynic philosophers wanted to divest of their possessions in order to avoid the disappointments and anxieties that unexpected loss can create. *Eudaimonia* required a placid mental state. For them, however, like their Stoic successors, there was no moral imperative to give their material goods to those in need. It did not matter where they went. The point was to get rid of them. It may even be that Cynics had no interest in helping the poor, since becoming poor was itself the goal.

As we have also seen, other Greek and Roman philosophers who talked about giving away goods urged generosity, but not to the truly poor. That would be a waste. The destitute lacked the personal character needed to make good use of funds. That's one reason they were poor in the first place. And looking at it from the perspective of the rich—the only perspective that philosophers much cared about—if wealth was simply flushed down the toilets of the impoverished, generous donors would have lost a valuable opportunity to advance their own status, honor, and social cachet among the people they most cared about. It was much better, then, to follow the time-honored tradition of giving money in acts of euergetism, providing resources for family members and friends who would eventually pay them back, giving gifts to clients who would reciprocate in other ways, and supporting municipal projects such as buildings or entertainments to the acclaim of the wider public.

For Jesus, it was completely different. Money was not to go (only) to family and friends. Where's the virtue in that? Funds should be given to the needy without any expectation of reciprocity. Banquets should be held for those who normally could not even get a decent meal, let alone give a return invitation. Excess money—or rather all the money—was to be given to the poor. They were the ones God favored (Matthew 4:43–47; Mark 10:20; Luke 6:30; 14:12–14).

These injunctions ultimately stem from Jesus's Jewish view of God. It is a "kingdom ethic" focused on the reality of the coming day of judgment and the utopian world that will arrive on its heels. The imminence of this climax of history radicalized Jesus's views: there was no time to wait and plenty of reason to give everything away. Treasure in heaven may be deferred gratification, but it is also money in the bank. In terms of its immediate effect, divestment for the sake of others is a concrete manifestation of love, the altruistic behavior God commands.

Forgiveness

There are numerous ways to show love to others, of course, and some do not require sharing material resources at all. Love is often manifest simply in how we carry out our interpersonal relationships. One of the most powerful expressions of love comes in acts of pure, heartfelt forgiveness.

It is important to recall that when talking about forgiveness, I am speaking of a process of reconciliation that involves a specific sequence of events: one person has knowingly and intentionally hurt the other, has come to regret it, felt remorse for causing harm, determined to reform their ways, acknowledged what they did, repented of it, and asked for forgiveness. The victim responds by accepting the request, forgoing further anger or retaliation of any kind, and allowing the relationship to be restored on the same terms as before the incident. This particular kind of forgiveness involves no penalty or payment, no retribution or revenge, no further requirement to make it right.

It may not come as a surprise that Jesus taught forgiveness, but the implications are startling. Jesus did *not* teach atonement. Jesus believed that God *forgave* sins. He did not demand a penalty, payment, or substitutionary sacrifice. If someone remorsefully confessed a sin (or, more often, multiple sins), repented, vowed to do better, and really meant it, God forgave them. That was the end of the story.

From this understanding of divine forgiveness, Jesus drew an ethical corollary. People should forgive those who sinned against them, that is, who intentionally harmed them in some way. This was not "unconditional" forgiveness. It was conditioned on genuine repentance and apology. But other than that, there were no strings attached.

Forgiveness in the Hebrew Bible

As might be expected, Jesus's views of forgiveness are deeply rooted in the Jewish tradition he inherited. But the Bible is a complicated book, presenting a variety of views on many issues; so too the Jewish tradition that came after it. Much of the Hebrew Bible and the later Jewish tradition, for example, stressed the importance of sacrifice for restoring a right relationship with God. That is different from forgiveness in the sense Jesus taught it.

The Israelite sacrificial system is notoriously complicated and, in many places, vague; scholars have long wrangled over how we should understand it. But the basic premise of atoning sacrifice is that God requires some kind of payment for a relationship broken by sin. This happened not only on the yearly Day of Atonement, as set forth in Leviticus 16, but also in some of the other sacrifices regularly performed in the temple.[28]

Other parts of the Hebrew Bible, however, embrace the idea of divine forgiveness without the need for sacrifice. In particular, forgiveness is a regular theme in the Psalms, found in some of the most powerful and poetic passages of Scripture, such as Psalm 51:

> *Have mercy on me, O God,*
> *according to your steadfast love;*
> *according to your abundant mercy,*
> *blot out my transgressions.*
> *² Wash me thoroughly from my iniquity,*
> *and cleanse me from my sin.*
> *³ For I know my transgressions,*
> *and my sin is ever before me.*
> *⁴ Against you, you alone, have I sinned*
> *and done what is evil in your sight,*
> *so that you are justified in your sentence*
> *and blameless when you pass judgment.*
> *⁵ Indeed, I was born guilty,*
> *a sinner when my mother conceived me. . . .*
> *⁷ Purge me with hyssop, and I shall be clean;*
> *wash me, and I shall be whiter than snow. . . .*
> *⁹ Hide your face from my sins,*
> *and blot out all my iniquities.*

Casual readers might be surprised that portions of the Hebrew Bible assume the need for atonement through sacrifice when others embrace forgiveness based on repentance alone. But such is the nature of Scripture, where multiple views come bound together between two covers. The same applies to the New Testament, of course. As we will see, Jesus taught forgiveness. But most of the New Testament authors taught atonement.

Jesus and Forgiveness

One of the key passages for understanding Jesus's teachings on forgiveness occurs in the Lord's Prayer, arguably the best-known and most widely memorized passage of the entire Bible. Different versions of the prayer are found in Matthew 6:9–13 (in the Sermon on the Mount) and Luke 10:2–4.[29] One of the differences involves the request for forgiveness.

The form of the request I learned growing up was: "Forgive us our trespasses as we forgive those who trespass against us." Later in life, I attended a church that instead said: "Forgive us our debts as we forgive our debtors." When I first heard this, I assumed the church was simply old-fashioned, maybe using the King James Version instead of a more accurate modern translation. But no, I was wrong. The version with "debts" comes from Matthew and the version with "trespasses" (also sometimes translated as "sins") comes from Luke. More or less. Luke's version actually gives a "mixed" form of the prayer that first mentions "trespasses" and then "debts": "Forgive us our trespasses as we forgive everyone indebted to us." Why then do some churches today say the word "trespasses" in both parts of the prayer, when that is found in *neither* passage, nor anywhere else in the New Testament? I suppose saying the word twice makes the prayer a bit more memorable.

In any event, both forms of the petition ask God to forgive our sins/trespasses/debts the way we forgive others indebted to us. Some philosophers have objected to likening the forgiveness of sin to an economic transaction. For them, "debt" is an incommensurate metaphor.[30] But the Greek word translated as "debt" simply refers to something that is owed to another. When someone "owes a debt to society," it does not usually mean they have refused to pay their taxes. It means they have done something that has broken the law or offended the social order. As a result, they need to "pay a price" for it, perhaps by spending time in jail or doing community service. Owing a debt to God means breaking his law and offending his divine order. That too comes with a price, but in this case, when God forgives, the debt does not need to be paid and there is no punishment or retribution.

This may not be a social strategy for anyone who prefers a judicial system that deters crime to one that leads to anarchy. But it is different when it comes to private, interpersonal relations. Forgiving someone who has committed a harmful act can be justified if you are willing to accept a genuine expression of regret, remorse, and promise of reform. The person has apologized and you have let her off the hook.

It is worth noting that the Lord's Prayer is not a promise to God to forgive others, since, or if, God forgives us. It is the other way around. We first forgive what others have done, and on those grounds we ask God to forgive us.

This concept of forgiveness differs significantly from the views of the Greek and Roman worlds. As we have seen, Aristotle discusses how an offender could be released from their moral debt only if they convinced the victim they had acted in ignorance or compulsion. He writes about this kind of response by using the Greek word *suggnome*, which means something like "come to the same view" or "have the same mind." This term is never used for "forgiveness" in the New Testament.[31] Instead we find *aphesis*, which means "a release" or a "pardon," based on the verb "to send away" (*aphiēmi*). The forgiver simply sends away the debt, gets rid of it, puts it out of the equation and out of mind.

Other important passages on forgiveness can be found in the Gospel of Matthew. After Jesus explains how a wrongdoer in the church should be shown the error of their ways, Peter asks, "Lord, how many times will my brother sin against me and I forgive him? As many as seven?" Jesus responds with characteristic but shocking clarity: "I don't say seven times but seventy times seven" (Matthew 18:21–22). It may sound hyperbolic, but in fact it's the opposite: Jesus appears to mean every single time.

He immediately illustrates his view with one of the great stories of the Gospels, the Parable of the Unforgiving Slave (Matthew 18:23–35). In the Roman world slaves could be paid by their masters for their labor; they could also borrow money and engage in other financial transactions. In this parable, a king has loaned money to various slaves, one of whom owed him "ten thousand talents" (18:24). This is Jesus at his hyperbolic best. A talent was a monetary unit based on the weight of silver, at that time worth six thousand denarii. A denarius was approximately the wage for one day's work by a manual laborer. In modern terms, if a laborer earns $7.25 an hour (the minimum wage here in North Carolina in 2025), a talent would be $348. The slave owes his master something like three and a half billion dollars.

Okay, it's a parable.

But it has a rather significant point. The slave falls to his knees and begs his master for more time to pay off the loan, and out of compassion the king forgives the debt completely. But the slave then goes to find a fellow slave who owes him 100 denarii ($5,800 in modern terms) and demands repayment. This other slave also falls to the ground and begs for time to repay. But the recently forgiven slave won't have it; he sends the fellow to prison until he can round up the money.

The other slaves are incensed and report to the master what has happened, with predictable results. He summons the unforgiving slave and attacks him: "You evil slave; I forgave that entire debt you owed me because you asked; why didn't you show mercy to your fellow slave as I did to you?" (He doesn't bother to mention the rather significantly different loan amounts.) In rage, the master hands the slave over to "the torturers" until he pays back his entire loan. And, well, good luck with that one.

Jesus ends the parable with a one-liner that clearly reflects the petition for forgiveness in the Lord's Prayer, but expressed negatively: "So also my heavenly Father will do to each of you, if you do not forgive another from your heart" (Matthew 18:35; see Matthew 6:12). The point reinforces what we learned from the Prayer: we need to forgive others with no strings attached when they acknowledge what they've done and ask for a pardon. If that is how we forgive, God will forgive us the same way.

Jesus's teachings of forgiveness are most powerfully and movingly encapsulated in an even more famous parable, "The Prodigal Son" (Luke 15:11–32). Although it is found only in Luke, it is characteristic of the other teachings of Jesus we have seen. On one level, the story serves as an allegory of how God treats his wayward children; on another, it models Jesus's insistence on human forgiveness based on repentance.

A man has two sons. The younger asks for his share of the inheritance in advance, takes it, travels to a distant land to lead a wild life, and wastes it all away. A famine strikes the land and, having no resources, the youth hires himself out as a farmhand to feed the swine. Things go from bad to worse and, on the brink of starvation, he considers eating the pig feed. Suddenly, he comes to his senses, realizing that even the hired help at his father's place have plenty of food. He decides to return home, acknowledge the wrong he has done, and beg for help—not to be restored to the family, but to serve as a hired hand.

His father sees him coming from a distance, runs up to him, and hugs and kisses him. The prodigal confesses he has sinned and is no longer worthy to be called his son, but the father calls his slaves and tells them to tend to him, dress him in the finest clothes, and prepare the "fattened calf" for a festive meal: "For my son was dead and he has returned to life; he was lost but now he is found" (15:24).

The story does not end there. When the older brother comes in from working in the field, he is outraged to learn the profligate is being feted as a returning hero and he refuses even to go inside. His father comes out to plead with him to join the feast, but he is hurt and feels slighted: he has obeyed his father his entire life and worked for years on the farm. In all that time, not once did his father allow him even a goat to sacrifice for a festive meal with his friends. Now this wastrel has burned through half the inheritance and returned from his wild living to celebrations. How is this fair? The father tries to solace him: "Son, you have always been with me and everything I have is yours. But we had to celebrate and rejoice, because this brother of yours was dead and has come to life; he was lost and has been found" (15:31–32).

Interpreters have long debated this parable. Some argue it is not really about repentance and forgiveness, since the father hugs and kisses the son without hearing a single word from his mouth. Where is the remorse, the regret, the request for mercy? Something can be said for this view, but on the other hand the prodigal is said to have "come to his senses," realizing he had done wrong, to have vowed to change, and returned—that is, he repented of his "sin." It is true that his confession comes *after* his father has welcomed him with open arms, but the father has done so precisely because he has seen him coming home and he knows what it means.

In recent decades, some interpreters have argued the story is not about the prodigal son at all but the sullen brother, who is jealous and unwilling to accept the happy news of his brother's reformation and return. There is certainly merit in this view as well: the story does shift at the end from the prodigal to the faithful son, who is, to be fair, surely justified in his jealousy and anger. But the account ends not with his sullen response but with his father's explanation: his other son has returned to his senses, realized his error, repented, and returned. That is a cause for forgiveness and celebration, not disdain.

The father's position reflects another key saying of Jesus. Elsewhere in Luke, Jesus and his followers are maligned by Jewish teachers for associating with the dregs of religious society: "Why do you eat and drink with tax collectors and sinners?" Jesus answers with a powerful metaphor: "Those who are healthy do not need a doctor, but those who are ill. I have not come to call the righteous but the sinners to repentance" (Luke 5:27–32). That is to say, those who are already doing what is right—whether upright Jews or the elder brother of the prodigal son—are living as they should; it is those who are not doing so who need to be brought back into God's good graces. Jesus's goal is to lead sinners to repent and return to God. When they do so, God will freely forgive them.

That is an occasion not only for celebration but also for ethical reflection. Throughout Jesus's teachings of forgiveness, we find two layers of thought, one connected with a person's relationship with God and the other with their relationships with others. Jesus sees the two as analogous and intertwined. God forgives those who repent of their sins and celebrates their return to him, and he expects people to do likewise. Those who refuse to forgive will not be forgiven. Those who do forgive can enter again into God's welcoming embrace.

In the chapters that follow, I will show how the expansion of Christianity led to the promulgation of this and other ethical views of Jesus, to the point that they reshaped moral thinking in the Roman world. But only in altered forms. Changes from Jesus's specific views were to be expected. Jesus was an Aramaic-speaking apocalyptic Jew from a rural backwater who expected the world as he knew it to come to a crashing halt in the very near future. It did not do so, and the vast majority of later converts to the Christian faith came from radically different cultures and held very different beliefs about the world. These necessarily affected their understanding of how to live in it. And so Jesus's ethics came to be transformed into softer versions. But even in altered forms, they would transform the moral sensibilities of the West and, in the end, simply become common sense.

Chapter Six

THE AFTERLIFE OF JESUS'S ETHICS

It is a historical and anthropological reality that the moral codes of highly developed cultures in different times and places are both broadly similar and strikingly different. Nearly all human societies have urged and celebrated love between parents and children; few of them have condoned pederasty—unlike fifth-century Athens at the "height" of ancient civilization.

As I have indicated, this combination of broad similarities and shocking differences is difficult to explain if humans have been provided with a moral compass from a power on high, but it makes perfect sense given evolutionary and social pressures. In order to survive virtually every conceivable environment and situation, individuals and groups have always had to look out for themselves *and* cooperate with others. Egoism and altruism are therefore both written into our DNA, but they came to be expressed in diverse ways depending on local circumstances. The resulting ethical norms and practices are therefore localized, but nonetheless strong. They are not rooted in an "objective" moral code.

In my experience, those who argue for "objective" morality almost always believe that their own sense of right and wrong has come directly from the Almighty, and that if anyone has a different sense, it is because they've become corrupted by modern culture, evil personal inclinations, or, well, liberal university professors. And since their own views are normative, they should be legislated.

This view presents us with a major irony: a hegemonic insistence on objective morality has repeatedly proved *harmful* to the welfare of others. It is the view that led Christians to force their own cultural and ethical values on other peoples, for example, by missionaries who considered African women indecent and immoral for not covering their breasts. Or, to bring the matter closer to home, by pillars of Christian morality who continue to insist that gay sex is "contrary to nature" and that the people who want to engage in it are driven by demons. I myself once thought that, and clearly remember from my fundamentalist days a tortured soul who pleaded with me to perform an exorcism.

It is also interesting to consider how conservative Christians today typically reject much of the moral vision of the biblical tradition, as do the rest of us. How many of us think the best way to remain pure from the corrupting influences of our environment is by slaughtering every man, woman, and child of the city where we want to live, as in Joshua 6 when the Israelites stormed Jericho?

When someone replies that this was a special situation, my response is that it is always a special situation. In special situations people often think it is a good thing to shoot their fellow employees, rape women captured in war, slaughter Native Americans, or bomb thousands of innocent civilians to demonstrate military seriousness and capacity. Those who argue for "objective" grounds for human interactions should at least realize that if such actions are "right" at some times but not at others, then necessarily those decisions can be made only through a personal evaluation of contexts and circumstances. That such evaluations are "subjective" should be obvious, since in many instances even those who subscribe to "objective" ethics cannot agree among themselves about the right course of action.

I am not, of course, arguing for an ethical free-for-all. Everyone who thinks deeply about the matter (which, admittedly, is not everyone) is reasonably well committed to their own sense of decency and morality. That too is part of our genetic makeup. I get it. Like everyone else, I too think my specific ethical code is superior to that of others. If I didn't, I would adopt theirs.

My argument in this book is that some aspects of what seems morally obvious for most of us today in the West derive from a cultural development that transpired because of the Christianization of our world. It is not that the followers of Jesus simply retained and propagated his ethical views. On the contrary, they altered them over time, often in significant ways. But one particular aspect of his teaching lived on: his insistence that we should behave altruistically even to strangers we may not like, appreciate, or respect. This basic ethical position came to be modified and modulated over time, because—again—of circumstances. But even in its evolved state, it would create a new common sense about how to be a good person that has endured for two millennia.

From Jesus to Christianity

Jesus's followers began to modify his ethical teachings soon after his death. Many of the changes were probably inevitable. During his public ministry, Jesus's small band of followers were lower-class Aramaic-speaking Jews who committed themselves to his understanding of the Jewish law and looked for the imminent appearance of the Kingdom of God. Within decades, their religion had spread outside the promised land, predominantly among Greek-speaking gentiles in urban areas scattered throughout the Mediterranean world.[1] There is reason to believe there were some 7,000 to 10,000 Christians by the end of the first century (out of an empire of 60 million); 140,000 to 170,000 by the end of the second century; and 2.5 million to 3.5 million by the end of the third.[2] Only a tiny slice of these were Aramaic-speaking Jews raised on the Torah and living in what was then called Palestine. The vast majority lived in other places and spoke different languages, they held varying understandings of the world, and they brought into their Christian communities different cultures, customs, and perspectives. Most of them had been raised with a different range of assumptions about what it meant to live ethically and they typically needed to confront different moral dilemmas from those of manual laborers in rural Galilee.

Naturally, many of their religious views changed radically at their Christian conversions. They (or presumably most of them) abandoned their polytheistic religions to worship the one God of Israel. They came to believe this

God was the creator and Lord of all and that the other gods either did not actually exist or were demonic forces. They believed that Jesus alone provided the path to eternal bliss after death and that he had revealed to them how to live in the meantime. Even so, they were not like Jesus's original followers in major ways: their cultural assumptions were rooted principally in Greek philosophical thought; they were growing as a worldwide church; and most of them realized the apocalyptic day of judgment was nowhere in sight.

They also had to deal with moral issues simply not in Jesus's purview. What would he have said about eating meat sacrificed to pagan divinities? Or about women speaking in church or deciding not to wear head coverings? What would he think about speaking in tongues during worship services? Or about Jewish followers sharing meals with gentiles? What would he have thought about gentile men not getting circumcised? How would he have decided which of the poor to help if a community of his followers had restricted funds and mutually exclusive options? We have no idea and neither did the early Christians. They just assumed one thing or another, and argued for it.

Three realities heavily influenced the ethical thinking of these early Christians. First, as Christian communities became larger, decisions had to be made about how to follow Jesus's instructions to help those in need. With limited resources, was it better to restrict charitable giving to fellow Christian faithful who were suffering from lack? They were, after all, members of a community lovingly committed to one another. Surely the faithful should be the target of alms when there was not enough to go around. On the other hand, would it not be more true to Jesus's teachings to help outsiders in even greater need? Jesus had pressed his followers to give to strangers. And doing so might incentivize them to convert.

Second, most gentile converts had previously never heard about the Jewish apocalyptic view that the world was soon to end with a resurrection of the dead leading to a glorious life for those saved here on a renewed earth. Many pagans did not believe in life after death at all. Those who did assumed it entailed the survival of the soul after the death of the body, as the disembodied soul ascended to the glories of the heavenly realms above or descended to the torments of the world below, as in Plato. This gentile notion that souls went directly to heaven and hell at death became standard among Christians in the early second century and played a significant role in their understanding of ethics. As a result, the urgency of Jesus's message became seriously muted and, correspondingly, his radical ethical demands softened. If we do not need to worry about the Kingdom arriving, say, next month, there are fewer reasons to sell everything we own and give to the poor. We have to think about the long-term implications of our actions.

Third, the ethical standards of the Greek and Roman world became at least as significant for acceptable Christian behavior as Jesus's own injunctions about self-giving love. Many Christian ethical guidelines for behavior simply embody ancient "common sense" about what it means to be a good person, rather than the radical views of Jesus himself. Even in the New Testament, ethical instruction often echoes pagan moral teachings, as in Paul's letter to the Romans, where he condemns "wickedness, evil, covetousness, malice, envy, murder, strife, deceit, gossip, slander, insolence, boastfulness, and disobedience to parents" (Romans 1:19–21)—all of them decried in pagan ethical writings as well. So too, many of the virtues celebrated throughout the writings of the New Testament were widely enjoined, such as being good, generous, kind, truthful, just, and helpful to others.[3]

That is not to say that the followers of Jesus simply abandoned his teachings to conform to the ethical standards embraced more broadly in their world. Jesus's distinctive emphasis on altruism to all, even strangers, differed markedly from what could be found in pagan cultures, and remained an important aspect of Christian exhortations to love, give, and forgive. But the times were changing and so too the teachings. We can see some of these shifts already in our earliest Christian author, the apostle Paul.

Ethics in the Writings of Paul

The apostle Paul was by far the most important figure in early Christianity, apart from Jesus himself. Nearly half the books of the New Testament claim to be written by him, another (Hebrews) was canonized because church fathers wrongly thought he wrote it, yet another (Acts) is largely written about him, and a number of the others engage with him and his views in one way or another. Paul was not one of Jesus's disciples. He was a highly educated Greek-speaking Jew from somewhere outside of Israel who, by his own account, once opposed the preaching of Jesus's followers with violence.[4] But three years or so after the crucifixion, he had a vision of Jesus that transformed him into one of Jesus's most devoted apostles (Galatians 1:13–17; 1 Corinthians 9:1; 15:8–9).

Paul believed God had specially commissioned him to take the message of Jesus to gentiles, in coordination with Jesus's original disciples, who preached to Jews. His distinctive contribution to the Christian message was that Christ's death brought salvation to all people, regardless of ethnicity. Even though Jesus was the Jewish messiah sent from the Jewish God to the Jewish people in fulfillment of the Jewish scripture, Paul preached that gentiles did not have to become Jewish to inherit salvation. Redemption came to anyone who believed in Christ's death and resurrection. Converts thus did not need to observe distinctively Jewish customs, such as circumcision, keeping the Sabbath, observing kosher food laws, and celebrating Jewish festivals. Such things were meant for Jews as God's original chosen ones, but now God had fulfilled his promises by bringing salvation to all (see Romans 2–3; Galatians 1–2).

One might think that if Paul did not urge his gentile converts to follow the demands of the Torah, he would instead insist they adhere to the teachings of Jesus. This is one of the great puzzles of Paul's writings: even though he devotes a good deal of attention to the question of how people should live and behave, he makes almost no reference to what Jesus said about it. In fact, he explicitly mentions only two of Jesus's ethical teachings: that a person should not get divorced and that ministers should be paid for their work (1 Cor. 7:14; 9:10).[5]

The reasons for this relative silence can be, and have been, much debated.[6] For our purposes, it is interesting that without quoting Jesus, Paul agreed with him that doing God's will meant engaging in active love, that is, altruistic behavior. Twice in Paul's letters he tells his readers that the entire law can be summarized in the statement of Leviticus 19:18: "You shall love your neighbor as yourself" (Romans 13:8; Galatians 5:14). Did he know that Jesus had also said that? It is certainly possible, but that would make it even more strange that he never points it out. Was it a fairly common sentiment among Jewish teachers at the time?

There is an intriguing irony connected with these two passages, since they occur in Paul's letters to the Romans and the Galatians, both of which argue that gentile Christians do not need to keep the Jewish law. But why then does he tell his gentile readers to love their neighbor precisely *because* it "fulfills the law"? This apparent discrepancy can possibly be resolved by recognizing that, on one hand, Paul insisted no one—Jew or gentile—could be reconciled with God by adhering to the dictates of the law, but only by faith in Christ. Indeed, for Paul, any gentile who thinks it *is* necessary to follow the Torah has completely misunderstood how salvation works.[7] At the same time, Paul believed the law shows how God wants people to behave, whether they are Jew or gentile. This God-given guidance is summarized in the commandment to love. Thus, those who belong to God by the salvation brought by Christ are expected to live out their newfound commitment by actively engaging in love for others. For Paul, it is not that a life of love brings salvation; salvation brings a life of love.

The importance of *agapē* pervades Paul's letters, but he does not share Jesus's laser-like focus on it. New issues had arisen and various forms of misbehavior needed to be addressed. What criteria were to guide ethical decisions? Where should followers of Jesus turn to know right from wrong? How could they know what God wants them to do in any given situation? To the surprise of many readers—and despite the passages in Galatians and Romans mentioned above—for Paul the answer is not simply "love." There are other, sometimes unrelated, grounds for his ethics.

This can be seen with particular clarity in Paul's first letter to the Corinthians, which deals almost entirely with ethical crises among converts in Corinth, a city on the isthmus dividing the northern and southern parts of modern Greece and a center of trade served by two major ports. Corinth is probably best remembered today for its rather checkered history, at least among strong advocates of so-called family values. Along with trade and industry, its economy was driven by commercialized pleasures enjoyed by elite Roman tourists who could afford its range of offerings. It is hard to know if the city's ribald reputation was deserved; some historians suspect it was based more on slander than reality. It was a famous Athenian, the comic playwright Aristophanes, who coined the verb "to Corinthinize," which meant to engage in sexually immoral behavior. In any event, most people who have heard of Corinth today know about it only from the two letters Paul addressed to the church there, which have not done much to improve its dubious reputation.

The Corinthian church consisted almost entirely of pagans Paul had converted (1 Corinthians 12:2). After Paul left for other mission fields, he got news of their "progress," and the news was not good. Serious divisions had arisen in the church, with leaders of different splinter groups claiming allegiance to one or another of the apostles (Paul, Cephas, Apollos; 1:10–13; 3:1–3). Worship services were chaotic, as members apparently competed for supremacy by "speaking in tongues" (14:1–33). Some women were participating in worship without being veiled (11:2–16), a very big problem for Paul.[8] At the weekly communion—an actual shared meal—richer folk were consuming all the food and drink, while poorer folk had little or nothing (11:17–34). These internal conflicts were even spreading to outside the church, with some members taking others to civil court. We do not know, alas, on what grounds (6:1–6).

Some of the tensions in the community related to ethical behavior arising from alternative theological views. One key dispute involved the status of the pagan gods, formerly worshipped by most, if not all, of the congregation. Did they actually exist? Some members, possibly the more highly educated, argued these other gods were merely idols, statues of wood or metal. But others believed they did indeed exist: they were demons trying to convince the unconverted of their power and beneficence. This difference in perspective led to a serious ethical dilemma. If a Christian ate in the home of a nonbeliever, or even wanted to host a special meal of their own, what were they to do with the reality that most meat on offer came from sacrificial animals originally offered to a god as part of a pagan ritual? One group claimed that since there was only one true God, there was no harm in eating the meat: you can't participate in the worship of a god that doesn't exist. The other side maintained that eating the meat meant participating in pagan practices and therefore demon worship. So, what to do?

In addition to these problems of unity, Paul also learned of instances of (what he considered) rank immorality in the Corinthian church. Some of the men were visiting prostitutes and had no qualms in letting it be known (6:12–19).[9] Another was cohabiting with his stepmother (5:1–2). At the other end of the spectrum, some church members were wondering if sexual relations could ever be right in any context, even if married. Aren't Christians supposed to be totally committed to God and his kingdom? How then can they be passionately involved with someone else, even a spouse? (7:1–7).

1 Corinthians provides Paul's blow-by-blow response to these various problems, most of which were nowhere near the radar screen of the historical Jesus and his group of Jewish followers in rural Galilee. Only twenty-five years had passed since his death, but major, new problems had arisen, and Jesus's teachings could not begin to address them all.

The "love commandment" was certainly relevant to some of these problems, and Paul occasionally alludes to it in creative ways. For example, on the issue of whether it was acceptable to eat meat that had been sacrificed to idols, Paul agrees with the group that maintained the meat was not really sacrificed to other gods, since they don't exist. He nevertheless argues that the meat should not be eaten. Why? For him it is not a question of knowledge but love (8:1–3). Those who eat the meat "knowing" other gods don't exist may influence fellow Christians who don't share that knowledge, pressuring them to eat the meat contrary to their conscience and beliefs. That is not a loving thing to do. So it is better not to eat the meat (8:1–13).[10]

We will see a good deal more about how Paul's appeal to love for seemingly unrelated issues (such as when it is right to speak in tongues) in the next chapter, when we consider his famous discourse on love in 1 Corinthians 13. But before coming to that, it is important to notice an important shift that has occurred between Jesus and Paul. Paul is concerned almost entirely about the community of Jesus's followers, the love of fellow believers for one another. He says virtually nothing about helping the stranger, the outsider, the hungry, the poor, and the needy beyond the Christian community. What would Jesus think about that? It is impossible to know, but the focus of ethical behavior has clearly shifted.

Even more striking, Paul often appeals to grounds for ethics other than *agapē*. For example, he lambastes the Corinthians for allowing the man sleeping with his stepmother to remain unpunished, insisting they follow the instructions of Moses: "Remove the wicked man from among you" (Deuteronomy 17:7; quoted in 5:13). At a stretch, this could be considered an act of love toward the man, since if he is removed from the community and "handed over to Satan" for "the destruction of his flesh" (whatever that means), it may lead in the end to the "salvation of his spirit."[11] But Paul's principal concern is not for the sinner himself but for the health of the community. He emphasizes that moral corruption in one part of the body easily spreads like cancer. The church cannot afford to have such corrupting influences in its midst. The man is to be expelled. It is certainly possible Jesus too would have advised casting sinners out of a congregation, but throughout the Gospels he is normally charged with being overly friendly with them (Matthew 11:19).

On a similar issue, Paul takes a completely different approach. Rather than ordering the Corinthian men visiting prostitutes to be removed from the community, he tries to reason with them. One could well imagine Paul appealing to the love commandment to condemn these men by arguing (as many would in the modern world) that a Christian who genuinely loves others would not contribute to their exploitation for the sake of personal sexual gratification. The loving thing to do, one could argue, would be to help prostitutes leave (what is for Paul) a life of sin and humiliation. That is not Paul's argument at all. His concern is that Christian men who have had sex with prostitutes have brought sin and corruption into the body of Christ, in a literal way that is both highly mystical and somewhat crass.

It is difficult for many modern readers to follow Paul's reasoning (1 Corinthians 6:12–20). Paul believed that Christians are all part of "one body," that is, "the body of Christ." Everyone who is baptized is united with Christ and together, as a community, they make up his "body." In a sense, they are Christ's physical presence here on earth. But more than that, for Paul, believers experience a mystical unification with Christ at baptism. When they are submerged in water, they are "made one" with Christ and put "into" Christ so that they are no longer within the alternative realm of sin (Romans 6:1–11).

Anyone who is "at one" with Christ is necessarily "at one" with all others who are "one" with Christ. There is complete unity, therefore, in the Christian body, the church. And that's the problem with having sex with a prostitute. When two people engage in sexual intercourse, they become "one" with each other, not only in a crass material way but also in a more mystical sense. Paul supports this view by quoting Genesis 2:24: "the two shall be one flesh." That means that the men who are "one with Christ" through their baptism are also made "one" with the prostitute in the sex act. Doesn't this make the prostitute "one with Christ," introducing her into his body? This body of Christ—comprised of all the baptized members of the church—is a holy temple. Bringing a prostitute into the body corrupts it. For Paul this is unthinkable. The body is the Holy Spirit's dwelling place. You cannot bring immorality and immoral people into it. So stop with the prostitutes.

You won't find *that* kind of logic in the teachings of Jesus.

Preserving the purity of the church is a major incentive for right behavior for Paul.[12] So too is maintaining its unity. The Corinthian leaders who claim spiritual superiority and allegiance to one apostle or another (Paul, Cephas, Apollos) are dividing the body instead of uniting it (chs. 1–4). One might expect Paul to deal with this particular problem by siding with the faction that agrees with him. Instead, he argues that *all* the factions are wrong.

Many of the problems in the Corinthian church are directly related to this issue of disunity: eating food offered to idols, chaos in the worship services, the inequalities on display at the Lord's Supper. The rollicking good time being had by the rich is not at all what this meal was supposed to be about; it was to be a remembrance of Christ sacrificing himself for the sake of others (11:18–22). This self-giving love was not simply to be remembered at the meal, it was to be reenacted. It was an occasion to reveal the unity of the body, not its divisiveness. And so, the conduct of the wealthier congregants was not just bad manners, it ran directly contrary to the Christian message and in opposition to the example of Christ himself. Paul indicates that God has responded to this conduct with the utmost seriousness, having made some members of the congregation ill and taking the lives of others (11:27–30).

Other views are more directly rooted in Paul's apocalyptic message. For one thing, like Jesus, Paul expected the end to come very soon. Unlike Jesus, he thought it would come with Jesus himself, soon to return in judgment. Paul expected to be alive when it happened. In both 1 Thessalonians 4:13–18 and 1 Corinthians 15:51–52, Paul includes himself among those who will be living at the time. This, then, is an "impending crisis" (7:26) and it has very serious ethical implications. For one thing, with so little time left, no one should worry about changing their social status, as if life in this world any longer mattered. Slaves should not seek their freedom. The married should not get divorced. The single should not get married. What would be the point? The end is soon. Paul allows one major exception to this rule. Even though he wishes that all other believers "were as I myself am" (7:7)—that is, single, celibate, and able to focus on the Christian mission—he concedes that someone who cannot control their sex drive should get married. "For it is better to marry than to burn" (With passion? In the day of judgment? Both? 7:9).

In some passages Paul's ethical reasoning is, at best, confusing. Why should women be veiled in church (1 Corinthians 11:2–15)?[13] Men do not have to be. And elsewhere Paul teaches that "in Christ there is no male or female" (Galatians 3:28). Apparently this is a conditioned equality. Women are equal with men as far as salvation is concerned, equally gifted with grace. But they are not to change their social status, not to be liberated from any outward sign of subservience to men by removing their veils. Paul does not argue this socially conservative view on the ground that since the end is near women might as well be content with their current lot. Nor does he mount the argument I always heard in my earlier days: that only prostitutes appeared in public without veils, so unveiled women in church could damage the Christians' already dubious reputation. Paul instead marshals other arguments for veiling, none of them about love and all of them a bit hard to understand. More than just about any other passage in Paul's letters, many interpreters get the impression that here he is tossing out every argument that comes to mind, hoping that one of them will stick.

He argues, for example, that the veil is important to show the subordination of women in the hierarchy of the genders: the husband is the "head" of the wife, just as Christ is the "head" of the man and God is the "head" of Christ (11:3). Presumably Paul means "head" as something like "the one who is in charge of" or "the one to whom one has to answer." He then states what seems to him to be an obvious point, that if a man prays with a covering on his head (meaning his real head), he "dishonors his head" (meaning Christ?), whereas if a woman prays with her (literal) head unveiled she dishonors her own head (her husband?). That, Paul says, is as bad as if she had her head shaved (11:5). And so a man "should not cover his head since he is the image and glory of God but the woman is the glory of the man" (v. 7). It is hard to see how that logic follows. To make matters worse, he concludes his case with what he appears to consider his most compelling point: "This is why a woman ought to have an authority [a veil?] on her head, because of the angels" (v. 10).

You will find various interpretations of this passage. Some honest scholars who have read it roughly a thousand times continue to say it is clear as mud. With respect to the (decisive?) appeal to angels, the two most popular interpretations are fundamentally at odds. Paul may be referring to the "good" angels who created the order and hierarchies of the world. In that case, women who pretend to have the same authority as men violate the natural order and create serious consternation in the angelic realms. Or they could be "bad" angels, such as the "sons of God" described in Genesis 6:1–4, who looked from above on beautiful women and descended to have sex with them. The veil, then, might be to hide the woman's attractiveness to keep angelic molesters away.[14]

Paul does not stop there, however. He goes on to argue for the veil because of what "nature itself teaches" (11:14). That is, he appeals to common sense. Paul points out that "nature" teaches that long hair is degrading for men, but glorious for women. Since God therefore designed women's heads to be covered (but not men's), he clearly wants them to wear veils.

Some of my students respond to this verse by asking if Paul had ever seen any of those pictures of the long-haired Jesus. For my part, as a male growing up in the late sixties and early seventies, nature never taught *me* that long hair was disgraceful. But I certainly learned it was when I went off to a Bible college that took Paul's common sense as . . . divinely given common sense. We had a strict code at Moody Bible Institute: men's hair could not come over the top of their ears.[15] Some churches were as strict as fundamentalist colleges. I once went to a Baptist church that had a barbershop on-site. Any long-haired freaky people who wanted to convert had to be clipped before they could be dunked in the baptismal tub onstage after the altar call.

An example like this makes it quite easy to show that what one person or group deems "unnatural" is completely natural to others. Yet arguments for "natural law" continue to be invoked today in discussions—and, indeed, legislation—involving gay and lesbian civil rights, trans issues, and non-normativity of all kinds.

This is just a sampling of Paul's ethical guidelines, but enough to show that ethics in early Christianity, starting with our earliest Christian author, was not only a matter of loving one's neighbor, the focus of Jesus himself. In fact, most of Paul's ethical guidelines do not map neatly onto Jesus's own teaching. Jesus urged his followers to help the poor and needy whoever they are, wherever they live, and whatever religion they embrace. Where is this in Paul?

My sense is that Paul would not have been at all opposed to this mandate to help strangers in need. He may well have endorsed it, though we have no clear indications he did. As we will see in the next chapter, he certainly campaigned for helping needy Christians in other places. But why does he never instruct the Corinthians to pool their resources to help the non-Christian destitute in their large city? Was it simply not an important issue for him? Even if we move beyond 1 Corinthians and examine the ethical instructions in Paul's other letters, it becomes clear that he is not overly concerned about those in physical need so much as about the communal lives of Christian converts. The times, they are a-changin'. And as often happens, they are returning things to an earlier state. Before the days of Jesus, pagans and Jews invariably privileged family, friends, and their own communities in their ethical concerns. Now, mutatis mutandis, Jesus's followers do so as well, but with one important difference: the "family" is their "brothers and sisters in Christ," the friends are their close Christian associates, and the communities are the churches throughout the Christian world.

Communal Ethics after Paul

As time goes yet further on, Christian ethics become both more conventional and increasingly focused on the community of believers. This becomes clear in letters written by unknown authors in the name of Paul years after his death, six of which appear in the New Testament itself.[16] Here I'll focus on just one of them, the letter to the Colossians.

The letter is allegedly written by Paul and his companion Timothy to the church in the Asia Minor city of Colossae. Much of the letter fits comfortably with Paul's own teachings, but there are differences as well, both in writing style and in the letter's theological concerns and perspectives.[17] A major problem addressed in the letter involves "false teachers" who are urging followers of Jesus to worship angels (along with God and Christ) and to continue observing aspects of the Jewish law. The unknown author insists they should do neither.

That does not mean Christians can live lawlessly. Quite the contrary, ethically upright behavior is essential for one's standing before God. The author devotes just over a chapter to explaining what this behavior entails. This list of dos and don'ts will sound familiar to anyone versed in the writings of Greek and Roman moralists. Christian believers are not to be involved with "sexual impropriety, unclean activities, passion, evil desire, and covetousness," nor "engage in anger, wrath, malice, slander, and foul talk" (3:5–8). In other words, church members are to be self-disciplined, an idea much at home in the world of pagan ethics. At the same time, the author gives a specifically Christian incentive for upright behavior: "The wrath of God is coming" (3:6).

There is also a decidedly Christian slant in his list of positive behaviors and attitudes. His readers are to embrace "compassion, pity, kindness, humble-mindedness, meekness, and patience." Humility and meekness are not widely touted in cultures of dominance. On the contrary, outside the New Testament, the Greek term I have translated as "humble-mindedness" typically conveys a negative sense of being "mean-spirited." The author goes on to paraphrase a teaching of Jesus: "Just as the Lord had forgiven you, so you should do as well" (3:13). In this case, the sequence of forgiveness is reversed: God is not said to forgive people who have already forgiven others (as in the Lord's Prayer); instead, divine forgiveness is the model for people to follow.[18]

The author ends his list of generalized injunctions by stressing the importance of love (*agapē*), which produces "perfect inner-cohesion" for the community (3:14). But this mutual love does not connote mutual equality. The author provides specific instructions for those occupying hierarchical social roles: wives/husbands, children/fathers (not mothers), slaves/masters. His injunctions to each member of these pairings show he assumes the hierarchies are natural and divinely instituted: in each case, the weaker partner needs to submit to the power and authority of the stronger. Wives are to *submit* to their husbands in obedience, while husbands are to *love* their wives and not make their lives "bitter." Children are to *obey* their parents in everything they require, since that is pleasing to the Lord, while fathers are not to *provoke* them. Slaves are to *obey* their masters in all they demand out of the fear of God and as a way of serving God; masters (literally: "lords") of slaves are to treat them *justly* and *fairly*, since they too have a Master (Lord) in heaven.

For the Christian household to function, everyone needs to understand their position in the power relations and behave accordingly. The author of Colossians expresses no concerns for the systematic problems built into social hierarchies; he accepts the status quo without question and insists that everyone embody the virtues appropriate to their position. To that extent, these are very conventional ethics indeed. But now they are also divinely sanctioned: the author insists that wives and slaves recognize their place and obey all orders, precisely because that is pleasing to God and will lead to a later reward.

Such teachings are not only more socially conformist than Paul's, they also represent a further step away from the concerns of Jesus. Nowhere does Jesus speak about the importance of social hierarchies. Instead, he subverts them, insisting his followers help the poor, the needy, and the outcast—issues never mentioned in the letter to the Colossians. The "Lord" may be front and center in this author's mind, but the historical Jesus's own ethical agenda is far removed from his concerns. He is addressing a community of believers in an altogether different world.

The heightened focus on inner-communal relations in Christian ethical discourse can be explained in part by the growing antagonism between church members and outsiders. Those not in the community of the saved were variably seen as either a threat or a target for conversion. Believers considered themselves a new social order, with spiritual fathers, mothers, brothers, sisters, and children that in many instances replaced the biological families they had abandoned. In some circles, Christians were instructed to "hate" their fathers and mothers (Luke 14:26; Gospel of Thomas 101) and to "remove themselves" from the world at large. Presumably, most individual Christians continued to love their biological families, friends, and neighbors. But animosities also arose even then, and the rhetoric of Christian leaders—whether or not it was regularly heeded by layfolk—stressed a fortress mentality of us versus them, with the "them" including close relations and former companions. As a result, the original Christian stress on acts of love became increasingly intramural, with the needs of insiders prioritized, sometimes exclusively.

That certainly is the case in some of the later writings of the New Testament. The Gospel of John, our last canonical Gospel, appearing some sixty years or so after Jesus's death, contains some of his best-known discourses. But in them he says surprisingly little about ethics, in contrast, say, to Matthew and Luke. This may be related to the fact that in none of Jesus's speeches in John does he speak about the coming Kingdom of God or the imminent appearance of a cosmic judge. As a corollary, Jesus does not urge his listeners to repent and return to God's graces by keeping his commands. The words "repent" and "repentance" never occur in John's Gospel.

Jesus's lengthy conversations and monologues in this account are almost entirely about his identity, about how he has come from heaven to reveal the truths about himself that can lead to eternal life. These, in turn, are topics he does not address in the earlier Gospels. And rather than urging his listeners to tend to the needs of the poor and marginalized, in John Jesus stresses the importance of community coherence. His followers need to love one another. He himself shows them how. At a climactic moment in the narrative, he assumes the role of a slave, washing his disciples' feet, telling them they need to do the same: "If I, your Lord and teacher, have washed your feet, you also ought to wash one another's feet" (13:14).

This a clear manifestation of *agapē*, loving service to others. But as usual in this Gospel, Jesus's injunction involves fellow believers. "I am giving you a new commandment: Love one another as I loved you," Jesus says. "By this everyone will know that you are my disciples: if you have love for one another"

(13:34–35). John sees this kind of commitment to the well-being of others as a mark of the Christian community. In contrast to their love for one another, they will be "hated" by "the world." Jesus tells his disciples they should take comfort in their persecution, because those outside "hated me first" (15:16). And since the world hates the Son of God, it "hates my Father also" (15:23), even though God sent Christ precisely because he "loved the world" (3:16). The contrasts then are complete: because Jesus's followers love him, God, and one another, they are hated by those who reject him.

John's stress on love within the community is nowhere combined with an injunction for Jesus's followers to reach out to those in need, to give their resources to the destitute, clothe the naked, or feed the hungry. In this context, if Jesus's followers do reach out to outsiders, it is to convince them to believe in Jesus for eternal life.

After the New Testament

Noncanonical writings from roughly the same time as John's Gospel also contain extensive ethical guidance. Around 100 CE we have a book known as the *Didache* (pronounced **Did**-ah-kay, meaning "Teaching") *of the Twelve Apostles*. The book does not claim to be written by the apostles, merely to represent their teachings.

The first section of the book provides succinct, rapid-fire ethical instructions organized as "the two paths, one of life and one of death" (1.1).[19] This appears to be an allusion to Jesus's saying in the Sermon on the Mount: "Enter through the narrow gate; for the gate is wide and the path easy that leads to destruction, and many are those who enter through it; but the gate is narrow and the path difficult that leads to life, and few are those who find it" (Matthew 7:13–14).

The *Didache*'s initial summary of the good but difficult path also echoes the teachings of Jesus: "This then is the path of life. First, love the God who made you, and second, your neighbor as yourself. And whatever you do not want to happen to you do not do to another" (*Didache* 1.1). The anonymous author then unpacks the meaning of these ethical demands, often by repeating words of Jesus without naming him or citing a Gospel source.[20] He begins simply by saying: "This is the teaching relating to these matters: Bless those who curse you, pray for your enemies, and fast for those who persecute you. For why is it so great to love those who love you? Do not the gentiles do this as well? But you should love those who hate you" (*Didache* 1:3)—words that seem straight from Matthew and Luke (Matthew 5:44, 46–47; Luke 6:28, 32–33, 35). So too do many other instructions: "If anyone slaps your right cheek, turn the other to them as well. . . . If anyone takes your cloak, give them your shirt as well. . . . Give to everyone who asks and do not ask for anything back" (*Didache* 1:4; see Matthew 5:39, 48; Luke 6:30).

Other teachings in the *Didache*, however, are not found in the Gospels and appear more closely tied to issues Jesus's followers confronted in later contexts: "Do not engage in pederasty, . . . do not practice magic, do not use enchanted potions, do not abort a fetus or kill a child that is born" (*Didache* 2.2). This is our earliest Christian condemnation of abortion, an issue not explicitly addressed in either the Old or New Testament. Along with the other injunctions in the verse, it appears to counter practices of "outsiders" to show the separate mores and moral superiority of Christians.[21] Even though murder was widely condemned throughout the Roman world, infant exposure and abortion were often practiced. Christian ethicists proscribed them, in part, to show the church's supreme commitment to the ethical life. So too the condemnation of pederasty (remember Plato's *Symposium* in chapter 2), magic, and potions—such things may have been practiced by pagans, but they were strictly off-limits for Christians, at least according to Christian rhetoric.

The idea that the followers of Jesus were to be morally superior to outsiders had been a standard feature of Christian discourse from the earliest years. We have seen this already in 1 Corinthians, where Paul is deeply concerned that the Christian community avoid behavior that might reflect badly on the gospel message. Thus his consternation about the man living with his stepmother, an immoral act "not even found among the gentiles" (1 Corinthians 5:1); the members of the church taking one another to civil court (6:1–8); and worship services so bizarre that outsiders might well think congregants had lost their minds (14:23). Over time, the emphasis shifted from avoiding scandalous behavior to promoting exceptional morality: followers of Jesus were to be a cut above the rest of the humanity when it came to ethical living. In no small part, this was to protect the community from accusations leveled against it by outsiders.

The Greek word for "defense" is *apologia*, and already in the New Testament we see traces of Christian apologetics, attempts to defend the faith from charges that it was illicit and dangerous. A particularly good instance can be found in the letter of 1 Peter, a book written in the name of Peter years after his death.[22] This unknown author was especially concerned about the harassment of Christians by outsiders. These were not imperial persecutions ordered by Roman authorities; such things came only later. This was local, grassroots opposition to the Christians for their refusal to participate in the social and religious life of their wider communities, which aroused suspicions.

The author of the letter instructs the Christians under attack to be ready to defend themselves: "Always be prepared to make a defense (*apologia*) to everyone who asks you for an account of the hope that is in you . . . while holding a good conscience so that, when you are slandered, those who revile your good conduct in Christ will be put to shame" (1 Peter 3:15–16). He repeatedly insists that followers of Jesus show their upstanding character to outsiders: "Preserve your good conduct among the gentiles so that when they slander you as evil doers they might see your good deeds and come to glorify God in the day of visitation" (2:12). Among other things, they are to be obedient to state authorities, so that everyone will see they are not persecuted for any actual wrongs they have done: "For it is the will of God that by doing good you may silence the ignorance of foolish people" (2:15).

This special need for Christians to engage in exemplary behavior became increasingly important with the passing of time. The early biblical intimations that Christians were sometimes seen as suspicious characters came to rather startling expression in the second Christian century, when opponents of Christians accused them of all sorts of deviant, nefarious, and downright dangerous activities.[23] Christians were seen as antisocial for refusing to participate in pagan festivals and public sacrifices, considered by nearly everyone else to be wholesome and happy communal affairs. More than that, Christians were known to be a closed and relatively secretive group. Church meetings were normally for believers only, and secrecy almost always breeds rumor. It did not help that Christians held their meetings at night or before dawn, and that they involved unusual rituals.

One of the most vivid and grotesque sets of charges leveled against Christians can be found in a book called *Octavius*, produced by a Christian of North Africa named Minucius Felix.[24] The book presents a fictitious debate between a Christian and a pagan. The characters and their actual debate may have been imagined, but the issues addressed were very real. The pagan, named Caecilius, explains some of the accusations occasionally made against Christians, and the Christian, Octavius, in turn refutes them. One particularly graphic depiction of Christian malfeasance involves the scandalous practices of their communal meetings. It appears that, historically, these charges derived from a seemingly reliable source: a highly placed Roman intellectual and public figure named Fronto, tutor of the emperor Marcus Aurelius.

Caecilius begins by explaining the Christians' secret and scandalous meetings:

> They recognize each other by secret marks and signs; hardly have they met when they love each other, throughout the world uniting in the practice of a veritable religion of lusts. Indiscriminately they call each other brother and sister, thus turning even ordinary fornication into incest.

On certain occasions these secret, incestuous activities take an even more remarkable turn:

> On a special day they gather for a feast with all their children, sisters, mothers—all sexes and ages. There, flushed with the banquet after such feasting and drinking, they begin to burn with incestuous passions. They provoke a dog tied to the lampstand to leap and bound towards a scrap of food which they have tossed outside the reach of his chain. By this means the light is overturned and extinguished and, with it, common knowledge of their actions; in the shameless dark with unspeakable lust they copulate in random unions, all equally being guilty of incest, some by deed, but everyone by complicity.

As if that is not enough, Caecilius claims the Christians' initiation rites involved ritual infanticide and cannibalism:

> The notoriety of the stories told of the initiation of new recruits is matched by their ghastly horror. A young babe is covered over with flour, the object being to deceive the unwary. It is then served before the person to be admitted into their rites. The recruit is urged to inflict blows onto it—they appear to be harmless because of the covering of flour. Thus, the baby is killed with wounds that remain unseen and concealed. It is the blood of this infant—I shudder to mention it—it is this blood that they lick with thirsty lips; these are the limbs they distribute eagerly; this is the victim by which they seal their covenant; it is by complicity in this crime that they are pledged to mutual silence; these are their rites, more foul than all sacrileges combined. (*Octavius*, ch. 9).

Scholars have long debated how such bizarre ideas of Christian behavior could have originated, usually on the assumption, which I share, that none of it could be true. It is sometimes argued that Christian liturgical practices came to be grotesquely distorted by rumormongers with limited knowledge but unlimited zeal. Christian meetings were indeed known to take place in the dark, since the church comprised believers at all socioeconomic levels and lower-class workers and slaves had to work during daylight hours. Moreover, members of the community did call one another "brother," "sister," "father," "mother," and "child." They were also known to greet one another with a "kiss of fellowship" and celebrate a ritual meal of bread and wine commemorating Christ's broken body and shed blood. So what is one to make of all that? Family members meeting kissing under the cloak of darkness? That's incest. Eating the "flesh" and drinking the "blood" of the "son of God"? That's murder and cannibalism.

Other scholars accept an easier solution: accusations of grotesque and inhumane behavior—in particular, killing babies and eating them—occur in a range of polemical texts from antiquity, always leveled at the nefarious and hated "Other." The same sorts of horrendous accusations can be found in pagan attacks against other pagans, pagan attacks against Jews, Christian attacks against heretics, and so on. There is a strong case for the view that Caecilius is simply regurgitating standard polemic, even if it is more scintillating to think that the charges were inspired by Christian ritual.

Whatever the origin of the accusations, how could Christians defend themselves against them? Indeed, how does anyone prove they have *not* been doing something? How do you prove a negative? If someone wants to believe a rumor, there is nothing on God's green earth to stop them. But Christian writers eventually emerged to deny the charges vigorously and make powerful counterclaims: Christians were the most moral human beings on the face of the planet. Anyone could see that simply by considering their ethical teachings and observing their daily lives.

This apologetic showcasing of Christian morality begins in the middle of the second century, when an increasing number of well-trained intellectuals converted to the faith and committed themselves to writing reasoned defenses—or "Apologies"—for it. Among the best known of the early Christian apologists are Justin of Rome (usually called Justin Martyr because of his demise), Tertullian of North Africa, and Origen of Alexandria, all three of whom went out of their way to defend Christians and celebrate their superior ethical behavior.[25] One of the lesser-known apologists was named Athenagoras, whose relative obscurity is unfortunate: his writings are terrifically interesting and exceedingly cogent in his refutation of pagan accusations against the faith. Only two relatively slim works have come down to us, one of which calls him a "philosopher from Athens" (hence his name). Otherwise we know precious little about him or his life.

His book *Petition for the Christians* is a straight-up defense of Christianity against charges leveled against it by pagan opponents. It dates to around 177 CE and is addressed to the emperors Marcus Aurelius and Commodus. There is almost no way, though, that the book would have actually made it into the hands of the rulers of the Western world, or that the author could have imagined it would. Much like Christian apologists today, Athenagorus was almost certainly preaching to the choir, providing his Christian readers with the logic and arguments they could use when encountering opposition from their pagan families, friends, and neighbors.

Most of the treatise defends Christians against the charge of atheism. This may seem a surprising accusation. Aren't Christians, of all people, the ones who believe in God? But it was a relatively common slander in the second and third centuries. The followers of Jesus were "without the gods" (the literal meaning of "atheist"), since they rejected all the divine beings worshipped in the world except their own. Athenagoras counters the charge by arguing that the Christian view of God is both right and true. There is only one God and the Christians are the ones who worship him, making the Christian faith superior to anything else on offer in the pagan world. Most readers today find his argument so sensible they don't see how there could be an opposition. That's the problem with "common sense" in different times and places.

The two other charges Athenagoras addresses involve Christian ethics, or rather, the horrendous Christian misdeeds already noted above. Athenagoras tries to prove attacks of cannibalism and incest are pure slander by arguing an empirical "reality": Christians are demonstrably more moral than any other people in the history of the planet, especially their pagan accusers. Athenagoras expresses incredulity that followers of pagan religions can accuse *Christians* of immorality. Just look at the Greek and Roman gods, worshipped even though tales about them constantly show off their adulteries and rapes and murders! Are these the models for decent behavior? Christians believe in a God who judges the righteous and reserves eternal fire for the wicked. Followers of Jesus are concerned for the welfare of society and for their own immortal souls. Of course, they are ethical.

Athenagoras then takes on the charges one by one. The claim that Christians are sexually licentious, he says, is laughable. Unlike Zeus, they have strict principles about passion and lust. It is against Christian rules for a man even to *look* at woman with desire. It is true they practice a ritual kiss during their worship services, but that is strictly regulated. Indeed, many Christians choose to live a holy life as perpetual virgins. Even married couples have sex only for the purposes of procreation. What's more, Christians insist on a single marriage: if a spouse dies, the surviving partner cannot remarry. That would be considered adultery.

Athenagoras insists that this strict regulation of sexual activity is unlike anything in the pagan world; for pagans to instruct Christians in sexual ethics reminds Athenagoras of the proverb about a "harlot" trying to "teach a matron." He reacts by turning the charge on his opponents: "Adulterers and pederasts, they revile us who live in self-denial or single marriage" (ch. 34).

As for brutal rituals for murdering babies and then consuming them, Athenagoras insists Christians are the least violent people in the empire. Even when attacked, they are instructed not to return "blow for blow" and are actually required to bless those who curse them. Christians do not even support legal homicide—that is, they oppose the death sentence. They are not allowed to watch "entertaining" murders in the arena, such as gladiatorial shows and animal fights (where wild animals are released to devour criminals). As to killing babies, Athenagoras argues it is unthinkable. Unlike pagans, Christians never "expose" their children, a widespread practice in which parents would leave an unwanted child in a public place, either to be taken up (usually to be raised in slavery) or to die. They don't even allow abortion—that is, destroy fetuses before they are fully human.

Of course, he avers, Christians cannot engage in cannibalism. They believe in a future resurrection of the body. In this treatise, Athenagoras is a bit vague on the logical connection between cannibalism and resurrection, but he does clarify his thinking in his only other surviving work, which defends the Christian belief in the resurrection of the dead. It was commonly thought in antiquity that the food a person consumed became part of their body during the process of digestion. This view raised some puzzling logical issues for Christians. In the case of cannibalism, when the bodies of both the cannibal and their victim were raised, who gets parts of the body that had been devoured? The person who originally had them or the one who ate them? In his treatise on the resurrection Athenagoras works to solve that problem, arguing that human flesh is digested differently from other foods so that it is always eliminated, never assimilated. But his point in the *Petition for the Christians* is that Christians themselves do not have to worry about the problem: they never eat anyone, let alone babies.

Throughout this short treatise Athenagoras has a simple line of defense: Christians go to radical extremes to observe God's sacred laws and, as a consequence, are far more moral than pagans. They're even more moral than the pagans' gods! Pagans may think adultery is bad; Christians do not lust. Pagans may condemn murder; Christians do not watch gladiatorial contests. Pagans may leave unwanted children to die; Christians do not even allow abortion.

Conclusion

In sum, as time went on, the followers of Jesus faced new challenges, leading them to shift their ethical emphases away from those of Jesus himself. The burgeoning Christian communities developed problems of their own, and a variety of ethical principles emerged in response. Moreover, as the apocalyptic urgency felt by Jesus faded, ethics became increasingly centered on behavior suitable for the long haul. Leaders of the churches did continue to stress the distinctive nature of Jesus's ethical principles, focused not on *eudaimonia* in this life or the importance of personal character for the sake of honor and status within one's community. They were about living for others. These others did tend to be those of their own Christian community—but it was a worldwide community. Active love was to be extended not only to those to whom one was personally related, biologically or socially, but to anyone in need, even strangers. An ideology of dominance shifted to an ideology of service. There was, to be sure, a reward for this kind of life in the world to come. Even so, this new ideal of service to others had salubrious results for society at large. For centuries, the hope for heaven would facilitate care for the hungry, homeless, elderly, friendless, outcast, marginalized, victimized, and lowly here on earth, as we will explore further in the chapters to follow.

Chapter Seven

LOVE AFTER JESUS

I often wonder how many people in our world consciously try to follow the teachings of Jesus. I certainly know a good number who do, some of whom do not identify as Christians. They are simply good-hearted, honest people who think Jesus's ethics provide important insights into how we ought to live: loving our neighbor as ourselves, treating others as we want to be treated, and caring for those in need. None of these people actually follows the literal teachings of Jesus. I've never met a non-Christian who has sold everything to give to the poor or who is completely unconcerned about where their next meal is coming from, since the kingdom is near. Then again, I've met only a couple of Christians who have gone that far.[1]

I do know many Christians who quietly go about the business of helping others, volunteering their time and giving to worthy causes for those in desperate need. Among these I am most impressed with the ones who do not showcase their great personal virtue. They just live the way they think is right, doing good for others even at some expense to themselves.

What I find depressing are the many, many Christians around us who are incredibly vocal about their commitment to Jesus's teachings even though they apparently either don't know what they are or ignore the ones most directly relevant to their lives. And not just the teachings of Jesus, but the teachings of the Bible as a whole. Why do some of those who insist most vehemently that our country should follow Christian teachings spend so much of their time pushing for social policies unrelated to anything in the Bible—or, even worse, precisely contrary to what it says? You would think these Bible-believers would at least read their Bibles.

This past week (as I write these words) a US congressional representative spoke passionately against a piece of proposed legislation that would require educational institutions not to engage in anti-Semitic discriminatory practices (that is, against Jews for being Jews). She vehemently protested that if this bill were to become law, she and other Bible-believing Christians would be convicted for "believing the Gospel that says Jesus was handed over to [the Jewish king] Herod to be crucified by the Jews."[2] My first thought was: God help us.

Which Bible do you suppose she was reading? Answer: no Bible. In three of the Gospel accounts of Jesus's trial (Matthew, Mark, and John) Herod makes no appearance at all. In the one account that does bring Herod into the trial, the Gospel of Luke, he meets with Jesus because the Roman governor Pontius Pilate can find no guilt in him and wants someone else to deal with the problem. But Herod too finds Jesus innocent and sends him back to Pilate, who then orders him crucified by his own soldiers (Luke 23:6–12, 15). Even here, then, Herod has nothing to do with Jesus's condemnation; it is a Roman who convicts him and Romans who crucify him. So why would this congresswoman complain that the proposed legislation would not allow her to affirm the "biblical view" that Jesus was "handed over to the [Jewish king] Herod to be crucified by the Jews"? One would imagine, or at least hope, it was out of sheer ignorance, not malicious forethought. But even if so, it was an ignorance rooted in her own mistaken views about Jews as literal Christ-killers.

I wish this kind of clueless and dangerous use of the Bible were a rarity in our world, but alas, it is oh so common. A frightening number of vocal proponents of biblical views do not appear to know they are simply weaponizing the Bible to promote their own social and political agendas. For years now our country has been torn apart by the question of abortion, with many of the arguments inevitably rooted in what the Bible, and especially Jesus, have to say about it—and, in particular, about when human life begins. Conservative Christian commentators are unanimous that the biblical view is that life begins at conception. But where does Jesus say anything about that? Nowhere. How about the rest of the Bible? There is no explicit mention anywhere about the status of the fetus as a human and no reference to abortion as murder. On the contrary, the several passages that do present "the biblical view" of the status of the unborn agree that the unborn is not yet fully human with human rights. Moreover the one passage that speaks of an induced abortion cites it as a procedure decreed by God to test a woman for infidelity.[3]

I myself do not use the Bible to decide modern ethical issues, and I would therefore never use the Bible to say whether abortion should ever be permitted. But if someone does choose to appeal to Scripture, they should at least learn what it says instead of assuming it affirms their own views.

What is most frustrating is that what the Bible does say—and specifically what Jesus teaches—is not simply overlooked in the raging debates about how we as individuals and a society should behave toward others, it is often completely reversed. What is the Bible's view about welcoming those from other lands into the country? The Old Testament repeatedly says that anyone who comes to live in the land of Israel should have all the rights and privileges of native-born Israelites: "When a foreigner resides among you in your land, do not mistreat them. The foreigner residing among you must be treated as your native-born. Love them as yourself, for you were foreigners in Egypt. I am the Lord your God" (Leviticus 19:33–34, NIV). And, what does Jesus himself say? Welcome the stranger, take care of the foreigner, give to *everyone* who asks of you, love your enemy.

One reasonable response to these teachings is that they are not practicable in our day and age. They may well have made sense when the world's population was smaller, but they can scarcely be considered viable policy now, in our country. I actually agree with that view. It does not make much sense to endorse social and political policies devised in vastly different circumstances over two thousand years ago. But then why do some Christian groups appeal directly to the Bible to bolster social agendas they favor—even if the issues show up in Scripture with striking infrequency (for example, "homosexuality") or not at all (for example, abortion)—but ignore the Bible's most basic and emphatic teachings connected with, say, immigration and care for the poor? Clearly, it is because they prefer exploiting the Bible to reading it.

This misuse of the teachings of Jesus and the rest of the Bible has been around for-roughly-ever. In the period of our interest, the early decades of the church, this kind of misuse made a minimal impact on society at large. The Christian church was a minuscule sliver of the Roman world during its first two hundred years and was not destined to start influencing state policy and legislation until toward the end of the fourth century.[4] It is nonetheless interesting to consider how Jesus's teachings were treated in this opening era of the church—especially how they were moderated and softened—since even in their altered forms they played a significant role in the lives of his followers. Eventually they transformed both the moral thinking and the social practices of the West.

This chapter focuses on Christian views and practices of love. The chapter that follows will consider two particularly meaningful ways of putting that love into action, through charitable giving and personal forgiveness.

Love in Christian Teaching after Jesus

We have seen that the English word "love" connotes a range of emotions and actions, as do the various Greek words for "love," and that often the English and Greek terms do not line up conceptually. The Greek words themselves often overlap in meaning and are sometimes used interchangeably. Only by looking at the context of a particular passage (in any author, not just biblical ones) is it possible to decide which particular concept lies behind the word. Still, throughout ancient Greek literature, references to affection between parents, children, and other family members often use the verb *stergō*; references to passionate relationships, especially but not only between sexual partners typically use *eraō*; close friendships between people who appreciated and were committed to each other, *phileō*; and affectionate esteem, *agapaō*.

With that in mind, it is interesting and possibly a bit surprising to find that *stergō* (either as a verb or in its noun form) never occurs in the reports of Jesus's teachings or, in fact, anywhere in the New Testament. Less surprising, perhaps, *eraō* does not either. *Phileō* shows up a good bit: twenty-five times in the New Testament as a whole, with twenty-one of them in the Gospels. But it is worth noting that when Jesus uses the term in Matthew, Mark, and Luke, it always indicates the *wrong* things people "love," for example, status or honor (see Matthew 6:5; 23:6; Luke 20:46).[5] John's Gospel uses it in a positive sense: God loves Christ, Jesus loves others, his followers love him, and so on (for example, John 5:20; 11:3; 16:27). Outside the Gospels the word is rarely used—for example, only once in Paul's writings (1 Corinthians 16:22).

Far and away, when New Testament authors talk about love they use the verb *agapaō* and its noun, *agapē*. When they do so, they nearly always change its nuance away from "affectionate esteem" to "active love," the kind of love that works in another's best interest, whatever one feels about them. The word becomes almost a synonym for "altruism." In their rhetoric and their claims about communal behavior, early Christians stressed the importance of helping others in need, even those outside their circles of family and friends. But there was a proviso: the recipients of these acts of love—even when they were distant strangers—were normally members of the larger Christian community, not outsiders at large. This was a change from the teachings of Jesus. Even so, at some point the vast majority of the Roman world's inhabitants would claim allegiance to the Christian faith, and in that sense nearly all "strangers" were also "insiders."

Paul's Chapter on Love

One can hardly talk about early Christian views of love without considering the views of the apostle Paul, especially his famous discussion in 1 Corinthians 13: the "love chapter," read at roughly 99 percent of all weddings ever held in America, although it is invariably misunderstood by nearly everyone wishing the happy couple many years of marital bliss. In rather poetic language Paul waxes eloquent on the importance of love (*agapē*) as the principal virtue of the Christian faith. The chapter begins with familiar words:

If I speak in the tongues of humans or angels, but do not have *agapē* I am a noisy gong or a clanging cymbal. And if I have the power of prophecy and know all mysteries and all knowledge and have all faith even to move mountains, but do not have *agapē*, I am nothing. And if I sell all my possessions and give my body over to be burned, but do not have *agapē*, I gain nothing.

Agapē is patient and kind, *agapē* is not jealous, it does not brag, it is not puffed up, it does not act shamefully; it does not seek its own way, it is not irritable, it does not hold resentments; it does not rejoice in what is wrong but revels in the truth; it bears all things, believes all things, hopes all things, and endures all things. (1 Cor. 13:1–3)

These are famously beautiful words. No wonder they regularly feature in the ceremony where two people pledge their love for life. One only hopes the couple pays special attention to the importance of patience and of avoiding jealousy, self-centeredness, irritability, and resentment.

Still, when Paul wrote this inspiring paean to love, marital bliss was the furthest thing from his mind. Anyone who reads 1 Corinthians carefully should notice this right away but . . . alas. I am constantly amazed that no one (even avid Bible readers) seems to notice that 1 Corinthians 13 comes between, well, 1 Corinthians 12 and 1 Corinthians 14, passages in which living happily ever after with one's adored spouse is nowhere in sight. The entire three-chapter passage is about how members of the church are supposed to use their spiritual gifts for the good of the Christian community.

To make sense of the passage I need to provide some background. One of the most striking features of Paul's letter to this deeply fractured Corinthian church is that he never addresses any of its leaders—a bishop, a priest, an elder, a deacon, a pastor, or anyone else in charge. There is a good reason for that. There weren't any church leaders. Like Paul's other churches, this was a "charismatic community," one that was run by the "gifts" (Greek: *charismata*) the Spirit of God had distributed among its members.

Paul understood that whoever joined the church through baptism was filled with the Spirit and given a spiritual gift that would contribute to the ongoing life of the community (1 Corinthians 12:13). People were given various gifts:

administration, healing, wisdom (knowing how to deal with complicated issues of faith in real life), faith (to perform amazing deeds), prophecy (to speak God's word), tongues (to converse with God in an unknown human or angelic language), the interpretation of tongues (to translate what was being said), and so on. These gifts were meant to build up the community and allow it to function effectively in the short interim between the resurrection and the return of Jesus, when he would inaugurate the future kingdom. During this brief period there was no need for church leaders: the Spirit led the church through the gifts distributed among its members.

In 1 Corinthians 12, Paul insists all these gifts were given by the Spirit for the "common good" of the entire community (1 Cor. 12:7–11). Not everyone could have a dramatic gift like prophecy, tongues, or healing. Paul likens the Christian community in Corinth to the human body: every part has a function, all parts have to work together, and even seemingly lesser parts are essential for the well-being of the whole.

Because some gifts are "greater" than others, as Paul himself acknowledges (12:31), spiritual competition had developed among members of the Corinthian community, leading to a good bit of chaos in their worship services. The ability to speak in tongues was particularly prized—it is, after all, a pretty amazing phenomenon—and apparently things had gotten out of hand. Multiple people were speaking in tongues during the service, not, in Paul's view, to serve the community, but for the sake of their own transcendent experiences and possibly to demonstrate their great spiritual abilities and superior standing before God (1 Cor. 14:26–33). Other "superior" gifts were obviously susceptible to similar problems, for example the Spirit-given ability to speak a message directly from God (prophecy), or to perform wondrous deeds beyond the ability of most mere mortals (faith healing and miracle working). We very much wish we knew what these entailed, or were believed to entail.

The problem of spiritual gifts in Corinth is so pronounced that Paul takes three entire chapters to deal with it. Chapter 12 discusses the variety of gifts and the need for everyone to use theirs for the good of the community without flaunting their spiritual superiority or being envious of those with "greater" gifts. Chapter 14 deals directly with the problem of speaking in tongues and provides guidelines for their use in a communal setting. Paul argues, for example, that only two or three people should speak in tongues in any meeting, one at a time, and only if an interpreter is present (14:27).

Wedged between these two chapters is chapter 13, the "love chapter." It too is about spiritual gifts, as clearly shown by its opening words. Every time I hear them read I wonder if anyone listening has any clue what they mean. Do they sound to you like they are addressing issues of conjugal bliss?

> If I speak in the *tongues* of humans or angels, but do not have *agapē* I am a noisy gong or a clanging cymbal. And if I have the power of *prophecy* and know all *mysteries* and all *knowledge* and have all *faith* even to move mountains, but do not have *agapē*, I am nothing.

What does all this talk of tongues, prophecy, knowledge, and faith have to do with a bride and groom? Nothing directly. These are spiritual gifts. Paul is saying that having them in excess is of no use unless they are being employed for the benefit of others in the community. The gifts are meant to help the congregation, not to exalt the self. They are to be instruments of *agapē*. The love chapter is about how members of the church are to use their *charismata*, their special "gifts of the Spirit," for the building up of their fellow members in the body of Christ.

This understanding explains the very end of the passage as well, which clearly is not referencing marital love:

> Love never fails. As for *prophecies*, they will pass away; as for *tongues* they will cease; as for *knowledge* it will pass away. For we know in part and we prophecy in part. But when the perfect come, that which is partial will pass away.
>
> When I was a young child, I spoke as a child, I thought as child, and I reasoned as a child. When I became a man, I did away with the things of childhood. For we now see in a mirror dimly, but then we will see face to face. Now I know in part, then I will fully know just as I am fully known. Now there remain faith, hope, and *agapē*, these three, but the greatest of these is *agapē*.

We are still in the realm of spiritual gifts: prophecy, tongues, knowledge. Paul insists these are temporary gifts meant to sustain the church through the brief interim period before "the perfect" comes—that is, before Christ returns in glory to bring a kingdom in which his people will no longer need these imperfect ways of hearing and knowing the will of God. When Jesus's followers enter that eternal kingdom, it will be like maturing from a young child to a full adult.

When Paul says "faith, hope, and love" alone remain, he is referring to the greatest gifts of all, those given to all believers, connecting the past, present, and future. Faith has already made Jesus's followers right with God; hope provides them with the assurance that the glorious kingdom of God is soon to come; and love guides their day-to-day existence in the present, as they live for others rather than for themselves. The "greatest of these is love" because when members of the community act in ways that benefit one another, they begin to reveal what life will be like in the kingdom. The church begins to experience the kingdom as members use their divinely endowed gifts from God to bring healing, insight, and knowledge of God to one another, building each other up and caring for one another's needs and concerns.

Christ as the Model of Agapē

For Paul and most other writers of the New Testament, the major motivation for living in *agapē* was the example of Christ himself. As the author of 1 John says, "We love, because he loved us first" (1 John 4:19). This Christian notion is closely tied to the view of the Hebrew Bible that the love of others follows from God's love of his people. For ancient Israelites, to portray God as the "God of the poor" or the "God of the oppressed" was not only to affirm a theological truism but also to express a historical claim: God delivered the children of Israel from their enslavement in Egypt and brought them to the Promised Land. He did this as an act of grace for those who did not deserve it. His concern for the needy was embodied in his interactions with them. And he expected his people to follow his example.

According to earliest Christian traditions, Jesus enacted the divine character of *agapē* in an even more radical way. He did not merely shower blessings from on high. He entered the world and gave his life for others, willingly experiencing the pains of crucifixion to provide salvation for those who were condemned to death. Early Christian authors focused on this example set by Christ in their ethical instruction. Nowhere is this expressed more clearly than in another stunningly powerful passage of Paul's writings, the famous "Christ poem" of Philippians 2:6–11.

Scholars have long thought the passage embodies a previously existing poem, either written by Paul himself or composed by someone else and in wider circulation before Paul inserted it into his letter.[6] The poem portrays Christ as a preexistent divine being in the heavenly realm who chose to become human and die on the cross. Because of his selfless act, God exalted him to an even higher position than he had before his appearance on earth, making him equal with himself in power and glory. Paul does not cite the poem to teach a lesson about incarnation, however, but to encourage his Philippian readers to imitate Christ's example.[7]

His introduction to the poem provides the key to its interpretation. Even though Paul does not use the word *agapē*, the concept of "self-giving love" is the clear focus. He exhorts his readers:

Do nothing from selfishness or conceitedness, but out of humility consider one another superior to yourselves. None of you should look after your own interests; look after the interests of others. Have the same mindset among yourselves that was also in Christ Jesus. . . .

He then explains what this mindset of Christ was:

Who, although he was in the form of God
Did not regard being equal with God
Something to be grasped after.
But he emptied himself
Taking on the form of a slave,
And coming in the likeness of humans.
And being found in appearance as a human

> *He humbled himself*
> *Becoming obedient unto death—even death on a cross.*

Ultimately, this act of sacrifice led to Christ's even greater glory. For in response to this act of altruism, God rewarded Christ beyond what anyone could imagine:

> *Therefore God highly exalted him*
> *And bestowed on him the name*
> *That is above every name.*
> *That at the name of Jesus*
> *Every knee should bow*
> *Of those in heaven, and on earth, and under the earth.*
> *And every tongue confess*
> *That Jesus Christ is Lord*
> *To the glory of God the Father.*

Even though Paul never quotes any of Jesus's teachings about the importance of self-sacrifice for others (in this letter or any other), the Christ poem powerfully conveys the message by citing Christ's own sacrifice as a model. Just as Christ forsook everything even to the point of death, his followers are to do likewise. In far more quotidian terms, they are not to focus on their own wants and needs. They are to give of themselves completely to others.

Paul as the Imitator of Christ

Paul elsewhere claims he practices what he preaches, modeling himself after Christ by suffering. He also insists this is the mark of all Jesus's true followers (2 Corinthians 11:13–31). Until Jesus returns, this world continues to be filled with pain and misery. Anyone who thinks becoming a follower of Christ will lead to a life of comfort and ease has misunderstood the Christian message. For Paul, being a Christian means suffering for others.

This message clearly runs at odds with what you may hear from your favorite televangelist or Prosperity Gospel preacher who assures you that God wants you to live the good life of wealth and luxury, that if you commit your life to Christ, he will provide you with (literal) riches beyond your imagination. It is no surprise this modern message is more attractive than Paul's. A gospel of pain is a tough sell in a capitalist society. It wasn't wildly popular in Paul's day either, even among his own converts. We know this from Paul's own letters, especially 1 and 2 Corinthians, both of which oppose teachers in the community who maintained that the glories of heaven were already available to the followers of Jesus as a reward for their faith. Paul responds to this view with polemical irony in a remarkable passage of 2 Corinthians, which explains why he, and not these false teachers, is a true apostle: he suffers more.[8]

Before explaining the passage, I need again to provide some background. After Paul wrote 1 Corinthians, he learned that much of his advice had gone nowhere. The divisions in the church continued and other apostles had come to Corinth proclaiming an alluring message: the blessings of the age to come were already available to believers now. These new emissaries held themselves up as evidence: they were eloquent speakers, with a charismatic presence and a powerful demeanor. Paul, they pointed out, was a physical weakling and a hopeless public speaker (2 Corinthians 10:10). Clearly, he did not understand or possess the power of Christ's resurrection.

It may be surprising that when Paul responds to these charges in 2 Corinthians, he does not merely agree with his enemies' assessment, but enthusiastically embraces it (2 Corinthians 10–12). His Christian opponents are right. He is pathetic by human standards. But, for Paul, this shows he is the true apostle of Christ. These "superapostles" (the sarcastic term he uses for them: 2 Corinthians 11:5) have precisely the wrong idea. Christ was not glorified in this world; he suffered horribly. So will his apostles. Paul is superior to the others because he shares in Christ's suffering in this wicked age. Only when Christ returns in glory will the evil powers that rule now be destroyed and the followers of Jesus be exalted. That means that anyone who is powerful and exalted now is manifestly siding with the godless powers still in control of this world. These others, then, are "false apostles, deceitful workers, disguising themselves as apostles of Christ." That is no wonder, says Paul, since "even

Satan disguises himself as an angel of light." So too "his servants," whose "end will correspond to their deeds" (2 Cor. 11:13–15).

To show that he, the suffering apostle, is the true servant of Christ, Paul provides a remarkable litany of his many horrible experiences while preaching the gospel. In comparison with these superapostles, Paul has undergone:

> Far more labors, far more imprisonments, far more beatings, often nearly unto death. Five times from Jews I have received the forty lashes minus one; three times I have been beaten with rods; once I was punished with stoning; three times shipwrecked and spent a night and day at sea; frequently on journeys, in danger from rivers, in danger from robbers, in danger from my own people, in danger from gentiles, in danger in cities, in danger in the wilderness, in danger to the point of death, in danger from false apostles, in labor and toil, often in sleeplessness, in hunger and thirst, often without food, in cold and exposure, . . . If I must boast, I will boast of the things that reveal my weakness. (2 Corinthians 11:23–30)

The repeated imprisonments, beatings, danger—and the stoning (!)—were all "for the sake of the gospel." That is, Paul accepted his pain and misery because it came as the cost of preaching salvation to those who needed to hear the message of Christ. He was suffering for others, as had Christ. That, of all things, was his "boast." He loved others—the Corinthians and his converts elsewhere—so much that he was willing to suffer horribly for them. And since he endured such pains, he, like Christ, would in the end be fantastically rewarded by God.

This, then, was at the heart of Paul's ethical message: like Jesus, he insisted that care for others should trump all personal considerations for well-being and contentment. Earthly *eudaimonia* was no longer in the picture. Serving others was the way to live.

Love after Paul

This focus on intra-community ethics continued long after Paul's day. I have already pointed out, for example, that the Gospel of John, written some thirty years after Paul's death, presents Jesus's ethical teachings quite differently from the earlier and more historical accounts of Matthew, Mark, and Luke. In John's Gospel, Jesus declares that his followers would be "hated by the world" even though they would be known as those who "love one another." Here, love is to be directed to fellow community members. "I am giving you a new commandment," Jesus announces, "that you love one another, just as I loved you, so you should love one another; by this everyone will know you are my disciples, that you have love for one another" (John 13:34–35).

A similar perspective can be found in the anonymous first epistle of John, named after the alleged author of the Gospel because of their extensive similarities in language and theme.[9] Whoever actually wrote the book has a lot to say about ethics within his Christian community. It was an ethics focused entirely on *agapē*. The word appears twenty-one times in the short five-chapter letter, more than in the entire Greek translation of the Old Testament; the verb *apapaō* occurs an additional eighteen times. As with the Gospel of John, love is to be expressed to others within the Christian community.

Here again the injunction to love is rooted in the belief that Christ died for sins. Jesus's followers "know love" because he "laid down his life" for them; they should therefore be willing to do the same for their Christian brothers and sisters (3:16). They are to "love one another because love is from God and everyone who loves is born of God and knows God; the one who does not love is not from God, because God is love" (4:7–8).

This love of others involves altruistic action that comes at a cost. "Those who have worldly goods and see a brother or sister in need, but close their heart to them, how does the love of God remain in them?" the author asks (3:17). The faithful should even be willing to die for one another (3:16). That is what Christ did, and anyone who does not love a fellow member of the community in this manner cannot love God. "This is the commandment we have from him: the one who loves God should love the brother or sister" (4:21).

Love Outside the New Testament

Christian writings outside the canon embody similar ideas, often contrasting the extreme self-sacrifice of Christians with the lives of outsiders not committed to *agapē*. One example comes in the letter of 1 Clement, sent in 95 CE or so from the Christians of Rome to the church of Corinth.[10] The letter addresses a serious problem that had arisen in Corinth, an ecclesiastical takeover in which the leaders of the church had been ousted by other members who assumed control. Was there a vote? A shouting match? Actual physical conflict? We don't know. However the transfer of ecclesiastical authority occurred, the Roman Christians were very upset and wrote their letter to urge the Corinthians to restore the original elders to their rightful positions.

It is a very long letter for such a direct purpose, but throughout its pages a key theme recurs: those who are committed to God are to serve others, not promote themselves. Followers of Jesus are to be humble, not power-hungry; committed to the welfare of the community, not to self-advancement. Over the course of the letter, the author provides numerous biblical and non-biblical models of this kind of altruistic behavior. In one particularly stunning example, he claims that "many" Christians in Rome have submitted themselves to voluntary incarceration to serve out the sentences of those in prison; many others have sold themselves into slavery for money to provide alms to the poor (1 Clement 55.2). These claims may be a bit hard to believe (can he really mean "many"?), but it is also hard to believe he is flat-out lying, since it seems to be a claim that could have been checked.[11]

Even if the author's claim is completely bogus or only partially true, he clearly assumes this kind of self-sacrificing behavior *should* be true, that is, that being a good Christian means living wholeheartedly by the dictates of *agapē*. The pinnacle of ethical behavior is to abandon personal well-being for the sake of others who are not even connected through family ties or friendship. It scarcely needs repeating: you won't find anything like *this* in Plato, Aristotle, Cicero, Seneca, Plutarch, Epictetus, or ... pick your Greek or Roman moral philosopher. Within seventy years of Jesus's life, the entire notion of what it means to live ethically had shifted decisively within the confines of the church from what had been found in the surrounding environment from time immemorial.

This ethic became a standard feature of later Christian writing. As just one additional example out of hundreds, consider the words of Dionysius, bishop of the large church of Alexandria in the middle of the third century. In a letter quoted by the church historian Eusebius, Dionysius discusses one of the truly horrible plagues on record, which he describes as "More terrifying . . . than any terror, more frightful than any disaster whatever." How did Christians deal with the disaster, as their fellow believers died around them in droves?

> Most of our brother-Christians showed unbounded love and loyalty, never sparing themselves and thinking only of one another. Heedless of the danger, they took charge of the sick, attending to their every need and ministering to them in Christ, and with them departed this life serenely happy; for they were infected by others with the disease, drawing on themselves the sickness of their neighbors and cheerfully accepting their pains. Many, in nursing and curing others, transferred their death to themselves and died in their stead. . . . The best of our brothers and sisters lost their lives in this manner. . . . Very soon the same services were done for them, since those left behind were constantly following those gone before." (Eusebius, *Church History*, 7.22)[12]

Again, these enthusiastic claims of death-defying altruism may be a bit hard to believe, especially the insistence that "most" Christians were doing this. But whatever the historical realities, the letter shows that Christian leaders believed Christians *should* behave in this way and claimed that many did. Followers of Jesus realized the right way to live in this world was to be ready to leave it, even in great agony, if that would benefit another.

Underlying this view was certainly an eschatological belief that living and dying like this would bring inestimable rewards in the life to come. It bears repeating that altruistic acts—even extreme ones—may have egoistic motivations. But with the rise of Christianity, the temporal and spatial loci of happiness shifted. In Christian rhetoric, at least, and presumably sometimes in actual practice, personal well-being, contentment, and satisfaction in this life did not enter into the question. On the contrary, the life of *agapē* entailed supreme sacrifice in obedience to God, even if the often unspoken assurance remained: *eudaimonia* abandoned now will lead to glory beyond all imagining in the world to come.

Evidence from Outside the Church

It may be easy to think these rhetorical claims of Christian self-sacrifice were nothing more than fictions invented by church leaders to showcase the moral superiority of the faithful. We do, however, have corroborating evidence that Christians (most of them? some of them?) did (sometimes?) behave differently from pagans adhering to traditional Greek and Roman views of morality. The most famous support comes in a lament of the last pagan emperor, Julian the Apostate (331–367 CE).

Julian was the nephew of the first Christian on the imperial throne, Constantine (272–337 CE).[13] After Constantine's death, his sons, also Christians, ruled the empire together or singly (they were often at each others' throats) until the death of the last one standing, Constantius II, leaving his cousin Julian heir to the throne. Like the rest of the ruling family, Julian had been raised a Christian. After assuming power, however, he revealed he had earlier converted to paganism—hence his sobriquet, "Apostate"—and he took steps to lead the empire away from Christianity and back to the traditional religions of Rome. At the end of a short reign (361–63 CE), Julian died of an ill-advised military action on the field. One can only speculate how the history of the West would have changed had he ruled forty years like his famously Christian uncle.

Because of his longtime involvement with the church before his apostasy, Julian understood its workings from the inside. As a ruler, he found it particularly irritating that Christians engaged in such open and well-known altruism in contrast to those adhering to the Roman religions of his day. There were still more pagans than Christians in the empire at the time, but the church was rapidly expanding and the attractions of this relatively new faith were now widely known. Julian believed that luring followers of Jesus back to the religions of Rome would require changes in pagan moral practices to match those found among Christians and Jews. This is clear from his well-known lament (in which he calls Christians "Galileans," since their religion started with the Galilean Jesus):

> Why do we not observe that it is their benevolence to strangers, their care for the graves of the dead, and the pretended holiness of their lives that have done most to increase atheism [i.e., Christianity]? . . . It is disgraceful that, when no Jew ever has to beg, and the impious Galileans support not only their own poor but ours as well, everyone can see that our people lack aid from us. (Julian, Letter 22)

At this stage, Christian altruism was obviously no longer exclusively intramural; Christians assisted the poor outside their ranks. Julian's remarks show the clear connection between Christian understandings of love and charitable giving. "Love" for the Christians was never about an emotion or passion; it was *agapē* in the new sense—giving to others to help them in their need.

Chapter Eight

CHARITABLE GIVING AND FORGIVENESS AFTER JESUS

Two weeks ago, I drove to our mountain house in western North Carolina to do some thinking and writing. I was not overly concerned about the weather. Hurricane Helene was heading toward the west coast of Florida and was projected to move north from there, with the mountains just outside the eastern edge of its path. I thought there would probably be some wind and a lot of rain, but not much else.

The storm unexpectedly veered east, and at 4:00 a.m. on September 27, 2024, it hit us head-on. For me, in a solid house built on the side of a forested mountain, it was not disastrous, just frightening. A mudslide buried the only road in and I was cut off from the rest of the world—no internet, no cell coverage, no way to get out. I had no idea how bad the devastation was until days later, when some of the roads were cleared and I could return home to Durham, which was practically untouched.

The storm was merciless. Over a hundred lives were lost just in North Carolina, with many homes and businesses swept off the map, thousands of others seriously damaged, water systems ruined, stretches of major highways wiped out. It will take a very long time just to get the basic infrastructure rebuilt and the livelihoods that go with them restored. Many neighborhoods and businesses may never return at all.

Now, as I write, some days removed from the storm, I am impressed and touched by the concern that has been and continues to be expressed not just by good people in the state of North Carolina but throughout the country and indeed the world: first responders moving into action, valiant local volunteers going door-to-door searching for survivors, those with basic provisions bringing them in however possible (transporting water by mule, state and federal government flying in supplies), national and international charities providing resources, organizations doing food drives, multitudes donating to disaster relief. There were, as usually happens, complaints, often aided by baseless rumors spreading quickly, that the government was ignoring or exploiting the situation. Even these rumors are sociologically interesting. They show the massive support we expect when we experience calamity: material assistance from people we don't know, from charities, from our government.

This is a modern phenomenon. In a crisis today, people feel a moral obligation to lend a hand, even to strangers who live hundreds or thousands of miles away.

I sometimes think about how news of such a calamity would have affected people in the Roman Empire. We know of horrible natural disasters from antiquity: epidemics (the horrible plague in Athens, fifth century BCE), devastating fires (Rome, 64 CE), volcanic eruptions that wiped out entire cities (Vesuvius, 79 CE), various earthquakes, droughts leading to horrendous starvation. At times there were indeed attempts to rescue victims and find survivors, at least those who were family members and friends.[1] And sometimes there was governmental support for the wealthy to rebuild their estates. But concern for the unknown poor and destitute—that is, for the vast majority of the population—was never on the radar screen.[2] There were no disaster relief organizations; no government-funded agencies; no public charities; no food banks; no collection points for needed resources; no fundraisers. People may have felt badly about the destruction when they heard of it. But there was little they would have done about it even if they could. Or even a sense they should.[3]

How times change. We begin to see the change already in the New Testament among the followers of Jesus.

It would be a mistake to think Christians after Jesus's death regularly followed his radical teachings literally. His demand to "sell everything and give to the poor" was almost universally abandoned until some three centuries later when the rise of monasticism provided notable and impressive exceptions. But from the beginning, Christian leaders did stress the importance of generous giving to provide for the needs of the poor. Moreover, the idea that everyone had *something* to give others took root early on. That is, unlike in most of the broader Roman world, charitable giving was not a reserve of the fabulously wealthy. Anyone with extra resources of any kind and on any level could help those who were worse off. Giving was democratized.

Paul and the Collection for Jerusalem

These features of Christian charity were evidenced already in the writings of Paul. One often overlooked feature of Paul's missionary endeavors is his resolute effort to raise funds from his gentile churches for the impoverished and struggling Jewish Christians in Jerusalem.[4] In Romans, his final surviving letter, Paul indicates he is set to travel to Jerusalem to deliver the donations he has raised for "those who are poor among the saints" (Romans 15:25–27). The monies, he tells us, have come from the generous giving of his churches in Macedonia and Achaia (modern Greece).

This collection is also mentioned in Paul's two earlier letters sent to Corinth (located in Achaia). He ends 1 Corinthians by explaining how the church was to take the collection: on the first day of the week (Sunday), everyone in the congregation was to put aside any surplus. The funds collected would be sent to Jerusalem through Corinthian delegates, possibly accompanied by Paul (1 Cor. 15:1–4). In his second letter, Paul devotes two chapters to the collection, exhorting his Corinthian converts to be generous (2 Corinthians 8–9).[5] He points out that the churches of Macedonia—presumably in Philippi and Thessalonica—had provided funds, despite being in rather hard straits themselves:

For in a great test of affliction, the abundance of their joy and their depth of poverty has overflowed in a wealth of liberality, for they gave as much as they were able, I can attest, and beyond their ability they gave, voluntarily, with many entreaties begging us to participate in the grace and fellowship of this ministry to the saints. (2 Cor. 8:2–4)

Paul is not simply stating a historical fact ("the Macedonians gave a lot"), but making an exhortation: "Just as you excelled in everything, excel in this act of grace as well" (2 Cor. 8:7). Paul then builds his case. The Macedonian Christians are not the only model to be followed. There is the example of Christ as well: "For you know the gracious act of our Lord Jesus Christ, that even though he was wealthy he became poor for our sake, so that you might become wealthy by his poverty" (2 Cor. 8:9).

Paul is clearly not talking about the historical Jesus leaving his palatial surroundings in rural Galilee to become an itinerant preacher, but about leaving his heavenly glory to come to earth to die for others. His followers too should give up whatever they have for the sake of others. The difference, of course, is that Paul is not asking his parishioners to give up absolutely everything (as Jesus did and demanded); they are to give from their surplus. As he says a few verses later, "In the present situation, your abundance will make up of their lack, just as their abundance has already been for your lack, so that there can be equality" (8:14).

This verse is key to understanding the deeper significance of Paul's collection. When he speaks about the Jerusalem saints having used their abundance to help the Christians of Corinth, he is decidedly not saying they provided financial support in a time of material need and that therefore the Corinthians should repay the favor. Paul is speaking metaphorically: the Jews have "shared" with gentiles the way of salvation, since God's plan to save the Jews has now been extended to all others. The Corinthian gentiles can repay this spiritual gift with much needed material support. That way there "can be equality."

The collection had strong symbolic significance for Paul. In many respects, Paul's entire mission focused on the unity of Jew and gentile in the church. God saves both on equal terms. There is no spiritual priority. Even though

Jews were the original chosen people, they rank no higher than others in the body of Christ. Conversely, even though most Jews rejected their messiah Jesus, gentiles are not superior in their acceptance of him. There is equality in the church, and the collection is meant to show it: gentiles and Jews are brothers and sisters in the faith.

Charity in the Writings of Luke

Other New Testament writings focus on the poor and needy as well, none more than the two-volume work of Luke-Acts. Readers have long recognized that the same author wrote these two books, the Gospel account of Jesus's life and the historical narrative of the mission of the church after his death.

More than the other Gospels, Luke emphasizes Jesus's concern for the poor, the hungry, the outcast, the estranged, the suffering—the "Other." Only in Luke do we find the parables of the Good Samaritan (10:25–37), the Prodigal Son (15:11–32), and Lazarus and the Rich Man (16:19–31), which we discussed earlier. Only here do we find Jesus praising the wealthy Zacchaeus for giving "half of his possessions to the poor" and repaying anyone he has defrauded "four times as much." This man may be a "sinner" and a despised tax collector, but he gives a huge amount of his resources to those in need. Jesus declares: "Today salvation has come to this house" (Luke 19:1–10).[6]

Similarly, only in Luke's version of Jesus's birth does his mother Mary praise God for bestowing honor on her, a lowly one: "He has taken the mighty from their thrones and exalted the humble, he has filled those who are hungry with good things and sent away those who are rich empty handed" (Luke 1:42–43). So too in Luke's version of Jesus's beatitudes, which, unlike Matthew's, focuses on those with material needs: "Blessed are the poor, for yours is the kingdom of God; blessed are those who hunger now, for you will be filled; blessed are those who weep now, for you will laugh" (Luke 6:20–22; contrast Matt. 5:3, 6). Jesus's concern for those in need is seen in his first public speech in Luke's account, again, found only here. Quoting the prophet Isaiah, he proclaims: "The Spirit of the Lord is upon me, because he has anointed me to preach the good news to the poor, he has sent me to proclaim release to the captives and sight to the blind, and to set free those who have been oppressed" (Luke 4:18–19).

This concern for those in need is found throughout Luke's second volume as well, the book of Acts. The account begins with an idealized portrayal of the harmonious unity of the earliest followers of Jesus just weeks after his death and resurrection. Already in chapter 2, on the day of Pentecost fifty days after the crucifixion, Peter preaches a sermon to Jews who have come to Jerusalem for the festival. Some three thousand convert on the spot. Once they are baptized, they immediately sell all their possessions and divide the funds to help those in need among them, sharing "all things in common" (Acts 2:43–45).

Soon afterward Peter preaches another sermon and five thousand "men" (so, not counting women) are converted. Once again, despite the large numbers of people involved, there is no trace of disharmony. Everyone is of the same "heart and soul" and no one holds any private property; all possessions are shared equally, with salubrious effect: "There was not a needy person among them; for everyone who owned fields or houses sold them and brought the proceeds and laid them at the feet of the apostles, and the funds were distributed to everyone, whoever had a need" (Acts 4:32–34).

These accounts are certainly not describing historical reality. The idea that over eight thousand Jews in Jerusalem converted to follow Jesus within a couple of months of his death is completely untenable. But the passage does highlight the priorities of Luke, which in many ways reflect those of the historical Jesus himself: material wealth is of no value before God and so should be of no value to his followers. What matters instead are the poor and needy. Those with funds should forsake their material goods to help those in want.

At least if they too are in the Christian community. Already in Acts' account of the earliest church we see its almost entirely intramural concerns. Christian converts are not using their resources to alleviate poverty in society at large, but to take care of their own—even if these men and women are otherwise strangers. Certainly, this in itself is a remarkable shift from ethical practices found nearly everywhere else in the Roman world apart from Judaism. At the same time, these Christian communities maintained that all believers were "brothers" and "sisters" in the faith. And so, in a sense, the Greco-Roman notion of family is what has changed: now it is the spiritual family in Christ that matters.

Charity among the Early Church Fathers

This concern for poor and suffering co-religionists remained a constant theme of the early church fathers in the decades after the New Testament. Around 150 CE, in a reasoned defense of the Christian faith, the apologist Justin Martyr indicates that the weekly meetings of the church in Rome involved not only the reading of Scripture, a sermon, prayers, and the eucharist, but also a collection:

> Those who are well off and wish, of their own choice, give whatever they choose, and what is collected is then handed to the leader of the church, who provides it to orphans and widows and to those who are in want because of illness or any other cause, and to those in prison, and those who are strangers who happen to be among us; in short he is the protector of all those who are in need. (Justin, *1 Apology* 67)

Some half century later, the church father Tertullian provides a similar account of his church in North Africa, indicating that once a month, those who chose would put in a small donation. The contributions were completely voluntary, he tells us, and went "to support and bury poor people, to supply the wants of boys and girls who have no resources or parents, and of old persons confined now to the house, and those who have suffered shipwreck; and to any in the mines or who are banished to the islands or shut up in prison for no reason other than their faithfulness to the church of God" (*Apology* 39).[7]

The idea that Christians with resources should give generously is also one of the major themes of the second-century apocalypse known as the *Shepherd of Hermas*, a book sometimes considered canonical Scripture in the first four centuries.[8] Hermas instructs his Christian readers to give "simply to all those in need, not wavering about to whom you should give or to whom not. For God wishes everyone to be given something from his own gifts" (*Shepherd*, 27.4). Those who fail to do so should consider the harsh condemnations to come on the day of judgment. If they delay, it may be too late and then "you will long to do good but there will be no opportunity." On that day, if "those in need" complain that the wealthy have ignored their plight, these rich Christians "will be shut out" of salvation (*Shepherd*, 17.5–6).

Hermas therefore argues that Christians with abundant resources are not to wallow in their wealth, but give to charity:

> Instead of fields, then, purchase souls that have been afflicted, insofar as you can, and take care of widows and orphans and do not neglect them. . . . For this is why the Master made you rich, that you may carry out these ministries for him. . . .
>
> This kind of extravagance is good and makes one glad; it has no grief or fear, but joy instead. And so, do not participate in the extravagance sought by outsiders; for it is of no profit to you who are slaves of God. (*Shepherd*, 50.8–10)

Despite such exhortations, we should not be too quick to assume that Hermas and other early Christian leaders argued for such charitable practices only for the good of those in need. The benefits to the rich themselves are patent throughout these pleas for generosity. Some scholars, in fact, have faulted Hermas for instrumentalizing the poor, treating them less as individuals than as a means of salvation, serving as tools for the wealthy to secure better fortune in the world to come.[9] It is certainly the case that Hermas directs his discussions of wealth to his community's affluent minority, and nowhere does he repeat Jesus's injunctions to the rich to "sell everything and give to the poor." Quite the contrary, for Hermas, the rich need to stay rich. The poor provide a useful long-term investment strategy for those looking to the eternal future.

This becomes clear in one of the most striking passages of the book, a metaphorical description of the symbiotic relationship of the rich and poor in the church (*Shepherd*, ch. 51). In a pseudo-autobiographical narrative, Hermas describes a walk he took through a field where he noticed an elm tree and a fruit-bearing vine growing up it. As he ponders the two plants, an angelic figure known as the "Shepherd" appears. Hermas tells his companion he is struck by how well suited the tree and vine are for each other, and the Shepherd states they are symbolic of the relationship of rich Christians and those who are poor. It is a puzzling claim, but the Shepherd explains. The vine bears fruit, but since it lies on the ground, the fruit quickly rots; the elm tree does not itself bear fruit, but the vine that attaches to it moves upward and thus bears more fruit that doesn't spoil. In that sense, the tree itself is bearing fruit. It is the mutual dependence of the two that produces a high yield; were they independent, one would bear fruit that goes bad and the other would bear no fruit at all.

That, says the Shepherd, is like the rich and the poor in the church. The rich person has money, but is "poor toward the Lord, since he is distracted by his wealth" (*Shepherd*, 51.5). He spends all his time and energy on his investments rather than devoting himself to worship and serving God. The poor person, on the other hand, focuses on worshipping and serving God, but barely has enough resources to survive. Wealthy Christians who endow funds on the Christian poor enable them to pray more for their benefactors, so that they too can be right before God. The more material resources the rich provide, the more the poor provide spiritual resources to the rich, and together they produce abundant fruit. Thus, for the Shepherd, riches are a very good thing, given by God to the affluent to further his purposes on earth.

It is an intriguing parable. But, of course, it requires the rich to retain most of their wealth. The idea that they should abandon everything for the sake of the poor never occurs to this author. One wonders what Jesus would say.

Clement of Alexandria

We know what later church fathers said. For some two hundred years, most of them were completely on board with this kind of reasoning. If the affluent members of the church gave all their wealth away, who would support *them*? And how would funds continue to fill the church coffers to help the poor and, well, pay the pastors? Nowhere does this line of thought come to more cogent and yet puzzling expression than in a treatise produced about half a century after Hermas by a prominent church theologian named Clement, from the large and influential church in Alexandria, Egypt. The writing is striking for several reasons, but most especially because it claims that a key biblical passage means the opposite of what it says.

Clement directs his treatise, *Who Is the Rich Man Who Can Be Saved?*, to the wealthy members of his congregation, basing his comments on the account of "Jesus and the Rich Man" we discussed in chapter 3. You will recall that in the passage, Jesus tells a rich man that to have "treasure in heaven," he must sell everything he owns and give the money to the poor. The man walks away, crestfallen. He simply can't do it. The disciples themselves are incredulous. Surely the wealthy, if anyone, are in God's favor? Jesus responds with that most memorable of lines: "It is easier for a camel to go through the eye of a needle than for a rich person to enter into the Kingdom" (Mark 10:17–25).

Clement's interpretation of the passage surely warmed the cockles of every affluent person's heart in his congregation.[10] He argues Jesus did not mean it. No one, Clement says, should think Jesus intended those words about camels and eyes of needles in a crass, material way. Instead, one must find "the meaning hidden in" them (*Who Is the Rich Man*, ch. 5).

What is it that Jesus wants the rich man to do? To cling to God, rather than to money. Clement points out that if the rich man had been fool enough to act on Jesus's words literally, he would have had nothing left. But abject poverty is not the way of salvation. Otherwise, everyone who is destitute would inherit the kingdom, and surely, for Clement, that cannot be right. Jesus, he says, does not order the man to engage in the "outward act" of giving everything away, but to do something "greater, more godlike, more perfect: to strip the soul itself and its disposition of its underlying passions" (*Who Is the Rich Man*, 12). Those who are rich can stay rich, so long as they are not passionate about their possessions. In fact, they *should* stay rich. That way they can help the poor. Clement is emphatic on this point: "Riches that also benefit our neighbors are not, then, to be renounced" (*Who Is the Rich Man*, 14).

Generous giving is thus very important for Clement. In part, that is because those who give a lot will receive a lot. Clement goes on to phrase this spiritual investment strategy in explicitly economic terms: There is a "great reward for our sharing, an eternal dwelling! Oh, what a great business! What a divine marketplace! A person buys immortality with money, giving away worldly things that are perishing to receive in exchange an eternal mansion in heaven" (*Who Is the Rich Man*, 32).

How good can it get for the rich? Luxury now and even more for all eternity.

Clement's interpretation may run precisely contrary to what the passage actually says, but even here a remnant of Jesus's basic idea remains, and remains revolutionary. Yes, the rich can keep most of their funds. But what they do give away is not to go to relatives, friends, clients, or municipal building projects but to those who are genuinely in need, at least in the church.

Anthony of Egypt, the Father of Monasticism

There may well have been Christians of the first two centuries who took Jesus at his word and sold all they had to give to the poor, but we don't hear much about them. Such people do start appearing on the scene near the end of the third century, none of them more famous than the ascetic figure commonly considered the "father of monasticism," Anthony of Egypt (251–356 CE).[11] Our principal source of information about Anthony is Athanasius, the great theologian and bishop of fourth-century Alexandria, who personally knew him and wrote his biography. For centuries Athanasius's *Life of Anthony* was one of the most popular noncanonical writings of all Christendom.[12]

Athanasius makes it clear that Anthony was not the first to take on abject poverty as part of his commitment to spiritual communion with God. He had predecessors whom he met and attempted to emulate. We know little about these people and it is hard to tell if any of them came from a wealthy background. But Anthony clearly did. His parents were rich Christians with extensive landholdings who died early, leaving Anthony the family inheritance.

Anthony was already an unusually devoted Christian in his youth, uninterested in developing a social life or pursuing his education. Some six months after his parents' death, his piety became yet more intense as he reflected on the Gospel stories of Jesus's disciples "leaving everything" in order to follow him (Matthew 4:21) and the account in Acts where the earliest converts sold "all their goods" and gave the funds to the poor (Acts 4:25). In particular, he was struck by the story of Jesus and the rich man, which he was not inclined to take metaphorically in the way of Clement. Anthony decided to obey Jesus's command.[13] He gave his family's lands to local villagers, sold his possessions, and gave the money to the poor. He placed his younger sister in a convent to be raised safely—presumably away from corrupting influences of the world—and took on a life of ascetic devotion: living alone, praying, fasting, and doing manual labor. He spent half his meager income on bread and gave the rest to the poor.

Athanasius tells us that Anthony would occasionally travel in search of holy men to learn better the ways of rigorous zeal. Eventually he went to a further extreme: moving to the desert to live in solitude (hence one of his sobriquets, "Anthony of the Desert"), eating only once a day (just bread, salt, and water) and often fasting for three or four days on end, spending entire nights in prayer, and when allowing himself to sleep, doing so on the hard ground.

One would think this kind of lifestyle could not be sustained for long, but Anthony lived to be 104. By 360 CE—four years after Anthony's death, when Athanasius wrote his biography—"anchorite" monasticism (monks living in isolation) had become a phenomenon. It is not that many thousands of Christians were divesting all their earthly goods to engage in rigorously ascetic devotion. But the monastic movement did become a hugely significant institution in Christendom and remained so for many centuries.

Historians have often puzzled over why this happened. Many have noted that the rise of lifelong self-imposed deprivation within the Christian tradition coincided with the cessation of persecution and martyrdom. The years 303–13 CE were particularly fraught for the Christian community within the Roman Empire. This was the time of the "Great Persecution" under the emperor Diocletian, when Christians who refused to abandon their faith could (in theory) be subject to torture and death. Not every Christian was under threat, of course, and imperial decrees ordering arrests and executions were not consistently carried out. In some parts of the empire, the orders had very little effect. But there were many instances of violent persecution and, in some areas, numbers of martyrs.¹⁴ These Christian martyrs took on an outsized significance within the wider community: they had given literally everything for their faith.

But the persecution ended abruptly in 313 CE, not long after the emperor Constantine converted to the faith. Christianity then experienced an earthmoving shift: what had been a violently persecuted faith was now imperially favored. That was naturally welcome news, but it deprived inordinately devoted Christians of a way to demonstrate their spiritual dedication in any radical way. If the faithful were no longer killed for their piety, how could they suffer for the cause?

The monastic movement provided a solution. Christians could follow Jesus's demands: ridding themselves of their worldly possessions and outdoing one another in their self-imposed hunger, sleeplessness, and isolation.¹⁵ These, then, were people who took Jesus at his word and gave up everything.

Basil the Great

So too did devoted Christians who did not live in isolation, as anchorites, but in monastic communities ("coenobitic" monks). An important development in such communities occurred in the middle of the fourth century, at just about the time Athanasius was writing his famous account of Anthony, a development with serious ramifications for the ethical investments and social commitments of the Christian church down till today.

A key figure in the movement was named Basil (later called "Basil the Great"), born around 330 CE into an affluent, prominent, and pious Christian family in Caesarea, the capital of the province of Cappadocia in Asia Minor.¹⁶ Basil's father provided his early schooling, preparing him for a vocation as a rhetorician; later he pursued his education in Constantinople and then Athens before returning to his home city to practice law and teach rhetoric. By then his father had died, and as the oldest son Basil inherited extensive landholdings in several provinces of Asia Minor. In his midtwenties, he tired of his chosen vocation and converted to an entirely new way of life. As he later wrote:

> Then I read the Gospel, and I saw there that a great means of reaching perfection was the selling of one's goods, sharing them with the poor, giving up all

care for this life, and refusing to allow the soul to be turned by any sympathy to things of earth. (Epistle 223, "Against Eustathius of Sebastia")[17]

Like Anthony before him, Basil saw the path to "perfection" in Jesus's words to the rich man in Matthew 19:21 as one to be taken literally. Spiritual perfection actually did require material divestment.

In 356 CE Basil sold a good deal of his property, shifted to a monastic lifestyle, and within two years had begun his own monastic community. Some eight years later he decided to move back into society, in part to engage in theological debates over Christ and the Trinity that were tearing the Christian community apart. He became a leader of the church in Caesarea and in 369 CE came to face a crisis that shaped his thinking and led to some of his most important writings on wealth and its legitimate use.[18]

The famine that hit Asia Minor that year was catastrophic almost beyond imagination.[19] The area had experienced a dry winter and spring. A drought ensued and crops did not grow, leading to massive unemployment (with no jobs in an agricultural economy), school closings, and eventually widespread starvation. In one of his sermons from the time, Basil refers to an unspeakable dilemma facing parents: With so little food, do they sell one or more of their children into slavery to buy food to keep the rest of the family alive? Or do they simply all go down together?

> Consider now the violent struggle that takes place between the desperation arising from famine and a parent's fundamental instincts. Starvation on the one side threatens a horrible death, while nature resists, convincing the parents rather to die with their children. Time and again they vacillate, but in the end, they succumb, driven by want and cruel necessity. (*I Will Tear Down My Barns*, 4)[20]

In other sermons, Basil lambasts the many wealthy in his congregation who "Fast, pray, sigh, and demonstrate every manner of piety, so long as it costs them nothing, yet would not part with a penny to help those in distress" (*To the Rich*, 3). For Basil, hoarding wealth while others are in need violates the very essence of the Christian faith, to "love your neighbor as yourself." He follows with an argument that is uncommonly simple and difficult to refute: "Those who love their neighbor as themselves possess nothing more than their neighbor." How could it be otherwise? Basil gives no wriggle room to anyone who imagines there may be ways to love a poor neighbor without actually sacrificing material resources—for example, by praying for those in need. He is quite explicit: "Care for the needy requires the expenditure of wealth" for "The more you abound in wealth, the more you lack in love" (*To the Rich*, 1). Indeed, "If you had truly loved your neighbor, it would have occurred to you long ago to divest yourself of this wealth" (*To the Rich*, 1).

Basil's sermons are meant not only to guilt-trip his affluent parishioners in this time of dire need, but also to help them think through the issue in Christian terms. What is the use of having far more wealth than necessary? Mortality is inevitable. As Basil puts it in one particularly clever rhetorical flourish: "What is the point of having acres and acres of land, fields, and orchards," when in the end, "all that awaits you is a six-foot plot of earth?" (ch. 6).

Basil subscribes to the kind of Christian communal sharing modeled by the earliest followers of Jesus in Acts 4:32–35. Those who hoard are robbers who "take for themselves what rightfully belongs to everyone" (*I Will Tear Down My Barns*, 7). As he says, "If we all took only what was necessary to satisfy our own needs, giving the rest to those who lack, no one would be rich, no one would be poor, and no one would be in need" (*I Will Tear Down My Barns*, 7). Those who refuse to do so are in danger of damnation. Basil reminds his congregation of Jesus's words to the "goats" in Matthew 25:41–43, the ones sent to the eternal flames because they did not provide for the hungry, thirsty, and naked: "Those who are under accusation in this passage are not those who have stolen anything," he writes, "these charges are rather leveled against those who have not shared with others" (*I Will Tear Down My Barns*, 8).

The Invention of Public Charities

Basil was instrumental in the invention of public charities for those in need, institutions virtually unheard of in the Western world prior to the fourth

Christian century. Today we take for granted that societies will provide hospitals, orphanages, food kitchens, poorhouses, and old persons' homes. But like every other human institution, these have histories, and in the West, they begin with the commitment of Basil and others like him to the commands of Jesus.

Andrew Crislip, a historian of early Christianity, has argued that institutional charity in the West began with health-care systems devised in fourth-century coenobitic monasteries, where monks lived in communities following established rules.[21] By design these communities were cut off from society at large. That made it impossible for monks to access the few health-care options otherwise available, whether to the wealthy, who alone could afford private doctors, or to everyone else, who could at least benefit from the home-care nursing of family members.

Not only did monks lack such traditional resources, their health-care needs were, in some ways, greater than average. Rigorously limited diets, fasting, and regular sleeplessness are obviously not conducive to physical well-being. Monastic health-care systems developed organically to deal with the problem. At first, the system was basic: a separate room for those who had become ill and expert physicians from the community who knew how to treat them. Over time these grew into established features of monastic life, creating a health-care system that was, in Crislip's words, "without precedent in antiquity," creating "the template for what would become known as the hospital in Late Antiquity."[22]

Basil was not the founder of the monastic system of health care, but as bishop of Caesarea, he developed, advanced, and popularized it through an institution called, after him, "the Basilias."[23] Unlike earlier monastic clinics, Basil's was a large facility, found not inside a monastery but alongside it, and open not just to the resident monks but also to outsiders, or at least to one particular set of outsiders: lepers.[24]

Of all those who suffered disease and disfigurement, lepers were widely considered among the most unfortunate. They not only suffered physically from a horribly painful condition of putrefying flesh, probably Hansen's disease, they were almost universally ostracized because of it. Reeking and grotesque, they were typically shunned by families, barred from public places, and left to fend for themselves. Survival meant begging, made difficult in many cases by loss of limbs. One physician from Basil's region, possibly two centuries earlier, wrote of lepers abandoned to dwell on mountainsides, with almost no help from their families or anyone else. "While some assist them in their hunger for a time, others help as little as possible because they want them to perish."[25]

Jesus, however, had commanded his followers to help everyone in need, even the lowest of the low. Basil took this command seriously. And so, as one ancient source explains:

> [Basil] formed a pious plan worthy of his brotherly love. After erecting immense houses and assigning to [the lepers] annual incomes which he procured from well-to-do persons whom his wise words had persuaded to make donations, he gathered all the infirm into this same place, calling its buildings "school-houses for the poor."[26]

This latter phrase is puzzling, but it appears to mean that the large facility was not only a place where these social outcasts could have their physical needs met with shelter, a bed, food, and medical attention, but also where they—as those who were "poor in spirit"—could have their spiritual needs addressed.[27]

This was the first full-scale operation designed explicitly to care for those in need. After Basil, such institutions began to feature more widely throughout the Christian world, especially in the western parts of the empire. Facilities had varying specializations: hospitals, poorhouses, and hostels for strangers all began to appear. By 400 CE or so we hear of each of these in a number of major urban areas, including Constantinople and Rome.

To reiterate: such public charitable institutions were nowhere to be seen in the Roman world prior to the Christian movement. Less than four hundred years after Jesus's death they started to become an expected feature of civilization.

Christian Charity and Altruism

Despite its novelty, in one respect the growing commitment of fifth-century Christian leaders to help those in need reflected a widespread feature of the pagan Roman world. As I noted earlier, the urban rich of the empire often had "clients" who attended to and served them—accompanying them in public, doing their bidding, openly praising them to others—in exchange for gifts of money and goods. This patronage system used the inevitable inequalities of social standing and wealth to the benefit of both parties, the disadvantaged client financially and the patron in status. As the empire turned Christian, the wealthy stopped funding municipal projects and began giving their resources instead to the church to assist the poor. But it was the leaders of the church, the bishops, who now controlled the funds. They decided how to distribute the resources and whom to help. In effect, they, not the donors, assumed the roles of patrons and came to be known as "lovers of the poor."[28]

We cannot assume that either the wealthy donors or the ecclesiastical distributors always engaged in these relief efforts out of purely altruistic motives. They were fully cognizant of Jesus's promise of "treasure in heaven." Still, whatever the ultimate motivations, no one should dispute the massive tangible difference effected by these later Christians, who had the means and the inspiration to make Jesus's demands into social realities. Basil's pagan ancestors from just two hundred years earlier would never have imagined institutions whose sole function was to help those in need; had it ever crossed their minds, they would have derided it as a kind of madness.

However one assesses the Christian message or the history of the church at large, such institutions have undeniably made an indelible mark on Western culture, providing life-saving and life-enriching benefits to millions of people over all these centuries. Where would we be without hospitals, orphanages, nursing homes, and charities dealing with disaster relief, poverty, literacy, homelessness, and hunger? As an agnostic/atheist myself, with regard to at least this particular offshoot of Jesus's teachings, I say: Thank God for Christianity.

Forgiveness

As I have pointed out, charitable giving is obviously not the only way to help those in need. Many acts of love are unrelated to material goods at all. The spirit needs love as much as the body. Recall the view of the pagan philosopher Epicurus: far worse than physical pain is mental anguish. A particularly intense form of anguish can come when we realize just how deeply we have hurt another by what we have done. So too, a particularly liberating act of grace comes when someone, whether an intimate or a stranger, forgives us when we express our regret and remorse.

Jesus taught a radical view of forgiveness fully rooted in his understanding of God. God forgives all those who turn to him in repentance and ask for pardon. He does not require sacrifices of atonement, payments for sin, or other penalties. This forgiveness is not "unconditional": it comes only on the basis of sincere repentance. But it is nonetheless an act of sheer grace.

The ethical corollary was that God's people should do the same for those who had "sinned against" them, hurting them through something they had said or done. If the offender expresses remorse and asks for forgiveness, it is to be graciously extended, with no retaliation, penalty, or punishment. Like God, we should "forgive our debtors" (Matthew 6:12).

The Great Reversal

Even though forgiveness based on repentance stood at the forefront of Jesus's teaching, things changed radically after his death. In one of the greatest ironies in the history of religion, Jesus's followers spread his message of salvation only after reversing it, insisting that God did not graciously forgive those who sincerely repented. He required an atoning sacrifice. That too had ethical implications.

The fact of this reversal is quite easy to demonstrate, even if it has flown under the radar of most readers and interpreters of the New Testament over the centuries. One need only look at what the earliest Christian writers actually say, and do not say, about Christ and salvation.

Our earliest author, Paul, stresses that his own views on the meaning of Christ's death and resurrection were shared with, and in fact had been inherited from, those who came before him. His most succinct expression of this gospel message comes in 1 Corinthians 15:3–5, where he reminds his Corinthian readers what he taught them when they converted. You will notice there is nothing about forgiveness here:

> For I handed over to you as of first importance what I had received, that Christ died for our sins in accordance with the Scriptures, that he was buried, and that he was raised on the third day in accordance with the Scriptures, and that he appeared to Cephas and twelve. . . . Whether it was I or they [the apostles], thus we preach and thus you believed. (1 Cor. 15:3–5, 11)

Why did Christ die, according to Paul? "For our sins." Why would that be necessary? Because sins require atonement. That is what the apostles before Paul had been preaching all along.

Paul expands his views in other passages, none more important than Romans 1–3. Here, at some length, Paul stresses why everyone needs to be reconciled with God: all people, both Jew and gentile, have sinned. No one is righteous; all live in ways contrary to God (1:18–3:20). What is more, keeping the Jewish law will not bring a restoration with God. God has instead provided a different solution. A right standing before God ("justification") comes "through faith in Jesus Christ for all who believe." Believers are "justified by God's grace as a gift through the redemption that is in Christ Jesus" (3:22–24). And how did Christ provide that redemption? By shedding his blood for others. God "put him forth as an atoning sacrifice through faith in his blood" (3:25).[29]

Paul develops this idea in several places, including two chapters later in Romans (I've put some of the key words in bold):

> Even while we were weak, at the right time Christ **died for the ungodly**. . . . God showed his love for us, because while we were sinners, Christ **died for us**. And now even more, since **we have been made justified by his blood**, we will be saved through him from the wrath of God. For if, when we were God's enemies, **we were reconciled to him through the death of his son**, by much more will we be saved by his life, now that we are reconciled. (Romans 5:6–11)

The relationship with God that had been shattered by human wrongdoing has been restored by the death of Jesus. Those who believe in Christ have been redeemed; they have been reconciled.

Where is "repentance" leading to "forgiveness" in all this? Nowhere. Neither here nor anywhere else in Paul's letters.

A study of the very words Paul uses in his writings proves enlightening. I have pointed out that our earliest Gospels (Matthew, Mark, and Luke) speak of God's "forgiveness" by using the Greek noun *aphesis* (a "sending away") and its verbal form *aphiēmi* ("to send away"). God "sends away" a person's sins, gets rid of them, disposes of them, when the person expresses remorse and repents. The noun ("forgiveness") is used altogether eleven times in these Gospels and the book of Acts. But it never occurs in Paul's letters. The verb ("to forgive") is even more common in these Gospels, occurring nearly 120 times, 40 of them in verses either spoken by or to Jesus about "forgiving sins." In Paul? It occurs just one time in connection with the forgiveness of sins, and even there it is not his own word: Paul is quoting an Old Testament passage that happens to use the term (Romans 4:7). He himself never talks about the forgiveness of sins.

It is interesting to consider why most readers have never noticed that whereas Jesus teaches the forgiveness of sins based on repentance—with no requirement for atonement—Paul, the apostles before him, and most Christian authors after him almost never do. I think there may be two reasons. The first is a bit in the weeds, involving a kind of academic shorthand scholars use when speaking about the "teachings of Jesus." When they use that phrase they are referring to the teachings of the *historical* Jesus, which are not necessarily the words Jesus is *recorded* as saying in the Gospels. That is, scholars are differentiating between the actual words Jesus likely spoke and the *reports* of his sayings in later writings about him. One of the primary tasks of New Testament specialists is to determine just which of the recorded sayings of Jesus he actually spoke and which have been placed on his lips by later storytellers. (It is clear that lots of sayings were invented for him, as anyone who reads the Gospel of Thomas, the Gospel of Mary, or the Gospel of Philip will quickly realize.) But this scholar-speak can create confusion for readers who are not accustomed to thinking in terms of what Jesus actually said versus what the Gospels indicate he said.

The reason this matters is that Jesus certainly does talk about dying "for" other people in the Gospels (see Mark 10:45 and his words at the last supper, Mark 14:23–24). If these were words he actually spoke, then he *would* have seen his death as an atonement for sins. But there are very good reasons for thinking Jesus did not say such things. One involves the issue I have been discussing: if Jesus really said an atoning sacrifice was necessary to appease the anger of God, it would have made no sense for him simultaneously to claim that God freely forgave people when they repented, just as we should forgive those indebted to us, without payment. The concepts simply do not gel.

The second reason it may be difficult to grasp the difference between "forgiveness" and "atonement" is that most people are not accustomed to differentiating between words and the concepts they convey. Words are the way we express concepts, but words themselves can be slippery, often ambiguous, vague, lacking in precision, and used in multiple and therefore confusing ways. Since people often use words loosely instead of precisely, it can be difficult to understand exactly what they are trying to say, that is, to understand what concept they are trying to communicate. This is not simply a modern phenomenon we confront when speaking English. It is true in every language, including the ancient Greek of the New Testament. A clear instance of the problem occurs when a New Testament author uses the words "forgiveness" and "atonement" in ambiguous ways, confusing readers into thinking the words are expressing the same concept.

A clear instance occurs in the book of Hebrews, written by an unknown author to stress the superiority of Christ to every aspect of the Jewish religion, which he sees as a mere foreshadowing of the salvation brought by Jesus.[30] In Hebrews 8–10 the author stresses the importance of the atoning death of Christ as a sacrifice for sins and says nary a thing about "forgiveness based on repentance." Readers are then naturally confused—possibly without realizing it—when the author indicates that Christ had to shed his blood for salvation because "without the shedding of blood there is no forgiveness of sins" (9:22).

Here is a prime instance of the conflict of words and concepts. The author does not mean "forgiveness" in the sense we have been discussing—a complete forgoing of anger without need of a payment. He is using it to refer to the absolution of sins that comes by the required payment of blood. So even though he uses the term "forgiveness," he uses it in a different way from the way Jesus does. For our discussion I am not interested in whether they use the same word, but whether they have the same concept. In fact, they have completely contrary concepts: for Jesus, God restores a relationship broken by sin by forgiving people, no payment required; for the author of Hebrews, he restores it only through a payment of blood. So, which is it? Does reconciliation come from forgiveness based only on repentance or does it require a bloody sacrifice? It depends whom you ask: Jesus or the author of Hebrews.

This author agrees with Paul and almost all the other authors of the New Testament. But how can that be? How did we get from the religion of Jesus focused on forgiveness to the doctrine of the church focused on atonement?

Why Jesus's Followers Abandoned His Teaching of Forgiveness

Many people today imagine that Paul "invented Christianity" by radically altering Jesus's teachings, turning the religion of Jesus into the religion about Jesus. I do not think that's true. As we have just seen, Paul himself indicates that his gospel of Jesus's death and resurrection was proclaimed by others before him. That makes sense. Paul had obviously heard of the Christian faith before he converted, three years or so after Jesus's death. He had persecuted Christians precisely because of what they were saying: Jesus was the messiah who died for the sins of others and was raised from the dead. Paul originally thought these people were both crazily wrong and blasphemous. That was why, in his own words, he "violently persecuted the church and tried to destroy it" (Galatians 1:13). But after he had some kind of vision of Christ, he became convinced Jesus's followers had been right. The reversal of Jesus's teachings from forgiveness to atonement therefore happened before Paul appeared on the scene.

When and why?

I think it must have happened right away, soon after Jesus's death and because of it. After the crucifixion, Jesus's disciples (all of them? most of them?) came to believe God had raised Jesus from the dead, and this belief led to a chain of realizations that quickly brought them to see that Jesus's execution had been part of God's plan for saving the world through an atoning sacrifice. To explain how this happened, we need to begin with what the disciples of Jesus thought about him before he died. There are good reasons for thinking they believed he was the messiah.

Most Jews in Jesus's day were not looking for a messiah any more than most are now. Among those who were, the messianic idea, as we have seen, was ultimately rooted in tales of the great King David, to whom God had promised an "eternal kingdom," that is, a dynasty that would last for all time (2 Samuel 7:12–16). Some time after the dynasty came to an abrupt end with the fall of Jerusalem to the Babylonians in 586 BCE, there emerged a notion of a future "messiah," an "anointed one" who would fulfill God's promises to David. A descendant would once again sit on the throne to restore Israel as a sovereign state.

Over time, views about this messiah developed. In Jesus's day, we know of various messianic expectations: some Jews thought the future savior would be a divine judge coming from above to destroy God's enemies in a show of force; others believed he would be a mighty priest who would rule the nation with his superior understanding of the Law of God; others, probably most, held to the traditional view that he would be a warrior-king like David.[31] These various expectations had one thing in common: the messiah, the deliverer of Israel, would be an exalted figure who would exercise God's power to destroy his enemies and rule the people of God.

There are good reasons for thinking that already during his lifetime, Jesus's disciples believed he was the future messiah. He may well have told them so.[32] He was executed for making that claim. The charge brought against him at his trial was that he called himself "king of the Jews" (or "the Judeans"; Mark 15:2, 18), and this was also the crime cited on the placard above his head (Mark 15:26). The Roman authorities would have had no interest in crucifying an obscure Jewish teacher urging his followers to love those in need and accept God's forgiveness. But claiming to be a king was a different matter altogether, a threat of insurrection.

If Jesus considered himself the future king, he would have understood this in the context of his broader apocalyptic preaching. His message was not that a military uprising would drive the Romans out of the Promised Land.

Indeed, he appears to have preached against taking up the sword.[33] Instead, he believed in a cosmic judge soon to arrive from heaven to destroy God's enemies and set up the glorious kingdom of God (Mark 8:38–9:1). And who would be appointed to rule this kingdom? Jesus appears to have thought he would be the one. He also appears to have told the twelve disciples they would rule with him. "You also will be seated on twelve thrones ruling the twelve tribes of Israel" (Matthew 19:28).[34] This must have been heady stuff.

The last week of Jesus's life, possibly not knowing that it was all soon to end, Jesus traveled with his disciples to celebrate the annual Passover feast in Jerusalem. He may well have wanted to take his message to the heart of the Jewish homeland at a time when large crowds would be gathered with religious fervor. The disciples may have been in high spirits, with great expectations for what was now to come.

But what came was not the kingdom. After several days, one of Jesus's inside circle betrayed him to the authorities. It may well be that Judas Iscariot did not simply tell them where they could find Jesus alone with no crowds around. (Would they really have needed an informer for that?) Perhaps he revealed the insider information that he and the rest of the twelve knew: that Jesus was calling himself the king soon to rule Judea.[35] Even if Jesus meant that in an apocalyptic sense, the authorities would have seen it as an incendiary political claim, when only the Romans could rule the land. They had Jesus arrested and turned him over to the Roman governor Pilate, who found him guilty and ordered him crucified.

Jesus's execution must have thrust a dagger through the hearts of the disciples. All their expectations—that the enemies of Israel would soon be destroyed, the Kingdom would arrive, Jesus would be appointed king, and they would be his co-rulers—were suddenly and decisively extinguished. Instead of overthrowing God's enemies, Jesus had been unceremoniously humiliated, tortured, and killed by them. The remaining disciples would have had to return home to their lives as poor day laborers. They may, in fact, have bolted in some haste: they were, after all, followers of a suspected insurrectionist. Our earliest Gospel, Mark, indicates they fled the scene of Jesus's arrest and made themselves scarce, possibly in terror for their lives (Mark 14:50).[36]

Then something unexpected happened. One or more of them saw Jesus alive again, or at least said they did. It seems almost certain, historically, that Peter claimed to have seen Jesus after his death, as attested in a letter by Paul, who personally knew him (1 Cor. 15:5). It seems likely that Mary Magdalene did as well, given the independent reports about her vision (Matthew 28:9–10; John 20:11–18). It is hard to know about all the others. In the Gospels, of course, all of Jesus's (now eleven) disciples are said to have seen him and come to believe in his resurrection almost immediately. Even these accounts, however, indicate that on virtually every occasion there were serious doubters. In one notable and rather puzzling version, we are told that the resurrected Jesus spent forty days with the eleven showing that he was again alive "with many proofs" (Acts 1:3). How many proofs would they need? And it took forty days? These "doubt traditions" may well represent a historical reality: possibly some (many?) of the disciples never did come to believe the reports others gave.[37]

Whatever one makes of the Gospel accounts, it is clear that, historically, some, possibly most, or maybe even all the disciples came to believe Jesus had been raised from the dead. That changed everything for how they thought about him. For one thing, it showed they had been right: he really was the Chosen One of God. The reported sightings did not make them think Jesus had experienced what we would call a near death experience. No, he had been gloriously raised from the dead, never to die again. But where was he now? Clearly not here. Right off the bat, his disciples came to think he had been taken up to heaven.

In the ancient world, Greeks, Romans, and Jews believed that anyone who ascended to the heavenly realms at the end of their life (or soon after) was not simply taken on a space journey, but was exalted and turned into a divine being, living among other divine beings in the world above.[38] The disciples believed that's what had happened to Jesus. He had been made God. He was not God the Father, Yahweh, the God of the Old Testament. But he was a divine being higher than the angels. Eventually, some of his followers came to think he had become equal with God himself.[39]

And he was returning for Act Two, not as a mere mortal but as the judge of the earth. Jesus had preached that a day of judgment was soon to arrive from heaven with the appearance of the Son of Man, who would wreak havoc on God's enemies and establish the kingdom of God on earth (Mark 8:38; Matthew 13:24–27; Luke 17:24–30). Now that the disciples believed Jesus was the Chosen One who dwelt in heaven, they realized he was himself the one who would bring that kingdom. Jesus was the Son of Man he had been predicting.[40]

This was a natural conclusion for the apocalyptic Jews who followed Jesus. But as soon as they drew it, an obvious conundrum appeared, the solution to which would change the world for all time. If Jesus was the future judge of the earth, the great king, the messiah—why did he die? Surely if he was the one God had chosen, his life must have been lived according to God's plan. But that must mean his death was also part of the plan. Why would God want his beloved Chosen One to be publicly rejected, humiliated, tortured, and executed?

We don't know how long it took for the disciples to come up with an explanation, but it may have been almost immediately. They were Jews living in the Roman world, and in that world, why did gods require living creatures to be killed? As sacrifices. In the law of Moses, why does God demand the death of animals? As sacrifices. Why then would God demand the death of his own son? As a sacrifice.

The Torah prescribes a variety of sacrifices that served various functions. Some atoned for sins, most importantly those performed on the Day of Atonement, Yom Kippur. The disciples eventually realized that the sacrifices in the temple foreshadowed the greatest sacrifice of all: the bloody death of the Son of God, sent to the world to bring atonement once and for all.

When Jesus's followers came to think this, they did not suddenly abandon Judaism to become Christians. Quite the opposite. They had been and remained Jews. They worshipped the God of the Jews, studied Jewish scripture, followed Jewish customs, adhered to the Jewish law, and observed Jewish festivals. But when they came to believe Jesus was the Jewish messiah, they realized their original messianic expectations had been wrong. Jesus was not the warrior-king some looked for, or any other figure of grandeur. He had died that others might live. His death is what brought redemption.

Well before Paul arrived on the scene, the followers of Jesus began advocating a new form of Judaism, different in at least one key way from what Jesus himself proclaimed. Jesus preached a radical message: that forgiveness came straight from God, graciously given upon a person's sincere repentance and earnest request. The temple and its sacrifices were not needed; no atonement was required. But soon after his death the disciples returned to a doctrine of atonement. True, the temple and animal sacrifices were no longer important. But for them, salvation did not come through repentance based on forgivness, as Jesus had taught. It came by his own atoning sacrifice.

It is particularly ironic that Jesus's contrary teaching of penalty-free forgiveness may actually have led to his death. Scholars have long maintained that the stories of Jesus's "cleansing of the temple" are rooted in a historical event, and that his actions there initiated the sequence of events that led to his arrest and crucifixion. According to our earliest accounts, when Jesus arrived in Jerusalem for the Passover feast, he entered the temple compound, overturned the tables of those exchanging currency, and drove out those selling sacrificial animals (Mark 11:15–19). He thus violently opposed the current sacrificial system and spoke out vehemently against it: the Temple was to be a "house of prayer," but the priests and their sacrificial cult had turned it into a "den of robbers." It was at this point that authorities started paying attention to Jesus (Mark 11:18). Over the next few days, he preached his apocalyptic message to gathering numbers of Jews: God was soon to destroy everything and everyone opposed to him, including the temple and those who ran it. To survive the coming onslaught, people did not need to participate in temple worship and sacrifices. They were to turn back to the ways of God, repent of their sins, and ask forgiveness. Those who did so would be spared.

This teaching, of course, ran precisely contrary to the beliefs and practices of the temple leaders, who had close connections with Jerusalem's Roman rulers.[41] The local authorities decided to intervene and remove Jesus from the public view. We know, of course, what happened next.

And so the irony came full circle. Jesus's teachings of atonement-free forgiveness led to his execution. His execution led to a new religion based on a belief in his resurrection. This belief in his resurrection led his followers to reverse his teachings of forgiveness by embracing the doctrine of atonement.

Atonement and Forgiveness in the Early Church

As Christianity developed over the centuries, the importance of atonement grew with time. Most Christian writers continued to maintain that only the death of Jesus could bring about a right standing with God.[42] There was a price for the sins of the world and Jesus paid it, making all those who had believed and been baptized reconciled with God. They alone would be "saved" on the coming day of judgment. Most of Jesus's followers believed it was coming soon. Paul expresses this belief some twenty to twenty-five years after Jesus's death in his earliest letters (1 Thessalonians 4:13–5:11; 1 Corinthians 15:51–52), and it is the view found in our earliest Gospel traditions (Mark 9:1; 13:30).

Eventually both the idea and the fervor it generated began to fade. Even so, the conviction that the end was near never completely disappeared from the Christian tradition; it existed on the margins for many centuries, and still is very much alive and well today.[43] But most Christians, in most places, most of the time, beginning as far back as the second century, have been convinced we are here for the long haul. That conviction brought some changes to Christian tradition relevant to our discussion of forgiveness.

Christian leaders as early as Paul had to deal with members of the church who now, after baptism, continued to live sinful lives. Once a person's sins had been atoned for, would Christ's death cover their *future* sins as well? Wouldn't there need to be some kind of atonement for later misbehavior? If not, then anyone reconciled with God by Jesus's death could lead whatever wild and licentious life they chose and still receive their heavenly reward. God couldn't simply forgive future sins without penalty, any more than he could forgive previous ones.

Paul never offers deep theological reflection on the problem. He simply urges sinners in his congregations to turn their lives around. Sometimes he pushes for punishment or threatens them with the loss of salvation (e.g., 1 Cor. 5:1–5), but he never provides a coherent solution to the problem, at least in any of the letters we have. Possibly he thought Jesus's imminent return obviated the need for a well-considered answer.

Writing later, the anonymous author of the book of Hebrews takes a dire view of those who return to sin after receiving redemption. They have lost their salvation: "For it is impossible for those who have once been enlightened, tasted the heavenly gift, and shared in the Holy Spirit to be brought back to repentance if they fall away, for they are then crucifying for themselves the Son of God again" (Heb. 6:4–6). In the same vein he says: "For if we willingly sin after receiving the knowledge of the truth, there is no longer a sacrifice for sins, but a fearful expectation of judgment and furious fire that will devour God's enemies" (10:26–27). He points out that according to Scripture, anyone who violates the law of Moses is to be executed without mercy. And so:

> How much worse do you suppose is the punishment for someone who has trampled on the Son of God and slighted the blood of the covenant that brought their sanctification and insulted the Spirit of grace. For we know who said, "Vengeance is mine; I will repay," and also, "the Lord will judge his people." It is a fearful prospect to fall into the hands of the living God. (Heb. 10:29–31)

Fearful indeed. But then what are Christians who habitually sin to do?

Some later church fathers, as one might expect, taught that sincere repentance could restore a sinner who'd already been baptized to God's good graces. Others took a different tack, arguing that post-baptismal sins required yet another atonement. Luckily, this time it would not require a human sacrifice. Christians could pay for their sins by giving their resources to those in need. Almsgiving and engaging in other acts of benevolence became a way to atone for post-baptismal sins, an idea ultimately rooted in views of almsgiving in Judaism.[44]

The idea can be found already in the *Didache* (written around 100 CE), which provides instructions to church members about charitable giving. "Do not be one who reaches out your hands to receive but draws them back from giving. If you acquire something with your hands, give it as a *ransom for your sins*" (*Didache*, 6:4–5). Closer to the end of the second century we have a rather more explicit injunction to the Christian faithful, in a sermon wrongly attributed to Clement, the bishop of Rome: "Giving to charity is good as a repentance from sin. Fasting is better than prayer, but giving to charity is better than both. . . . For giving to charity lightens the burden of sin" (2 Clement 16:1–4).

No one in the early centuries of the church dealt with the issue more clearly than Cyprian, a mid-third-century bishop of the large church of Carthage, whose letters and treatises address numerous issues confronting the growing Christian community. Most of the problems Cyprian addresses are practical rather than doctrinal, though his theological beliefs clearly affect how he resolves issues of Christian behavior. One of these issues involves church members who have returned to lives of sin. Cyprian is emphatic that any believer who has been baptized has been "purged by the blood and sanctification of Christ." Christ's atoning work does not, however, cleanse sins committed later. Still, God has not left Christian sinners without hope: those who have dirtied themselves and "become foul" still "may once more be cleansed." It happens, once again, by charitable giving: "By almsgiving we may wash away whatever foulness we subsequently contract" (Treatise 8, *On Works and Alms*).[45]

Some sins, of course, are worse than others and, for Cyprian, require additional cleansing agents. Dealing with sin always requires repentance, but repentance needs to be sincere and demonstrated through a public show of humility. That may not be part of the teaching of Jesus, but now, over two centuries later, we are starting to find the idea of "penance" for sins committed after baptism.

For Cyprian and other church leaders, falling from the faith was a particularly inexcusable sin and required extraordinary acts of repentance. Apostasy had become a major issue, especially during the reigns of the emperors Decius (249–51 CE) and Valerian (253–60 CE), the first Roman emperors to require all Christians to sacrifice to the Roman gods on pain of torture and death.[46] Many refused and paid the price, including eventually Cyprian himself, who was martyred in 258 CE. Others succumbed, however, and once persecution passed, many apostates sought to be restored to the church. But how could they return to the grace of God after willfully turning away from it? For

Cyprian, it would not be easy. In his treatise, "On the Lapsed," written at the conclusion of the reign of Decius in 251 CE, Cyprian directly addresses those who had fallen: "Do you think that God will easily have mercy on you when you have declared him not to be your God?" (*On the Lapsed*, 35). No, it will take a great deal to be welcomed back into God's good graces: days of grief; sleepless nights of prayer; constant lamentations, stretched out on the ground in sackcloth, ashes, and filth; fasting; a diligent doing of "righteous works, by which sins may be purged; frequently applying oneself to almsgiving, by which souls are freed from death" (*On the Lapsed*, 35). What is more, those who had fallen away must abandon their wealth; their estates are to be sold and the proceeds given away. To return to God's graces will take an absolute, full-on, no holds barred commitment. Only then will God be merciful.

Interpersonal Forgiveness in a World of Atonement

An obvious question about Christian ethics is whether the early disciples changed their views of *interpersonal* reconciliation at the same time they reversed Jesus's understanding of reconciliation with God. Does the Lord's Prayer really mean: "Accept Christ's atonement for our sins, as we accept atonement from those who sin against us"?

The issue is complicated in part because many transgressions involve not only individuals but communities, and communities that advocate mercy still need to enforce justice. If a thief, rapist, or murderer could simply apologize for what they did and be forgiven without penalty, what would deter future offenses, a perpetual state of communal harm, exploitation, and total chaos? Possibly an initial offense could be forgiven along the lines Jesus prescribed, but repeat offenses would require something further. Yet Jesus insisted a person be forgiven not seven times but seventy times seven. Would a criminal system based on Jesus's views require a culprit to commit 490 murders before receiving a sentence?

Early Christian sources, of course, are far more interested in social arrangements among Jesus's followers than in society and judicial systems at large. It is clear that interpersonal forgiveness was indeed practiced in early Christian communities. Consider this passage found in the Gospel of Matthew:

> If your brother or sister sins against you, go and point out the fault when the two of you are alone. If you are heeded, you have regained that one. But if you are not heeded, take one or two others along with you, so that every word may be confirmed by the evidence of two or three witnesses. If the person refuses to listen to them, tell it to the church, and if the offender refuses to listen even to the church, let that one be as a gentile and a tax collector to you. (Matt. 18:15–17)

Scholars have long maintained this passage does not come straight from Jesus himself, since it presupposes the existence of a Christian "church," which did not come into existence until after his death. Jesus anticipated something different: a glorious kingdom in which Israel would rule and there would be no more evil or suffering. But, as one old saw has it, "Jesus expected the kingdom, but what he got was the church."[47]

The passage in Matthew indicates that a Christian harmed by a fellow member of the church is to confront the offender. If the person pays heed, then they are reconciled. "Heed" does not mean simply to "hear the words that are spoken," but also to agree and respond positively. That is, the person apologizes for the wrong they did, bringing reconciliation (the person is "regained"). If the person responds negatively, then one or two other members of the community are to be brought in to discuss the fault. If the person still refuses to repent and apologize, and does so yet again when confronted by the entire congregation, they are to be cut off from the community. In this view of things, just as God punishes sin by cutting off sinners and removing them from his ambit, so too the community. But anyone who repents is brought back into good standing, no other penalty assessed.

One can probably assume this was the rhetoric accepted and sometimes put into practice in Matthew's community some fifty years after Jesus's death. We find something similar in an interesting passage in the book of James involving a ritual of healing that presupposes the widespread view that sin and illness were closely linked.[48]

> Is anyone among you sick? They should call for the elders of the church and have them pray over them, anointing them with oil in the name of the Lord.

> The prayer of faith will save the sick, and the Lord will raise them up, and anyone who has committed sins will be forgiven. (James 5:14–16)

The term "repentance" does not occur here, but it seems to be implied. The sick realize their problem and bring in their spiritual leaders, who are persuaded to pray over them and anoint them with oil, leading to physical healing and its corollary, spiritual forgiveness. There is no further charge or penalty. It should be pointed out that in this case the sick have indeed paid a price for their sins: God has made them ill. But once they repent, that is the end of matter.

Forgiveness without further payment continues to be taught in church writings well beyond the New Testament period. To pick just one example, we find the following instruction to church elders in a letter written by the bishop of Smyrna, Polycarp, to the church of Philippi sometime in the first part of the second century:

> The presbyters should be compassionate, merciful to all, turning back those who have gone astray . . . not severe in judgment, knowing that we are all in debt to sin. And so if we ask the Lord to forgive us, we ourselves also ought to forgive. (Letter of Polycarp 6:1–2)

If we pay close attention to such passages, we come to the somewhat strange conclusion that Christian writers *did* insist that followers of Jesus imitate God's own example when it comes to love and charity, but not forgiveness. God requires an *atonement* for transgression. Christians, though, should *forgive* one another. Perhaps the Lord's Prayer would be more correctly worded something like: "Redeem us from our sins through atonement since we forgive without atonement those who sin against us."

Conclusion

The Christianization of the Roman Empire thus produced mixed results when it came to public and private morality. Jesus's own teachings of God's gracious forgiveness without atonement were quickly lost. But throughout history, many of his followers have followed his instruction to forgive others without payment or retribution, or at least try to do so. And possibly the world is a better place for it. But most people continue to think a personal affront or damage requires penalties, or at least some kind of payback. And even then that may not suffice. Many people feel they *should* forgive someone who has harmed them; but how many hundreds of times have we heard "I just can't"?

The major ethical changes brought by Christianity came, then, as the Christian populations of the West began to adopt Jesus's teaching of altruistic love, even to strangers, and its concomitant material expression in new practices of charitable giving. Here I think there really was a revolution. In our (still) predominantly Christian world, most people do feel they should love others who are in need, even if they are strangers, and at least do something to provide some help, for example by doing volunteer work or donating hard-earned money for disaster relief or to institutions dealing with hunger, homelessness, and the myriad other personal and social problems our world confronts. Not everyone does that, of course. Many don't. But many do and even more think they should. That part is good.

Moreover, this shift in ethical thinking led to the formation of remarkable institutions whose sole purpose was to heal the sick, feed the hungry, provide housing to the homeless, and care for those who were widowed, orphaned, or elderly. These shifts may not have played a large role in governmental policy for a very long time—essentially until the modern period—but they certainly do now.

Even so, as many readers will have been thinking, it would be a huge mistake to think this change in moral sense and behavior provides an unmitigated affirmation of the "goodness" of the Christian tradition and its superiority to all that came before it or that now exists alongside it, in either other religious traditions or the growing humanism of the West. It is true that many devout Christians insist that morality itself was brought into the ancient world through this new faith, making the world and everyone in it unconditionally better. But many agnostics, atheists, and followers of other religions maintain the opposite, that Christianity has done unnecessary and inconceivable harm, that without Christianity we would not have had crusades, inquisitions, wars of religion, and pogroms against Jews that led to the Holocaust. Which is it?

My view is that both sides of the argument are making simplistic and overgeneralized claims about a deeply complicated and entangled set of issues. One way to express the complexity is to ask not which side is right, but whether either of them is wrong.

Conclusion

ALTRUISM IN THE CONSCIENCE OF THE WEST

The only time anyone in my family could remember hearing my devout grandfather use foul language was in August 1935, when Franklin Delano Roosevelt signed the Social Security Act into law. The act changed how the country dealt with those who needed assistance by providing federal aid to Americans in need: unemployment and health insurance, retirement benefits for the elderly, financial assistance for widows with children, support for the disabled. The benefits were funded through taxes: those with sufficient means would funnel some of their hard-earned resources through the government to help others. My grandfather was vehemently opposed to it. He was not a big fan of the New Deal or the [expletive deleted] president who pushed it.

It is not that my grandfather was hard-hearted and didn't care for the poor. On the contrary, he was a devoted Christian committed to the teachings of Jesus and deeply concerned for others. But like many Americans at the time, he had been born and raised a rugged individualist and believed that "governmental handouts" were not only unfair to hard-working taxpayers but also did more harm than good, precisely for the people that liberal soft-hearted politicians were trying to help. People should work for what they got. When times were hard, it would be better for them, in the long run, to figure out for themselves how to survive, rather than rely on someone else to do the work for them. And so, as strange as it may seem to those of us who support such legislation, he actually was an altruist. In his view, some ways of helping only led to harm.

Most people are altruistic in one way or another—it is simply part of what it means to be human. Without altruism the human species would not have emerged, survived, and thrived. Nor would any of the prehuman species we count as our biological ancestors. Without some level of sacrificial cooperation, no social group can succeed in the competition for resources. This is not just a modern biological theory but a documented social and historical reality. For as long as we have had records—and for all time before we had records—human cultures have engaged in mutual assistance even at a personal cost.

But there is altruism and there is altruism. And as we've seen, the kind of altruism embedded in governmental assistance to the poor, as crystallized in some ways in the Social Security Act of 1935, would not even have been conceivable in the worlds of antiquity. That did not change much even with the conversion of the Roman Empire in the centuries after Constantine. This kind of charity is a modern phenomenon, made possible by excessive wealth generated by industrial and postindustrial societies that created the middle class. But it is *driven* by a Christian ethic that understands that altruism is to be extended to the "other"—not just friends, family, potential friends, and beneficiaries of one's private patronage, but anyone in need, even strangers.

This ethic is part of our psyche today because the Western world became Christian and, in some measure, adopted the views preached by the religion's founder and his earliest followers. Over the centuries the rhetoric and practice of helping those in need became deeply imbedded in society and on an individual level came to be internalized by a majority of Christians everywhere. What it means to be Christian, and what it means to be a human raised in a Judeo-Christian culture, is to help those in need, whether we know them, or want to know them, or would like them if we did. Not everyone *has* that common sense, of course, and the impulse to help can take very different forms depending on whether you're, say, a rugged individualist or a soft-hearted liberal. But for most people in the West, it is part of what it means to be human.

What Good Has It Done?
The Christian Movement in Retrospect

Throughout this book I have been trying to explain and even celebrate some of the good brought into the Western world by the Christian movement over the past two thousand years. For many Christians, this may seem rather obvious: of course the "good news" is good and has done good. But few people, even the most devout, know the details. I hope my book will help them appreciate some of the specific contributions the Christian faith has made to our culture. (Christians invented *hospitals*?) I also hope they will recognize the world of good outside of Christianity—before, during, and after the Christianization of the West. In my experience, many of those who are most committed to the Christian faith think of the ancient pagan world—as well as the modern non-Christian world—as godless, immoral, harmful, and soul-destroying. But it is hard to read Aristotle, Seneca, or Epictetus without wishing more of our fellow citizens would think such deep and coherent thoughts about life and meaning, what it is to be a good person, and to find contentment—and then change their lives accordingly.

Just as numerous Christians think in broad, generalizing terms about how their faith brought goodness into the world, it has become almost de rigueur among non-Christian critics of Christianity, especially those who were once believers themselves, to attack the faith, saying nothing good about it and attributing to it nothing but evil. It is indeed very easy to detail the horrors brought to our world by those claiming to do the sovereign will of the Christian God: the savage destruction of pagan art and architecture in late antiquity; the violent pogroms against Jews leading eventually to the Holocaust; the bloody Crusades and ongoing violence against Muslims; the horrible tortures and forced conversions of the Inquisitions; the pious justifications of war and slavery; the ongoing hatred and violence in our own time against the "other" because of their race, gender, sexual orientation, ethnicity, place of origin, or most anything else.

Many Christians will defend the faith by saying that none of this represents "true Christianity." They are right that none of it is true to the teachings of Jesus, but they are wrong to say it is not Christianity. It is Christianity. These are things done in the name of Christ by his followers against those who have not believed in him or have not held the right beliefs about him or were different in some other way. We forget, or possibly never knew, there were prominent Nazi theologians, including renowned scholars of the New Testament, who were faithful and active members of their churches and believed that Christ was on their side in their hateful agendas and actions.[1] It is harder to overlook the many Christians today who advocate radical nationalism, racism, sexism, homophobia, Islamophobia, anti-Semitism, the slaughter of civilians, and the burning of the planet—all claiming Christ is on their side.

Even as a Christian I saw these problems, and I think it is a mistake for Christians today to refuse to recognize them.

At the same time, I also know there is another side, and it too needs to be given full credit, not as a way of mitigating the horrors but as a way of seeing that very few religions, philosophies, or ideologies are thoroughly, incontrovertibly, inherently evil, just as none is thoroughly, incontrovertibly, inherently good. The reason for this reality is, or at least should be, obvious: ideologies are believed and enacted by humans, and humans are both terribly flawed and filled with great moral potential.

I often get asked, usually by non-Christians, whether I think, on balance, the Christian faith has done more good or evil in the world. I always reply that the question is unanswerable. There are no cosmic scales or AI-generated algorithms to provide an approximate, let alone decisive, answer. History is long, religion is complex, and good and evil are variable, coming in shades and degrees. What I will say, even to my non-Christian friends, is that even if we were preternaturally able to look at all the specific effects of the Christian faith in just about every time and place, we would find the same generalized answer: in addition to the terrible suffering that the Christian faith and those who follow it have created and are still creating, there is also a lot of good. We are remiss if we fail to notice it.

Much of the good brought to the world by the Christian faith has involved an important shift in the understanding of what it means to be a good person, a moral agent, and truly human. Unlike what could generally be found in the Greek and Roman worlds, the Jewish tradition that Jesus inherited and embraced stressed acting in love not only toward family members, friends, and those who could become friends but even complete strangers, especially needy members of the community. Jesus, possibly like other Jewish teachers before him, universalized this principle. God was the God of the whole world and everyone in it. To be right with God meant to live for others, whoever they were, whatever they looked like, wherever they lived or came from. Love of all, especially those in need, was paramount, even if it required some sacrifice. Even if it required the ultimate sacrifice.

The followers of Jesus believed his own life and death were models to be followed. It is true that few Christians in the decades, centuries, and then millennia after his death adhered to his teachings literally.[2] But, on the whole, they have thought that living for others was an essential element in being a thinking and moral person. It is very difficult to quantify the impact of this shift in ethical perspective, not just on individual lives but also on the social and political agendas of the Western world. We can, however, see the concrete results all around us. It was the Christian movement that led to the creation of public hospitals, orphanages, old persons' homes, poorhouses, private charities, and governmental programs dealing with disaster relief, poverty, hunger, and homelessness.[3] Whether or not these institutions would have evolved in some other way based on other influences is impossible to know; what we can say is that they were Christian interventions.

Equally if not more important changes occurred on the personal level, in our moral vision of what it means to live in this world. I obviously do not mean that everyone in the West became and remains a committed altruist. After reading this morning's news, I think a strong case can be made otherwise. There are more than enough people all around us, now as always, and in scarily increasing numbers, even among those who most loudly proclaim their commitment to Christ and his teachings, who do not share an altruistic impulse toward strangers (or even family members), who live in complete isolation from others or, worse, who seek society in order to dominate it, striving for their own good at all costs and showing zero concern for the welfare of others—from the solipsistic tyrant to that egomaniacal narcissist who lives next door.

But that is not most of us. Most of us continue to sympathize with those who are in pain or turmoil or danger. We want to help those in need, even if we don't know who they are. We see it not just as something we ought to do, but something we want to do. If we choose not to do much or anything at all, we sometimes feel pangs of guilt and regret.

Why is that? The sense that we should help strangers in need did not come from our prehistorical ancestors, nor from the Greek and Roman worlds at the foundation of our civilization. It came from the social pressures asserted on the Western world by the moral instruction of early Christians based principally on the teachings of Jesus. Eventually, it came to be simply how people thought and felt, part of our psyche. Jesus, in the end, transformed the moral conscience of the West.

NOTES

INTRODUCTION

1. Certainly, without some form of cooperation and assistance our species would not have survived, let alone thrived, for some three hundred millennia. Here I am speaking of altruistic behavior specifically toward strangers. Of the many books on the evolutionary biological and psychological issues involved with altruism, nearly all of them controversial (there are large disagreements in both fields), among the most interesting and useful are Elliott Sober and David Sloan Wilson, *Unto Others: The Evolution and Psychology of Unselfish Behavior* (Harvard University Press, 1998); Robert M. Sopolsky, *Behave: The Biology of Human's at Our Best and Worst* (Penguin Books, 2017); and Lewis Dartnell, *Being Human: How our Biology Shaped World History* (Vintage, 2023). See also chapter 2, note 2.
2. When I say it is "common" sense, I certainly do not mean it is the "universal" sense. One measure of how thoroughly Western culture has been ethically Christianized in this way is the emphasis on altruism to strangers in thoroughly secular modern ethical movements such as "effective altruism," which is not ostensibly rooted in religion, yet advocates for doing the greatest amount of good (for complete strangers) in the most cost-efficient ways. Among the leading proponents of the view have been William MacAskill and Peter Singer. See MacAskill, *Doing Good Better: How Effective Altruism Can Help You Help Others* (Avery, 2015), and Singer, *The Most Good You Can Do: How Effective Altruism Is Changing Ideas about Living Ethically* (Yale University Press, 2015). For serious critiques of the enterprise of effective altruism, see the collection of essays in Carol J. Adams, Alice Crary, and Lori Gruen, eds., *The Good It Promises, the Harm It Does: Critical Essays on Effective Altruism* (Oxford University Press, 2023).
3. My initial foray into the topics I deal with in this book began in 2018, when working on my book *Heaven and Hell: A History of the Afterlife* (Simon & Schuster,

2020) and its academic corollary, *Journeys to Heaven and Hell: Tours of the Afterlife in the Early Christian Tradition* (Yale University Press, 2022). Early in my research for these projects (especially focused on charitable giving in early Christianity), I decided that this would be my next book. But in 2019, Tom Holland's terrific study, *Dominion: How the Christian Revolution Remade the World* (Basic Books), appeared. I, naturally, thought my thunder had been (inadvertently) stolen. But in fact, not. Holland and I agree on a lot of things, but our foci, concerns, and breadth of coverage are quite distinct. His is an impressively expansive discussion of wide-ranging themes over the entire course of two millenia. Mine, as will be seen, is not that at all.

4. See my book, Bart Ehrman, *Lost Christianities: The Battles for Scriptures and the Faiths We Never Knew* (Oxford University Press, 2003).
5. Some readers may think of possible exceptions, such as military hospitals and occasional grain doles. I'll be dealing with these later in the book.
6. One might object that a widespread interest in the "other" could not be expected before the technologies of mass communications. It is a bit hard to sympathize for the millions of people starving in Somalia if you've never heard of Somalia, don't know there are millions of people there, or are not keeping up with the recent tragedies on the ground. There is obviously a good bit of truth to that view, but it is also important to remember that mass communication is a remarkably recent phenomenon. The moral obligation to help the unknown "other" was firmly entrenched in the Western psyche a millennium and a half ago.

CHAPTER ONE: DOES ALTRUISM EXIST?

1. Just as in *alternative* ("other" choice/possibility) or *altercation* (dispute with "another").
2. There is a large body of scholarship devoted to just about every aspect of altruism: what it is; how it is to be understood; whether it refers to actions or motivations or both; how it came to develop/evolve among living species and humans in particular; whether it is actually possible; how it relates to egoism; if there is scientific evidence for it; and on and on. For a solid beginning I would suggest three relatively brief articles (with bibliographies): Richard Kraut, "Altruism," *Stanford Encyclopedia of Philosophy*, ed. Edward N. Zalta (Fall 2020), https://plato.stanford.edu/archives/fall2020/entries/altruism/; John Doris, Stephen Stich, and Lachlan Walmsley, "Empirical Approaches to Altruism," *Stanford Encyclopedia of Philosophy*, ed. Edward N. Zalta (Spring 2020), https://plato.stanford.edu/archives/spr2020/entries/altruism-empirical/; David Konstan,

"Altruism," *Transactions of the American Philological Association* 130 (2000): 1–17.

3. Though not, as I've indicated, if these others are unconnected to us genetically or socially. See Sober and Wilson, *Unto Others*.
4. Charles Darwin, *On the Origin of Species*, based on the first edition (Capstone, 2020; original 1859), 174.
5. Richard Dawkins, *The Selfish Gene*, 4th ed. (Oxford University Press, 2016).
6. Thomas Hobbes, *Leviathan*, ed. C. B. Macpherson (Penguin, 1981; original 1651), 15.
7. Doris, Stich, and Walmsley, "Empirical Approaches," 1.

CHAPTER TWO: THE ANCIENT QUEST FOR HAPPINESS

1. And was that ever a shock. I didn't even know how to begin class. I knew it wasn't with prayer, but . . . what then?
2. For the reasons, see my book *God's Problem: How the Bible Fails to Answer Our Most Important Question—Why We Suffer* (HarperOne, 2014).
3. For religion in the Roman world at the time of early Christianity, see the excellent overviews of James Rives, *Religion in the Roman Empire* (Blackwell, 2007), and Mary Beard, John North, and Simon Price, *Religions of Rome, Vol. 1: A History* (Cambridge University Press, 1998). For a briefer overview, see my book *The Triumph of Christianity*, 74–104.
4. See my discussion of the terms "pagan" and "paganism" in Ehrman, *Triumph of Christianity*, 76–78. In this book I will be using the term "monotheism" in a broad sense to refer to religions that insisted on *worshipping* only one God, rather than the belief that there *was* only one God.
5. The major exceptions were the various "mystery cults" focused on one or another divinity such as Isis, Mithras, or Demeter. Unfortunately, we are poorly informed about what these various cults entailed and how they were practiced. They really are still "mysteries." But it does appear they involved the worship of one or another god or goddess who could personally enable their devotees to enjoy a better life in this world and also to secure a happier existence in the world to come. For a useful overview and collection of the relevant ancient texts in translation, see Marvin Meyer, ed., *The Ancient Mysteries: A Sourcebook of Sacred Texts* (University of Pennsylvania Press, 1999).
6. See the full discussion of Sober and Wilson, *Unto Others*, chs. 1–5, 17–194.
7. Some scholars have made concerted efforts to discover how morality worked on the ground among the great majority of the ancient population who were not among the cultural elites. It is a difficult undertaking, since nearly all our

relevant evidence is literary, written by and/or for educated elites. There may be some ways around the problem, however, as explored in a now-classic work by Kenneth Dover, *Greek Popular Morality in the Time of Plato and Aristotle* (Basil Blackwell, 1974), and more recently by Teresa Morgan, *Popular Morality in the Early Roman Empire* (Cambridge University Press, 2007). Morgan's book is particularly relevant to our interests here, since she deals with how non-elites thought and talked about morality in the first two centuries of the Roman world. Even though most of our literature comes from upper-class elites, Morgan proposes that "non-elite" views also survive in certain genres, especially fables, proverbs, popular moralizing sayings, and short anecdotes of people who should be imitated. She subjects such works to a full analysis and finds many similarities and differences between popular morality and highbrow philosophy. For the issues of altruism that I am focusing on here, many of the similarities are particularly interesting: that wealth can corrupt those who have it and, as a consequence, lead to harm for those who do not; that it is important for those with resources to be generous in their giving, but also the sense that recipients of this largesse are most commonly friends, family, and others of one's "own sort"; that hierarchies of power (that is, the realities of domination) are both inevitable and natural; and so on.

8. For introductory-level discussions of ancient moral philosophers, good starting places are Julia Annas, *Ancient Philosophy: A Very Short Introduction* (Oxford University Press, 2000), and Anthony Kenny, *Ancient Philosophy* (Clarendon Press, 2004). For outstanding discussions of all the relevant topics, with bibliographies, see the articles in the *Stanford Encyclopedia of Philosophy*, easily available online at https://plato.stanford.edu, including the overview in Richard Parry and Harald Thorsrud, "Ancient Ethical Theory", *Stanford Encyclopedia of Philosophy*, ed. Edward N. Zalta (Fall 2021), https://plato.stanford.edu/archives/fall2021/entries/ethics-ancient/. For more in-depth discussions see Christopher Boronich, ed., *The Cambridge Companion to Ancient Ethics* (Cambridge University Press, 2017), and the justifiably celebrated full-length treatments of Julia Annas, *The Morality of Happiness* (Oxford University Press, 1993), and Martha Nussbaum, *The Therapy of Desire: Theory and Practice in Hellenistic Ethics* (Princeton University Press, 1994).

9. Named after either his father or, more likely, his son, both named Nicomachus. See chapter 3, note 14.

10. As found earlier as well, including in Plato, *Symposium*, 204d–205a.

11. Need I point out: in the patriarchal world of antiquity, the male adult was the ultimate concern.

12. Matthew R. Christ, *The Limits of Altruism in Democratic Athens* (Cambridge University Press, 2012), 1–2. He later elaborates, based on his careful analysis: "A fairly consistent pattern emerges from our survey of helping behavior in diverse spheres: Athenians show little proclivity toward helping those outside their kin and circle of friends in substantial ways." Moreover, "To the extent that wealthy men helped less fortunate men, this may have most commonly taken the form of loans rather than outright gifts, and even this limited form of help may have been confined largely to their intimates" (pp. 25–26).
13. He devotes two entire books of the *Nicomachean Ethics* to this and other issues connected with friendship. We'll be considering some of the key details later in chapter 3.
14. See the lengthy discussions of Julia Annas, *Morality of Happiness*, and Martha Nussbaum, *Therapy of Desire*.
15. See Julia Annas, *Morality of Happiness*, and Martha Nussbaum, *Therapy of Desire*. For useful articles on the two major schools, see David Konstan, "Epicurus," *Stanford Encyclopedia of Philosophy*, ed. Edward N. Zalta & Uri Nodelman (Fall 2022), https://plato.stanford.edu/archives/fall2022/entries/epicurus/; Marion Durand, Simon Shogry, and Dirk Baltzly, "Stoicism," *Stanford Encyclopedia of Philosophy*, ed. Edward N. Zalta & Uri Nodelman (Spring 2023), https://plato.stanford.edu/archives/spr2023/entries/stoicism/. For Cynics, see William Desmond, *Cynics* (University of California, 2008).
16. See the recent translation of Pamela Mensch, *Lives of the Eminent Philosophers: Diogenes Laertius*, ed. James Miller (Oxford University Press, 2018). The other major source for understanding Epicurean teaching is his later devotee, the Roman Lucretius, in his long poem *On the Nature of Things*, a paean to Epicurus and his views with some distinctive twists of the poet's own. For modern discussions of Epicureanism, in addition to the works cited in notes 6 and 14, see the range of articles in Philip Mitsis, ed., *The Oxford Handbook of Epicurus and Epicureanism* (Oxford University Press, 2020).
17. Lucretius (note 16) provides a detailed explanation in his book *On the Nature of Things*, where he notes that since atoms are necessarily falling at the same speed in straight perpendicular, in theory they can never collide. But for some inexplicable reason they occasionally swerve out of line, leading to collisions and combinations. The "swerve" is one of the most distinctive and peculiar aspects of Epicurean thought.
18. In addition to the works cited in notes 8 and 15, see the various articles in Brad Inwood, ed., *The Cambridge Companion to the Stoics* (Cambridge University Press, 2003).

19. Some Stoics insisted that this applies to all people: men and women; slaves and free. The debates about women are particularly interesting given the overwhelmingly patriarchal prejudices of virtually the entire ancient world. Other perspectives come to the fore in the teachings of one of the most famous philosophers of the early Roman empire, Musonius Rufus, a Stoic philosopher who was the teacher of the yet-to-be-more-famous Epictetus. We regret very much not to have any of his writings, but we do have a number of sayings that later writers quoted and several lectures allegedly transcribed by one of his followers. In two of these he makes his views of women and the philosophical virtues quite clear: "That there is not one set of virtues for a man and another for a woman is easy to perceive." He goes on to explain that women in their daily lives, just as much as men, need to be trained and proficient in prudence, self-control, justice, and courage. To some degree these are simply human virtues, endowed at birth; but for them to become an ingrained part of a person's character requires training, and so, he concludes, "The same type of training and education must, of necessity, befit both men and women" (Musonius Rufus, "Women Too Should Study Philosophy").
20. I am not saying that the author of the prologue was influenced *only* by Stoic thought. A good deal of what he says about the Logos alludes, for example, to Genesis 1, where, in the Greek version the author was using, God creates the world by means of his "word" ("And he *said*, 'Let there be light'"), and the word brings into existence light and life. But Stoic thought as well seems to be in play in John's prologue. Some Jewish thinkers—notably Philo—were quite comfortable seeing intriguing connections between the words of Scripture and the teachings of Greek philosophers.
21. That has certainly happened to me. For over fifty years I've been extremely happy I got hepatitis the summer of 1972 before my senior year in high school, bringing my baseball career, such as it was, to an ignominious end. For the rest of the summer I had to refrain from all physical activity, but I was not the kind of kid who could sit around doing nothing. To stave off boredom I decided to spend my time working on the debate topic for the coming fall. I enjoyed debate for the same reason I enjoyed sports: it was highly competitive. But I had never thrown myself much into it before then. Still, it was something I could do sitting down, reading, taking notes, and preparing "evidence" for that year's resolution.

It wasn't long before I even found it entrancing. Once I recovered from hepatitis I continued to work like a fiend on debate and loved it. In the short term, it paid off: I had some incredibly gifted colleagues on the team and, with me bringing up the rear, we won the state debate tournament. But of more importance for me in the long term, I realized I actually *liked* academic work and was good

at research and ... I am certain that if that hadn't happened, I would never have become a scholar. Thank God for hepatitis.
22. The Greek word used here, *prohairesis*, sometimes translated as "moral purpose," is a favorite word of the Stoic Epictetus, but it is difficult to express in English. Literally it means something like "choosing one thing ahead of another" or "a chosen course of action."
23. The irrational fear of death is a theme Seneca deals with in a number of his letters to Lucilius; see for example Letters 24, 30.
24. See the works cited in notes 8 and 15.
25. Apollodorus of Ephelus in Diogenes Laertius, *Lives of Eminent Philosophers*, 7.121.
26. There have been long debates about whether Diogenes's teacher Antisthenes should instead be considered the "founder" of the Cynic movement. For biographies of both, see Diogenes Laertius, *Lives of Eminent Philosophers*, book 6.
27. See Gerald Downing, *Christ and the Cynics: Jesus and Other Radical Preachers in First-Century Tradition* (Journal for the Study of the Old Testament Supplement Series, 1988); John Dominic Crossan, *The Historical Jesus: The Life of a Mediterranean Jewish Peasant* (HarperSanFrancisco, 1991).

CHAPTER 3: LOVE, CHARITY, AND FORGIVENESS IN THE GREEK AND ROMAN WORLDS

1. For example, Oxford philosopher Richard Swinburne, *The Existence of God* (Clarendon Press, 2004), with whom I once had a particularly infuriating on-air debate on the related issue of the morality of suffering and the problem it causes for belief in God. You can find it here: https://www.youtube.com/watch?v=hrrcb1WcfzM&ab_channel=BartD.Ehrman. A more balanced view is presented in an article written (I realized) by my philosophy teacher at Wheaton College (with whom I disagree on the point; for what it's worth, he would not recognize me from Adam), Stephen Evans, coauthored with David Baggett, "Moral Arguments for the Existence of God," *Stanford Encyclopedia of Philosophy*, ed. Edward N. Zalta & Uri Nodelman (Winter 2022), https://plato.stanford.edu/archives/win2022/entries/moral-arguments-god/.
2. See Robert Wright, *The Moral Animal: Why We Are the Way We Are: The New Science of Evolutionary Psychology* (Vintage, 1995); Sober and Wilson, *Unto Others*; and just about any evolutionary biology textbook, such as David Buss, *Evolutionary Psychology: The New Science of the Mind*, 6th ed. (Routledge, 2019).
3. Whether parts of the account are fiction or not is irrelevant to my point, since even if invented they represent the author's and readers' common sense.

4. I am using the translation of Richard Crawley, revised by Robert B. Strassler, in *The Landmark Thucydides* (Touchstone, 1998). For a relevant selection of key passages from the account, see Gregory M. Reichberg, Henrik Syse, and Endre Begby, eds., *The Ethics of War: Classic and Contemporary Readings* (Blackwell, 2006), 3–17.
5. Just within the New Testament we have clear instances of a dominated person dominating someone yet weaker, in Matthew's parable of the unforgiving slave (Matthew 18:23–34). The book of Revelation fully accepts the ideology of domination. One of its leading assumptions is that the powerful should dominate, but the power is in the wrong hands. Christ and his followers should have total domination, not the Roman empire. See my book *Armageddon: What the Bible Really Says about the End* (Simon & Schuster, 2023). A humorous tale of domination can be found in Lucian of Samosata's dialogue, Timon, which shows how the dominated comes to love dominating once he strikes it rich.
6. The classic study of the meaning of love (*agapē*) in early Christianity, which many of my generation (wrongly) chose to pillory, was Anders Nygren, *Agape and Eros*, 2 vols., transl. Philip S. Watson (SPCK, 1932, 1938). A classic exploration of the command to love in the writings of the New Testament is Victor Paul Furnish, *The Love Commandment in the New Testament* (Abingdon, 1972). For a recent and more detailed scholarly analysis is Oda Wischmeyer, *Love as Agape: The Early Christian Concept and Modern Discourse*, trans. Wayne Coppins (Baylor University Press, 2021).
7. Aristotle makes the contrast explicit in several places, for example, in Aristotle, *Nicomachean Ethics*, 8.4.11, 8.6.2, 9.1.1.
8. For Aristotle, see note 7; for Plato see *Symposium* 183c.
9. For a fuller discussion, see Andrew Lear, "Ancient Pederasty: An Introduction," in *A Companion to Greek and Roman Sexualities*, ed., Thomas K. Hubbard (Blackwell, 2014), 102–27.
10. We also have ancient discussions of male adult homosexuality and (to some extent) lesbianism, but they do not feature in the dialogue. See Thomas Hubbard, ed., *Homosexuality in Greece and Rome: A Sourcebook of Basic Documents* (University of California Press, 2003).
11. Translation by Alexander Nehamas and Paul Woodruff in John M. Cooper, ed., *Plato: Complete Works* (Hackett, 1993).
12. These "essences" are commonly referred to as the Platonic "forms" or "ideas."
13. Socrates does not deliver the final speech of *The Symposium*. After he concludes, a new figure appears at the party, Alcibiades, who is cajoled into providing a speech praising Socrates and his personal character in relation to the issue of *eros*. Most

readers have seen this final speech as a secondary anecdotal conclusion to the dialogue, but Martha Nussbaum, one of the great interpreters of Plato, makes a strong case that it is in fact the climax and that Alcibiades provides a convincing counter to Socrates's view by celebrating not the detached ascent of the soul to the knowledge of a universal and disembodied truth, but the deeply personal and particular understanding of true passion that only comes by experience, thus more like poetry than philosophy. Her reading is brilliant and nuanced, but in the end, I do not find it completely convincing. I read the Alcibiades scene as analogous to the myth or Er at the end of the Republic (and other myths in Plato), a crucial supplementary explanation of Plato's vision in an ironically different (seemingly contradictory) mode, a *story* that grabs the emotion rather than *dialectical reasoning* that compels the mind.

14. Aristotle's father and son were both named Nicomachus; the latter appears to have edited this work and so it was named after him. Among the other writings of Aristotle, two focus on ethics, the shorter *Eudemian Ethics* (probably written earlier, but covering many similar topics) and the "Great Ethics" (*Magna Moralia*), which is shorter still and may have been written by someone else. For a solid overview of Aristotle's ethical works and views, see Richard Kraut, "Aristotle's Ethics," *Stanford Encyclopedia of Philosophy*, ed. Edward N. Zalta & Uri Nodelman (Fall 2022), https://plato.stanford.edu/archives/fall2022/entries/aristotle-ethics/.

15. I am using the translation of Robert C. Bartlett and Susan D. Collins, *Aristotle's Nicomachean Ethics* (University of Chicago, 2011).

16. Some modern scholars have argued that Stoics held views of altruism very similar to those that emerged in the Christian tradition (without using the word *agapē*). See, for example, Runar M. Thorsteinsson, *Roman Christianity and Roman Stoicism: A Comparative Study of Ancient Morality* (Oxford University Press, 2010), and the highly nuanced analysis of Troels Endberg-Pedersen, *Paul and the Stoics* (Westminster John Knox, 2000). As I have indicated, I agree that Stoics maintained that "reason" not only infuses all reality but is especially present in humans and that, as a consequence, "humankind"—not just oneself—should and ought to be a focus of ethical concern. But it is abundantly clear in our surviving Stoic authors that this metaphysical understanding of "reason" never led to active, loving engagements with the bulk of humanity, the poor, and the destitute. Possibly in principle it should have done, but Stoic discussions of the recipients of love—for example, in reflections of who is "worthy" to receive material benefits, gifts, attention, and favor—make it clear that only a select few deserve active attention: Stoics such as Seneca who reflect on generous

interactions with the "other" and "humankind" almost always refer only to a certain narrow class of others. When discussing ancient views of altruism, it is always important (though rarely done) to consider the serious demographic realities on the ground connected with poverty, class, social dislocation, and their implications, as I will explain below. See further note 23.

17. I will be dealing with apparent exceptions, such as the Roman grain dole, below. See pages 68–69.
18. Occasionally the urban poor received some beneficences as trickle-down from the wealthy urban elite, as I will explain in a moment. These material awards came only to them, the city dwellers, and only to the freeborn adult male citizens among them, not to the vast bulk of the population living outside the city. When historians point out that provisions of cheap grain were sometimes made available (for purchase) in the city of Rome and a few other major cities, they are referring to this slice of the population, not to those who lived in other urban areas and not to the great masses who never set foot in a city. See my further discussion on pages 68–69.
19. For some of the most compelling studies of the economic realities in the Roman world, see Peter Garnsey: *Famine and Food Supply in the Graeco-Roman World: Responses to Risk and Crisis* (Cambridge University Press, 1988); William V. Harris, *Rome's Imperial Economy* (Oxford University Press, 2011); Walter Scheidel and Steven J. Friesen, "The Size of the Economy and the Distribution of Income in the Roman Empire," *Journal of Religious Studies* 99 (2009): 61–91. Some alternative perspectives can be found among the essays collected in Margaret Atkins and Robin Oxborne, eds., *Poverty in the Roman World* (Cambridge University Press, 2006).
20. I am using the data, somewhat simplified, provided in Scheidel and Friessen, "The Size of the Economy," 82–85.
21. For a contrary view, see note 23.
22. For a fine biography, see James Romm, *Dying Every Day: Seneca at the Court of Nero* (Vintage, 2014).
23. Some scholars treat ancient charitable giving more generously, maintaining that there were indeed instances of the wealthy giving to those in need generally, not just to relatives, friends, and clients. In addition to the works cited in note 16, see Daniel Caner, *The Rich and the Pure: Philanthropy and the Making of Christian Society in Early Byzantium* (University of California Press, 2021), who suggests that authors like Seneca insisted "on giving to anyone who was poor and needy" and that generally philosophers maintained that philanthropy "could be extended to unfamiliar groups" (pp. 42–43). In my view, this is a flaw

in his otherwise superb analysis. In almost every case that Seneca and other ancient philosophers of wealth speak of giving money to those in need who are not family, friends, or clients, it is only to those of the same socioeconomic class, not to the destitute, unless there is some other mitigating circumstance. It is not a concern for poverty or the poor per se. Seneca does indicate that money can be given to a slave, but only if the slave is highly intelligent and perceptive—that is, in Seneca's thinking, a slave who has an extraordinary head on his shoulders. He is not suggesting resources be given to most household slaves or indigent free persons. That much is clear simply by reading the reference Caner cites (Seneca, *Benefits*, 4.29.2).

24. Paul Veyne, *Bread and Circuses: Historical Sociology and Political Pluralism* (Allen Lane, 1990; French original, 1976), 5.
25. The classic study of giving is Marcel Mauss, *The Gift: Forms and Function of Exchange in Archaic Societies*, trans. Ian Cunnison (Free Press, 1954); fine summaries of ancient euergetism can be found in John M. G. Barclay, *Paul and the Gift* (Eerdmans, 2015), 1–65, and Peter Lampe, "Social Welfare in the Greco-Roman World as a Background for Early Christian Practice," *Acta Theologica* 23 (2016): 1–2, the latter of which can serve as an abbreviated and informed update of the groundbreaking classic, Hendrik Bolksestein, *Wohltaetigkeit und Armenpflege im vorchristlichen Altertum* (Bouma's Boekhuis, 1967; original 1939).
26. The term (or its French equivalent) was coined by A. Boulanger in 1923; see Veyne, *Bread and Circuses*, 10.
27. A rather glaring instance is in the overly generous-to-the-elite reading of A. R. Hands, *Charities and Social Aid in Greece and Rome* (Thames and Hudson, 1968).
28. See the impressive study of Garnsey, *Famine and Food Supply*.
29. Harris, *Rome's Imperial Economy*, 51–52.
30. See the examples scattered throughout Garnsey, *Famine and Food Supply*, 167–243.
31. Harris, *Rome's Imperial Economy*, 33.
32. I say "broadly" (that is, throughout the empire) since, as I've stressed, the uneven distribution of wealth was sometimes seen as a problem within Jewish communities as well.
33. See the valuable study of Princeton historian of late antiquity Peter Brown, *Poverty and Leadership in the Later Roman Empire* (Brandeis University Press, 2002). Among other things, Brown stresses that "to be a 'lover of the poor' became a public virtue" within Christianity (p. 1), in stark contrast with the Roman world that preceded it, where the rich provided funds for their cities, "never to the poor" in desperate need: "A rich man was praised for being a *philopatris*, 'a lover of his home-city,' never for being a *philoptôchos*, a 'lover of the poor'" (p. 5.) Even private

giving (to individuals), focused on "one's fellow citizens" and "dependents" rather than the "poor" (p. 11).

34. As we will see, there were precedents in Judaism when it came to human relations with God, for example in the Hebrew Bible, where a psalmist pleads to God for forgiveness (e.g., Psalm 51). But most transgressions between humans required reparation, and restored relationships with God required sacrifice.

35. Charles Griswold, *Forgiveness: A Philosophical Exploration* (Cambridge University Press, 2007); David Konstan, *Before Forgiveness: The Origins of a Moral Idea* (Cambridge University Press, 2010); Martha Nussbaum, *Anger and Forgiveness: Resentment, Generosity, Justice* (Oxford University Press, 2016). See also the essays in Charles Griswold and David Konstan, eds., *Ancient Forgiveness* (Cambridge University Press, 2012).

36. Hannah Arendt, *The Human Condition*, 2nd ed. (University of Chicago Press, 1988; original 1958), 238.

37. Konstan, *Before Forgiveness*, 22–58.

38. This includes the Stoics, who otherwise, in some ways, embody some of the ethical principles found among the Christians. See note 23.

39. Thucydides, *Peloponnesian War*, 5.89.

CHAPTER FOUR: THE JEWISH ROOTS OF JESUS'S ETHICS

1. See my book *Lost Christianities: The Battles for Scripture and the Faiths We Never Knew* (Oxford University Press, 2003).

2. Some of the foundational studies, still worth reading, are Jules Isaac, *Jesus and Israel*, trans. Sally Gran, ed. Claire Hachet Bishop (Holt, Rinehart & Winston, 1971; French original, 1948); Marcel Simon, *Verus Israel: A Study of the Relations between Christians and Jews in the Roman Empire, 135–425*, trans. H. McKeating (Oxford University Press, 1986; French original, 1964); Rosemary Ruether, *Faith and Fratricide: The Theological Roots of Anti-Semitism* (Seabury, 1974); John Gager, *The Origins of Anti-Semitism: Attitudes toward Judaism in Pagan and Christian Antiquity* (Oxford University Press, 1983).

3. In addition to laws focused on how to worship God and behave together in community are numerous laws connected with ritual "purity." Certain substances and activities could make a person impure before God, for example, touching a corpse, menstruating, having a semen emission. These were not considered "sins," but defilements that required cleansing rituals to put a person in a pure state in order to worship God properly. Because they are not closely tied to ethics per se, I will not be discussing them at length here.

4. The law itself does not distinguish between cultic and ethical laws—the law is the law. But it is clear that some of the laws have to do directly with how to worship God and others with how to treat members of the community.
5. Sometimes, as in Herodotus, this is expressed less as a "rule" than as a personal life policy.
6. Some scholars have claimed that Jesus was the first to phrase the Rule positively: "Do to others as you want them to do to you," but that is not true. One positive expression of it, for example, comes over three centuries before Jesus in the writings of the Greek orator Isocrates, who expresses it in a variety of ways (see *To Demonicus*, 1.41; 2.24, 38; 3.61; 4.81).
7. For further similarities of Jesus's teachings with others of his day, see my discussion of Tobit on p. 121. Some of the most significant studies of almsgiving in Judaism before, during, and after the time of Jesus show striking similarities with his views and those of his followers. See especially Gary A. Anderson, *Charity: The Place of the Poor in the Biblical Tradition* (Yale University Press, 2013), and Gregg Gardner, *Wealth, Poverty, and Charity in Jewish Antiquity* (University of California Press, 2022). Gardner in particular shows the parallel developments in the early centuries CE, for example in the notions of giving without any expectation of repayment, of giving as an atonement for sin, and of rewards in the afterlife for charitable giving in this world.
8. I will discuss them briefly in the next chapter. For an overview, see Bart D. Ehrman and Hugo Mendez, *The New Testament: A Historical Introduction to the Early Christian Writings*, 8th ed. (Oxford University Press, 2024), 72–78.
9. Apocalypticists, including Jesus and his followers, appear generally to have believed in annihilation, not eternal torment. This destruction is sometimes called an "eternal punishment" not because it will be eternally felt, but because it will never be reversed. See my discussion in Bart Ehrman, *Heaven and Hell: A History of the Afterlife* (Simon & Schuster, 2022), 147–67.
10. The book of Daniel is set in the sixth century BCE, allegedly written by a Judean exile in Babylon at the time; scholars have long known, however, that it was actually composed in the 160s BCE by an author claiming to "foresee" the events that would happen after the exile. For a full discussion, see John Collins, *Daniel: A Commentary on the Book of Daniel*, Hermeneia (Fortress Press, 1994).
11. See the miracles allegedly performed by Vespasian in Tacitus, *Histories*, 4.81. In many ways far more interesting are those narrated about the Baal Shem Tov, since they are based in part on the testimony of his personal secretary, whose son-in-law wrote them down later. See my discussion in Bart Ehrman, *Jesus before*

the Gospels: How the Early Christians Remembered, Changed, and Invented the Stories of Their Savior (HarperOne, 2016), 95–100.
12. Within the New Testament there are also quotations of Jesus in 1 Corinthians 7:10–11; 9:14; 11:22–24, written prior to the Gospels, and in Acts 20:35, written later. There are also, of course, noncanonical Gospels that quote his teachings. Especially important among these is the Gospel of Thomas. For an introduction and recent translation, see Bart D. Ehrman and Zlatko Pleše, *The Other Gospels: Accounts of Jesus from Outside the New Testament* (Oxford University Press, 2014), 155–73.
13. There are some exceptions in the Gospels where Jesus does encounter non-Jews, for example, Mark 7, where he meets with a woman from Syro-Phoenicia, and John 4, where he has a long conversation with a Samaritan. These are unlikely, however, to be historical accounts.
14. Mark's Jesus stresses that following him does not lead to glory, but to public humiliation, shame, torture, and death (Mark 8:34–39). No wonder few people in the narrative, or who read the narrative, want to take him seriously. In John the message is conveyed through a kind of symbolic act (John 13:1–20). On Jesus's final evening with the disciples, he takes a basin of water and a towel, and one by one washes their feet, the work of a household slave. Peter refuses to allow Jesus to humble himself in this way, but Jesus insists he must do so and that Peter must allow him. Jesus is the slave of all, even his disciples. He then instructs them to behave the same way. It is not the leaders who matter but the followers, not the masters but the slaves.

CHAPTER FIVE: LOVE, CHARITY, AND FORGIVENESS IN THE TEACHINGS OF JESUS

1. Richard Hays, *The Moral Vision of the New Testament: Community, Cross, New Creation: A Contemporary Introduction to New Testament Ethics* (HarperSanFranciso, 1996). Hays also has a lengthy discussion of homosexuality, which he opposes on the ground that it is condemned univocally in both the Hebrew Bible and the New Testament. Naturally many other fine scholars disagree up and down the line. See, among others, Dale Martin, *Sex and the Single Savior: Gender and Sexuality in Biblical Interpretation* (Westminster John Knox, 2006). I need to note that eighteen years after Hays's book was published—just a few months ago—he indicated he had changed his mind on homosexuality and expressed regret for his earlier statements. See his book, coauthored with his son, Old Testament scholar Chris Hays, *The Widening of God's Mercy: Sexuality within the Biblical Story* (Yale University Press, 2024).

2. The word can have other meanings; it is used twenty-one times in the Gospels, but to refer to such things as the "kiss" of Judas when he betrayed Jesus or for people who love the wrong kinds of things, for example, popularity or status.
3. Scholars among my readers will realize how I'm simplifying things here to keep the matters clear. All devout Jews, for example, thought it was important to keep the Law as much as possible. But some emphasized aspects of legal observance to an extreme more than others, particularly in relationship to other desiderata advanced by other groups (see my discussion on pages 106–10). For a longer overview, see Ehrman and Mendez, *The New Testament*, 72–78. For fuller discussions of Judaism in the period, see especially Shaye Cohen, *From the Maccabees to the Mishnah*, 3rd ed. (Westminster Press, 2014), and E. P. Sanders, *Judaism: Practice and Belief, 63 BCE–66 CE* (SCM Press; Trinity Press International, 1992).
4. For an overview of the key issues and a discussion of the relevant passages connected with sacrifice, see Gary Anderson, "Sacrifice and Sacrificial Offerings (OT)," in the *Anchor Bible Dictionary*, vol. 5, ed. David Noel Freedman (Doubleday, 1992), 870–86.
5. We know of one such community, Qumran, where the Dead Sea Scrolls were discovered, but there were certainly others. Some Essenes did live in villages, towns, and cities, but unfortunately we have only scant information about them or their practices.
6. For a fine overview, see James Vanderkam, *The Dead Sea Scrolls Today*, 2nd ed. (Eerdmans, 2010).
7. Many scholars have speculated whether Jesus was closely associated with the Dead Sea Scroll community, since he had similar apocalyptic views. This seems unlikely, since the very essence of his mission differed from theirs. The Essenes were intent on separating themselves from all the impure influences of the world at large; Jesus was known for going the other direction, associating openly with "tax collectors and sinners" and insisting that it was the unrighteous who needed to be "healed." The similarities in their apocalyptic views are more likely due to the fact that such views were more widely held among Jews at the time, not just Jesus and the Essenes.
8. Some scholars have argued Jesus was indeed in favor of armed resistance to the Romans. This was originally argued by Hermann Samuel Reimarus, in the first book ever published that approached the historical Jesus from a historical-critical perspective; see the translation and edition of Charles Talbert, *Fragments from Reimarus: Consisting of Brief Critical Remarks on the Object of Jesus and His Disciples as Seen in the New Testament* (Fortress, 1970); more recently it is the view argued by Reza Aslan, *Zealot: The Life and Times of Jesus of Nazareth*

(Random House, 2014). Most critical scholars have not found the case persuasive; see my discussion in Bart Ehrman, *Jesus before the Gospels* (Harper One, 2016), 167–71.
9. For a fuller discussion of Jesus's views about violence and the coming Son of Man, see my discussion in *Jesus: Apocalyptic Prophet*, 141–82.
10. See especially Furnish, *The Love Commandment*.
11. This is an issue raised by moral philosophers since the Enlightenment, most pointedly, early on, by Immanuel Kant, in *Metaphysical Foundation for Morals*.
12. Many readers think the love between David and Jonathan went far beyond friendship. Some of the relevant texts certainly seem to suggest sexual passion; but, as one would expect, it is a matter of debate (see 1 Samuel 18–20).
13. A number of the sayings found in Matthew's Sermon are also scattered throughout different chapters of the Gospel of Luke.
14. One indication that Luke has taken a known parable of Jesus (one that he actually said) and fit it into his narrative is that it does not flow organically from the context (so that Luke did not invent it for the occasion). Most people who read the passage have not noticed one of its oddities: Jesus allegedly tells it in response to a question that it does not answer (see note 18).
15. The significant differences in Luke's account have led some scholars to suggest that he is not simply editing Mark's passage, but is possibly providing an alternative form of the story from another source.
16. A "lawyer" in the New Testament is not a professional who does your mortgage or defends you in court, but a Torah scholar.
17. For a thorough discussion of the Samaritans through the ages down to the present, see Reinhard Plummer, *The Samaritans: A Profile* (Eerdmans, 2016).
18. There's another perplexing feature of the parable that again is not widely noticed. The lawyer has asked Jesus who the neighbor is that he is supposed to love, and one would expect that the answer will be that it is the Jewish man who was robbed and beaten and is in need. But after Jesus tells the parable it turns out that the *Samaritan* is the neighbor, the one who helps rather than the one who is helped. As I indicated earlier, this bit of confusion is part of what has led scholars to suspect that Luke had inherited the story and used it to make his point, even though it doesn't quite work: it is not a story about how loving one's neighbor means helping even an enemy in need, but about how one's enemy can act like a neighbor (which was not the lawyer's question).
19. Jesus does not appear to be referring to eternal torment here, but to an eternal annihilation that is never to be reversed. See my discussion in Bart Ehrman, *Heaven and Hell: A History of the Afterlife* (Simon & Schuster, 2025), 154–66.

20. There are, of course, a large number of books devoted to the questions of charitable giving in the teachings of Jesus, as based on his Jewish heritage, and in the Christian church through the ages. Some of the more recent and influential are Peter Brown, *Through the Eye of a Needle: Wealth, the Fall of Rome, and the Making of Christianity in the West, 350–550 AD* (Princeton University Press, 2012); Peter Brown, *The Ransom of the Soul: Afterlife and Wealth in Early Western Christianity* (Harvard University Press, 2015); David Downs, *Alms: Charity, Reward, and Atonement in Early Christianity* (Baylor University, 2016); Richard Finn, *Almsgiving in the Later Roman Empire: Christian Promotion and Practice, 313–450* (Oxford University Press, 2006); Gregg E. Gardner, *Wealth, Poverty, and Charity in Jewish Antiquity* (University of California Press, 2022); Roman Garrison, *Redemptive Almsgiving in Early Christianity* (Sheffield Academic Press, 1993); Susan R. Holman, ed., *Wealth and Poverty in Early Church and Society*, Holy Cross Studies in Patristic Theology and History (Baker Academic, 2008); Helen Rhee, *Wealth and Poverty in Early Christianity* (Fortress, 2017); and Paul Veyne, *Bread and Circuses: Historical Sociology and Political Pluralism* (Allen Lane, 1990; French original, 1976).

21. On the importance of the verse to the later Jewish and Christian traditions, and for the development of the practices of charitable giving more broadly, see especially Anderson, *Charity: The Place of the Poor in the Biblical Tradition*. Anderson focuses especially on the books of Tobit and Sirach (parts of the Apocrypha in the Protestant tradition); he explores as well the developments within rabbinic Judaism comparable to Christian traditions at about the same time in late antiquity, for example, "Giving alms is equal to keeping all the commandments in the Torah" (Tosephta, *Peah*, 4.19).

22. Luke does not present it as a historical event, but as one parable in the context of a long sequence of others told in this part of the Gospel. See my discussion in *Heaven and Hell*, 199.

23. The parable in its current form almost certainly does not go back to Jesus himself—in particular because of the ending, which is predicated on the recognition that Jesus has already been raised from the dead (see my discussion in *Heaven and Hell*, 197–203); but its perspective on wealth lines up well with Jesus's own views, as seen in the other passages I am discussing here.

24. Both Matthew and Luke acquired this story from Mark. Luke makes only a few changes, Matthew many more; but the key lines I discuss are virtually the same among the three.

25. This is an interesting way of putting the question, since in the Old Testament the term "inheritance" usually refers to acquired property; the "property" that man is looking to "inherit" is the eternal "Kingdom of God" that Jesus has been

proclaiming. People today rarely think of the kingdom as an earthly territory, since they imagine "heaven" as an ethereal state for disembodied souls above. For Jesus and other apocalyptic Jews, the kingdom was to be an actual place here on earth that the resurrected bodies of the righteous would enter.
26. Some people reconcile the passage with Paul by pointing out that Jesus says the man must follow him, taking that to mean faith in Jesus is essential. But Jesus tells him to become his follower only *after* doing what is necessary for treasure in heaven.
27. Downing, *Christ and the Cynics*; Crossan, *The Historical Jesus*.
28. For an overview of the key issues and a discussion of the relevant passages, see Anderson, "Sacrifice and Sacrificial Offerings (OT)."
29. Most people who read Luke do not expect to find his version missing some of the key petitions familiar to everyone who has learned the prayer, including "Your will be done, on earth as it is in heaven," and "deliver us from evil."
30. Griswold, *Forgiveness*, 59–62.
31. The word does occur once in the New Testament, but not in reference to "forgiveness." Paul uses it in 1 Corinthians 7:6 to refer to a "concession" he is making.

CHAPTER SIX: THE AFTERLIFE OF JESUS'S ETHICS

1. Many scholars have maintained that the Christian church was largely or even mainly comprised of Jews even at the end of the first century, but the evidence does not support the view. Somewhat ironically, Jesus's followers had a far harder time convincing fellow Jews that Jesus was the messiah than persuading pagans to abandon their gods to follow the God of Jesus. The gentile dominance of the church already in the first century is attested in nearly all the books of the New Testament, from the letters of Paul, to the book of Acts, to books that give strong indications of being directed mainly to gentile audiences: Mark, Luke, John, 1 Peter and 2 Peter, Revelation, etc. By the second century, Jewish-Christian believers were on the margins of the larger Christian movement and were portrayed as heretical in their views and quaint in their practices by the church leaders on record. I discuss the various aspects of the early Christianization of the empire in my book *The Triumph of Christianity* (Simon & Schuster, 2018).
2. After that, the religion grew geometrically until it more or less had taken over the empire by the end of the fifth century. See my book *Triumph of Christianity*, 287–94.
3. This is one of the major theses demonstrated by Wayne Meeks, *The Origins of Christian Morality* (Yale University Press, 1993).

4. The book of Acts claims Paul was from Tarsus, but he himself never mentions it.
5. Paul does have other sayings that appear to reflect Jesus's teachings in the Gospels (e.g., that people should pay their taxes; Romans 13:6–7), but he does not indicate Jesus said them. That may seem surprising, since attributing them to Jesus would almost certainly provide his injunctions with even more cachet. But possibly Paul had learned these sayings from other Christians and didn't realize they went back to Jesus himself.
6. Did he have no real occasion to mention them? That seems unlikely, given their relevance for many of his own instructions. Did he assume his readers knew them already? Did he himself not know much more? He was, after all, writing before the Gospels, and he did not spend significant time with the other apostles until years after his conversion (Galatians 1–2). For an overview of the issues, see Ehrman and Mendez, *The New Testament*, 429–33. An excellent fuller treatment is in Victor Paul Furnish, *Jesus According to Paul* (Cambridge University Press, 1993).
7. Paul never tells Jews to stop keeping the law, and he probably would never have done so. God gave the law to the Jews and presumably planned for them to keep it. But for Paul that is not because it brings salvation. Christ alone does that.
8. Apparently "in Christ" and "in the church" were two different things for Paul. Women may have been equal as parts of the body of Christ, but for Paul they were not to behave in ways inappropriate to women in their social world.
9. Was this because Christ had "set them free"?
10. Paul deals with the same issue in 10:1–30, but in a rather confusing and seemingly inconsistent way, arguing that the pagan gods really are demons, so that eating the meat involves worshipping evil divinities.
11. Scholars debate what Paul has in mind. Some think, for example, that if the man is expelled from the church he will return to the realm of Satan, realize the error of his ways, feel terror for his soul, repent of his sin, and return to God's good graces. Others think Paul is telling the Corinthians to impose a death curse on the man that (somehow) might lead to his postmortem salvation. For an important discussion of the problem and Paul's response, see Dale Martin, *The Corinthian Body* (Yale University Press, 1995), 168–74.
12. See Dale Martin, *The Corinthian Body*, 139–97.
13. There is a good deal of debate about the passage in the scholarly literature, not just on the less-than-obvious logic of Paul's arguments but also on the actual situation he is addressing. Traditionally it has been considered a question of whether women should wear veils—and that's the view I continue to find most persuasive. But some scholars maintain he is instead referring to coiffures. For

a now-classic discussion, see Elizabeth Schuessler Fiorenza, *In Memory of Her: A Feminist Theological Reconstruction of Christian Origins* (Crossroad, 1983), 226–33.
14. See the discussion in Dale Martin, *Corinthian Body*, 229–49.
15. My roommate and I circumvented the rule by having our girlfriends give us perms. When we left campus for the summer, and the perm was no longer permanent, we already had the long hair we wanted.
16. The "disputed" Pauline letters are Ephesians, Colossians, 2 Thessalonians, 1 and 2 Timothy, and Titus. For reasons scholars have argued these are not actually by Paul, see my book *Forged*, 92–114.
17. See my discussion in Ehrman, *Forged*, 112–14.
18. The author uses a different word for "forgiveness" here, *charizomai*, instead of *aphiēmi* (see page 133). But the concept appears to be the same or at least very similar.
19. It is widely recognized that the Didache falls into three sections, from three different sources the unknown author used. The notion of the "Two Ways" of ethics in chapters 1–6 can be found in other Jewish and Christian writings as well, including the Epistle of Barnabas.
20. It has long been a matter of scholarly debate whether the author actually had access to any of our Gospels or instead cited sayings of Jesus he had heard or seen elsewhere.
21. See chapter 7, note 3.
22. For a discussion of the authorship of the book, see the discussion in *Forged*, 66–68; 70–77.
23. See my discussion in Ehrman, *Triumph of Christianity*, 188–94.
24. See C. W. Clarke, *The Octavius of Minucius Felix* (Newman Press, 1974). I have taken quotations from this edition.
25. See Ehrman, *Triumph of Christianity*, 206–16.

CHAPTER SEVEN: LOVE AFTER JESUS

1. These were all Eastern Orthodox monks living in monasteries.
2. Widely reported in the news; see, e.g., https://www.nytimes.com/2024/05/02/us/politics/antisemitism-jews-republicans-democrats-congress.html.
3. With regard to the status of a fetus—fully human or not?—the key passage comes just after the Ten Commandments, in Exodus 21:22–26. In this law, if a man fighting another inadvertently strikes and hurts a pregnant woman standing nearby, there is to be a penalty. If she dies, he is to be executed. Anyone who takes

a human life is to pay with his own life: "an eye for an eye and a life for a life." But if she survives and the fetus dies, the penalty is different: the offender is to pay a fine to her husband. In other words, in this case the offender is understood not to have taken a human life, but to have destroyed the property of the wife's husband, and so must pay restitution, just as if he had killed his neighbor's ox.

The only intentionally induced abortion mentioned in the entire Bible is in Numbers 5:11-32, which describes a ritual a woman is to undergo to determine whether the child she has conceived is her husband's. That is, it is a test for adultery. The priest is to provide her with a drink/potion which, if she has been unfaithful, will cause an abortion. It needs to be stressed, this is a law given by God that requires an abortion for an illegitimate child. No other passage of Scripture speaks of abortion.

The passages frequently cited in the modern debates to argue that the fetus is indeed a full human are not relevant to the question, as can be seen simply by reading them carefully. A leading example is the much-quoted Jeremiah 1:5: "Before I formed you in the womb I knew you." Doesn't this clearly show that Jeremiah was a full human being at the point of conception, while still in the womb? On the contrary—look more closely. He is talking about his existence *before* conception. That is when God first "knew him." Anyone who takes the verse literally needs to subscribe not to the full humanity of the fetus but to the pre-existence of the soul, prior to birth.

The reality is that, like all such verses, this one speaks in metaphorical language. The authors of such passages did not believe in souls existing in a netherworld waiting to become human or nor did they provide a biblical answer to the philosophical and scientific question of when life begins. They are declarations and celebrations of God's sovereignty: He knew everything about the author and always had known it, even before the author attained consciousness.

4. For the rate of growth of the Christian church, and the influence it asserted in its early centuries, see my book, Bart D. Ehrman, *The Triumph of Christianity: How a Forbidden Religion Swept the World* (Simon & Schuster, 2018).
5. As noted, the word can also mean "kiss" and is used in the account of Jesus's betrayal where Judas Iscariot kisses Jesus (see Matthew 26:48).
6. No Greek would classify the passage as a poem since it is not set in poetic meter (e.g., dactylic hexameter or iambic trimeter). But it is similar to Greek translations of Hebrew biblical poetry, such as found in the books of Psalms or Proverbs, which is also not metrical, but sets forth parallel or developing ideas from one line to the next, using highly exalted language to do so (as opposed to Paul's normal prose).

7. Among the reasons for thinking this was a preexistent poem that Paul inserts in the letter is its elegant poetic style, unlike the prose of the surrounding context, and his *use* of the poem not to promote his theological views of Christ's incarnation and exaltation (its own emphasis), but to advance an ethical agenda about the need for love. That is to say, Paul is using a known theological poem to draw out some of its unspoken ethical consequences.
8. Scholars have long recognized that 2 Corinthians comprises at least two different letters that have been spliced together: chapters 10–13 come from a harsh letter Paul wrote the church following 1 Corinthians, after he realized they were turning against him; chapters 1–9 come from a conciliatory letter he wrote later, once their relationship was restored. For more information and a discussion of the evidence for this view, see Bart Ehrman and Hugo Mendez, *The New Testament: A Historical Introduction to the Early Christian Writings*, 8th ed. (Oxford University Press, 2026), 384–87.
9. Hugo Mendez has recently mounted a strong argument that the author of this letter is impersonating the author of the Gospel. Neither one of them identifies himself as John. See his book *The Epistles of John: Origins, Authorship, Purpose* (Cambridge University Press, 2025).
10. Although traditionally ascribed to Clement, an early bishop of Rome allegedly appointed to his position by Peter, the book itself never mentions Clement, let alone claims he wrote it. There are good reasons for thinking the letter was written around 95 CE, right around the time of the Gospel of John. For fuller explanation, see my introduction to 1 Clement in Bart D. Ehrman, *The Apostolic Fathers*, vol. 1, in the Loeb Classical Library (Harvard University Press, 2003), 21–25.
11. The author does not directly indicate who the beneficiaries of these acts of self-sacrifice were, whether outsiders or fellow Christians. But since the raison d'être of the letter is to show how Christians are to behave toward one another, it seems likely he is referring to Christians who sacrificed themselves for fellow believers.
12. Translation of G. A. Williamson, revised by Andrew Louth, *Eusebius: The History of the Church from Christ to Constantine*, Penguin Classics (Penguin, 1989).
13. See my discussion in Bart D. Ehrman, *The Triumph of Christianity: How a Forbidden Religion Swept the World* (Simon & Schuster, 2019), 247–50. For a fuller account, see Julian Murdoch, *The Last Pagan: Julian the Apostate and the Death of the Ancient World* (Sutton, 2003).

CHAPTER EIGHT: CHARITABLE GIVING AND FORGIVENESS AFTER JESUS

1. The most famous incident involved the famous Roman scholar and author Pliny the Elder, who commissioned a rescue mission during the eruption of Vesuvius and died in the attempt. The mission was not to rescue as many people as possible, as would happen typically today, but to evacuate his friends.
2. As might be expected, there were occasional ad hoc governmental interventions when large swaths of the populace were displaced and homeless—for example when Nero opened up places of refuge on the Campus Martius and in gardens in Rome, with some some food supplies, after the great fire of 64 CE. Like the occasional grain doles, though, these were in large part attempts to calm the surviving masses (because of rumors that Nero wasn't concerned? Or suspicions that he had ordered the fire?) rather than any demonstrable concern for the suffering of those burned out of house and home per se. See the discussion of Joseph J. Walsh, *The Great Fire of Rome: Life and Death in the Ancient City* (Johns Hopkins University Press, 2019), 56–57.
3. Of course there was far less they *could* have done about it, lacking our communication and transportation systems, modern technologies of collection and distribution, and economic wherewithal. That was a world in which only a small percentage of the population enjoyed surplus resources that could be spared to assist others. On the other hand, there was an incredibly wealthy imperial structure and massively affluent individuals who could have changed the social order if that had been either imagined or desired.
4. See Bruce W. Longenecker, *Remember the Poor: Paul, Poverty, and the Greco-Roman World* (Eerdmans, 2010). An interesting assessment of Paul's collection in relation to comparable (secular) collections of funds in the Greco-Roman world can be found in John S. Kloppenborg, *Christ's Associations: Connecting and Belonging in the Ancient City* (Yale University Press, 2019), 245–64. For a full and erudite study of Paul's understanding of giving, see John M. G. Barclay, *Paul and the Gift* (Eerdmans, 2015).
5. Scholars have often proposed that these two chapters actually come from different letters of Paul that have been spliced together by a later editor. Chapter 9 seems to take up the subject anew, as if Paul has not been addressing the issue already for an entire chapter and, seemingly without need, repeats some of the same material.
6. It is important to recall that here I am discussing how Luke *portrays* Jesus; I am not addressing the question of what the historical Jesus actually said and did.

7. Translation of S. Thelwall in *Ante-Nicene Fathers*, vol. 3, ed. Alexander Roberts and James Donaldson (Hendrickson, 2004; original 1885), slightly altered.
8. It is included among the books of the New Testament in the famous fourth-century Codex Sinaiticus and was sometimes quoted as a Scriptural authority by church fathers at the time. Translations are my own; see Ehrman, *Apostolic Fathers*, vol. 2.
9. See Steven J. Friesen, "Injustice or God's Will: Early Christian Explanations of Poverty," in *Wealth and Poverty in Early Church and Society*, ed. Susan Holman (Baker Academic, 2008), 31–34.
10. For this explanation of Clement's understanding of the passage I am relying on my earlier discussion in Bart D. Ehrman, *Journeys to Heaven and Hell: Tours of the Afterlife in the Early Christian Tradition* (Yale University Press, 2022), 122–23.
11. He is widely known by other names as well, such as Anthony the Great, Anthony the Anchorite, and Anthony of the Desert.
12. For an excellent discussion of the major aspects of early Christian monasticism, see the collection of essays in Bernice M. Kaczynski and Thomas Sullivan, *The Oxford Handbook of Christian Monasticism*, pt. 1 (Oxford University Press, 2020).
13. At first he gave (only) most of it away, but eventually he took Matthew 6:34 seriously to heart and rid himself of what was still left over.
14. See the discussions of imperial persecutions in Bart D. Ehrman, *The Triumph of Christianity*, 198–217, and Candida Moss, *The Myth of Persecution: How Early Christians Invented a Story of Martyrdom* (HarperOne, 2013), 154–59.
15. See the interesting article by John Wortley, "The Spirit of Rivalry in Early Christian Monachism," *Greek, Roman, and Byzantine Studies* 33 (1992): 383–404.
16. For a good overview, see C. Paul Schroeder, "Introduction," in *On Social Justice: St. Basil the Great* (St. Vladimir's Seminary Press, 2009).
17. Translation of Blomfield Jackson, *St. Basil: Letters and Select Works*, Nicene and Post-Nicene Fathers, series 2, vol. 8 (Hendrickson, 2024; original 1895), 263.
18. Susan R. Holman, *The Hungry Are Dying: Beggars and Bishops in Roman Cappadocia* (Oxford University Press, 2001).
19. The three of them formed a kind of triumvirate, known collectively as the Cappadocian Church Fathers, most famous for their roles in establishing the traditional doctrine of the Trinity.
20. All translations are from Schroeder, *On Social Justice*.
21. Andrew T. Crislip, *From Monastery to Hospital: Christian Monasticism and the Transformation of Health Care in Late Antiquity* (University of Michigan Press, 2005). See as well the earlier work of Timothy S. Miller, *The Birth of the Hospital in the Byzantine Empire*, 2nd ed. (Johns Hopkins University Press, 1997).

22. Crislip, *From Monastery to Hospital*, 9, 100.
23. See the fuller treatments of Susan R. Holman, *The Hungry Are Dying: Beggars and Bishops in Roman Cappadocia* (Oxford University Press, 2001), and Richard Finn, *Almsgiving in the Later Roman Empire: Christian Promotion and Practice, 313–450* (Oxford University Press, 2006).
24. There have been debates about the scope and purpose of the Basilias. One long-held view was that it was a much larger facility serving a wide range of needs, with inpatient medical facilities, trained physicians and nurses to tend to the sick (of all kinds) who could not afford private care; kitchens with hired staff and servants to provide meals to feed the hungry and destitute; baths, storehouses, workshops, stables; hospice care for the elderly; facilities to house, feed, and educate orphans; and special facilities for lepers. This view has been convincingly challenged by the most recent and authoritative account of Daniel Caner, who argues that earlier scholars had let their imaginations shape their narratives rather than carefully sorting through the actual evidence. The ancient sources portray the Basilias as a "leprosarium" (a facility for lepers), not a more expansive charity. This does not minimize its importance, however, but rather magnifies it, showing Basil's laser-like focus on those in greatest need, the lowest-of-the-low, who were denigrated even by the impoverished. Caner, *The Rich and the Pure*, 55–57.
25. Quoted in Caner, *The Rich and the Pure*, 56
26. Translation of Caner, *The Rich and the Pure*, 56.
27. Caner, *The Rich and the Pure*, 57.
28. As early Christianity scholar Helen Rhee puts it, "There was a notable shift from patronage of wealthy lay leaders in household settings to patronage of bishops and other clergy in a more formalized church structure. . . . The clergy largely took over the official roles of patrons." Clear evidence of this shift can be seen in early church writings that describe (and prescribe) the regulations governing church offices, such as the *Didascalia*. See Rhee, *Loving the Poor, Saving the Rich: Wealth, Poverty, and Early Christian Formation* (Baker Academic, 2012), 140.
29. The rare term Paul uses here for "atoning sacrifice" (*hilastērion*) has been translated variously over the years, sometimes, for example, as "propitiation," to indicate that Jesus's death satisfied God's wrath against sinners, or as "expiation," to indicate that Christ's blood covered over and so hid from sight the sins of others. The term itself refers to the "mercy seat" on the ark of the covenant in the Old Testament, where sacrificial blood was spread. However it is expressed in English, it refers to a bloody sacrifice necessary to deal with the problem of human sin.
30. For an overview of the themes and perspectives of the book of Hebrews, see Ehrman and Mendez, *The New Testament*, 482–89.

31. See John Collins, *The Scepter and the Star: Messianism in Light of the Dead Sea Scrolls*, 2nd ed. (Eerdmans, 2010).
32. See my fuller discussion in Bart Ehrman, *The Lost Gospel of Judas Iscariot: A New Look at Betrayer and Betrayed* (Oxford University Press, 2006), 158–63.
33. In part my view is based on the overwhelming emphasis of Jesus's teachings in multiple traditions: "Love your neighbor as yourself." "Love your enemies." "Love those who persecute you." "Blessed are the peacemakers." "Render unto Caesar the things that are Caesar's." "The one who lives by the sword will die by the sword." Throughout independent accounts of Jesus's life he is shown to promote loving and submissive nonviolence. I decidedly do not think these sayings were invented by later Christians who wanted to pacify their Roman enemies by insisting that their crucified messiah was peace-loving even though he was not. See my discussion in Bart Ehrman, *Jesus before the Gospels: How the Early Christians Remembered, Changed, and Invented the Stories of Their Savior* (HarperOne, 2016), 167–71.
34. There are solid reasons for thinking this is an authentic saying of Jesus, in particular because it is very difficult to believe a later Christian storyteller, after Jesus's death, would have placed the saying on his lips. In it he indicates that *all twelve* of his disciples would rule with him in the future kingdom, but one of the twelve he was addressing was Judas Iscariot. After Judas's betrayal led to Jesus's crucifixion, no one thought he, the betrayer, would be one of the future rulers. And so, it is not likely to have been a saying invented by a later follower, but to have come from Jesus himself. See my fuller discussion in Ehrman, *Jesus, Apocalyptic Prophet*, 217–19.
35. For this understanding of Judas's betrayal, see my book *The Lost Gospel of Judas Iscariot*, 153–69. We don't know why Judas betrayed him; numerous explanations are possible: Was he disgruntled? Did he want to force Jesus's hand to rouse the Jewish crowd? Did he simply want the cash?
36. Whether for Mark they remained together as a group cannot be determined. After the arrest, Peter alone is mentioned—possibly trying to learn what was happening to Jesus. Peter is clearly in fear, since he denies knowing Jesus three times (Mark 14:66–72). After that neither he nor the others are mentioned, except insofar as the women are said never to inform them that Jesus has been raised from the dead and is to meet them in Galilee (16:7–8).
37. For a discussion of the doubt traditions and whether, historically, all the disciples did come to believe Jesus had been raised from the dead, see my book, *How Jesus Became God: The Exaltation of a Jewish Preacher from Galilee* (HarperOne, 2014), 189–92.

38. For example, Romulus the founder of Rome, or nearer Jesus's own day, Apollonius of Tyana. See my book *How Jesus Became God*, 25–38 (for Greek and Roman examples), and 76–82 (within Judaism).
39. It is mystifying that in recent years conservative Christians (and others) have come to think that the New Testament portrays Jesus himself as Yahweh. That simply is not true; Christ *prays* to the Lord God (Yahweh) of Israel, is said to have been sent from him, is said to represent him, and is said to have been made equal to him at his exaltation (e.g., Philippians 2:6–10). But the fact he is made equal with him shows that he is a different being. Moreover, being equal with God/Yahweh is not the same as being *identical* with him.
40. That is why, years later, in the Gospels Jesus uses the term Son of Man for himself. His followers identified him as the coming Son of Man and so naturally had him speak of himself in those terms.
41. The Gospels sometimes portray Jesus's opposition to the temple, its priestly leaders, and the sacrificial cult in far more subtle ways. Early in Mark's Gospel, for example, Jesus encounters a paralyzed man and says to him, "Your sins are forgiven." The Jewish leaders take offense and claim he has committed a blasphemy, since only God can forgive sins (2:1–12). But it is important to note that Jesus does not say, "I forgive your sins." He pronounces to the man that forgiveness has taken place, but in the *passive* voice: God has forgiven the man's sins. What grants him the authority to make such an announcement? Within Judaism, this was the function of the priests in the temple based on sacrifices. On this, see E. P. Sanders, *Judaism Practice and Belief, 63 BCE–66 CE* (Fortress Press, 1995), 273–74. Jesus then is not claiming to be God in the passage. He is usurping the role of the priests and the temple sacrifices.
42. I say "most Christian writers" because some quite famously maintained that the death of Jesus had no bearing on salvation. That is true, for example, of some groups of Gnostics who maintained that it was Jesus's secret teachings, not his death, that brought salvation. So too, for example, the Gospel of Thomas, saying 1.
43. See my book *Armageddon: What the Bible Really Says about the End* (Simon & Schuster, 2023).
44. See Peter Brown, *Ransom of the Soul*, 96–99.
45. Translation of Ernest Wallis, *Cyprian*, in Cleveland Cox, ed., *Fathers of the Third Century*, vol. 5 of The Ante-Nicene Fathers (Hendrickson, 2004; reprint of 1886 original), 476.
46. See my discussion in *Triumph of Christianity*, 201–4.
47. Strikingly, among all four Gospels, the term "church" appears only twice, both times in Matthew—here in this passage and two chapters earlier in Jesus's

comment to Peter: "On this rock I will build by church" (Matthew 16:18). These are almost certainly sayings put on Jesus's lips by Matthew or by one of his sources. The quip comes from French New Testament scholar Alfred Loisy, who wrote: "Jesus foretold the kingdom, and it is the church that came." See Loisy, *The Gospel and the Church*, trans. Christopher Home (Isbister, 1903), 166.

48. For other passages, see Mark 2:1–12, where the paralytic's disability is connected with sins, and 1 Corinthians 11:27–30, where members of the church who have not observed the Lord's Supper properly have been punished by illness or death.

CONCLUSION: ALTRUISM IN THE CONSCIENCE OF THE WEST

1. See especially Susannah Heschel, *The Aryan Jesus: Christian Theologians and the Bible in Nazi Germany* (Princeton University Press, 2008).
2. On the question of whether the widely held sense that early Christians were routinely, systematically, and brutally persecuted see Moss, *The Myth of Persecution*, esp. 127–62.
3. It may seem obvious to some readers that these institutional changes would have appeared anyway, without Christian involvement. I am not so sure, both because of the deeply embedded cultural assumptions in that world prior to Christianity and because of the unusual social and cultural forces that brought changes after the West became predominantly Christian. In any event, whether something else *would* have made the necessary social, political, cultural, and economic interventions necessary, it was Christianity that did so.

INDEX

Aaron, 106
abortion
    contemporary politics of, 164–65
    early Christian condemnation of, 155, 161–62
    Hebrew Bible references to, 242–43n3
Abraham, 122–23
Acts (New Testament)
    charitable giving concept and, 185, 186, 192, 195, 201, 206
    Jesus quoted in, 236n12
    Paul's writings and, 141, 241n4
adiaphora ("things that make no difference"), 35
afterlife, ancient Greek and Roman concepts of, 15, 29, 36. *see also* apocalypticism
agapē (active love)
    Christ as model of, in New Testament, 171–73
    in Christian teaching after Jesus, 143, 146, 151–54, 166–67
    early use of term, 61
    in Jesus's teachings, 102
    New Testament scholars' interpretation of, 48, 101

Agathon, 50
agnosticism, 13–14
Alcibiades, 230–31n13
Alexander the Great, 23, 39, 85
almsgiving, 121, 210, 235n7
altruism, 5–12. *see also* ethics and happiness in ancient thought; love, charity, and forgiveness in ancient thought
    actions as, 8–10
    agapē as, in Christian teaching after Jesus, 166–67
    Christianity and impact on, 3, 219–22, 250n3
    defined, 5
    differing perspectives, contemporary, 217–19
    effective altruism movement, 223n2
    egoism vs., 5, 8
    evolution and, 9–10, 223n1
    forgiveness and, 71
    in Jesus's ethical teachings, 96–97
    Jesus's understanding of, and day of judgment, 102–3
    love and, 49–50, 52, 58–61

altruism (*cont.*)
   love in Ten Commandments and, 110–15
   moral obligation to strangers as, 1–3
   motivation for, 8–12
   as obligation, 8, 12
   others and, in ancient Greece, 21–23
   Paul's teachings on, 142
   political perspective and, 217–19
   runaway car example and, 5–8
   Stoics on, 231–32n16
   as "tribal," 47, 74–76
Amos, book of, 120
Amos (Hebrew prophet), 80, 81
Analects (Confucius), 82
ancient Greece. *see also* ethics and happiness in ancient thought; love, charity, and forgiveness in ancient thought; *individual names of Greek philosophers*
   altruism in, and view of others, 21–23
   Athenian culture, 20–22, 46, 50, 144, 227n12
   ethics of ancient Romans and transition from, 23–25
   on forgiveness, 133
   Greek-speaking gentiles as Jesus's followers, 139–41
   love concepts of, 49–57, 102
   polis (city) concept of, 20, 23
   polytheism of, 14–17
   sungnōmē (forgiveness), 73
ancient Rome. *see also* ethics and happiness in ancient thought; love, charity, and forgiveness in ancient thought; *individual names of Roman emperors*
   ethics transition from ancient Greek thought, 23–25
   on forgiveness, 133
   polytheism of, 14–17
Anderson, Gary A., 239n21
androgyne concept, 53–54
animal sacrifice
   Jewish practices (in time of temple), 106
   pagan practices, 16
   Paul on, 144
Anselm, 17
Anthony of Egypt, 191–92, 194
anti-Semitism, 77–78, 99–100, 164
aphesis ("a release"/"sending away"), 133, 201
Apocalypse of John (book of Revelation, New Testament), 77, 99, 100, 230n5
apocalypticism. *see also* resurrection; salvation
   annihilation vs. eternal torment concepts, 235n9, 238n19
   heaven and hell concepts of early Christians, 140–41
   historical context of Jesus's teachings and, 84–88, 91–93, 107–8
   Paul's apocalyptic message, 147–48
   Son of Man, 87, 109, 118–19, 207
Apollos, 144, 147
Apology (Tertullian), 187
Aquinas, 17
Arendt, Hannah, 72
aretē (virtue), 21, 32, 52, 58–61
Aristophanes, 53, 54, 144
Aristotle
   altruism in ancient Greece and, 21–23

INDEX

on ethics and *eudaimonia*, 17–21
on forgiveness, 73, 133
influence of, in time of Jesus, 60–61
on love, 50, 57–60
Nicomachean Ethics, 18, 57–60, 231n13
Politics, 20
Roman thought and influence of, 23–24
Stoicism and influence of, 32
Athanasius, 191–92
atheism, 160
Athenagoras, 159–62
Athenian culture, 20–22, 46, 50, 144, 227n12
atonement vs. forgiveness, 71–72, 130
Augustine, 17

Baal Shem Tov, 89
Babylonians
  ideology of dominance and, 45
  temple (Jerusalem) destruction by, 82, 85, 105, 109
baptism
  "body of Christ," 146–47
  sin and, 209
Basilias, 196, 247n24
Basil the Great, 193–97
Beatitudes (Jesus), 123, 185
Ben Sira (Jesus son of Sirach), 82–84, 110, 120
Bible. *see* Hebrew Bible; New Testament
Bread and Circuses (Veyne), 66–67
Brown, Peter, 233–34n33

calamity, charity as response to, 1–2, 181–83, 245n3. *see also* charitable giving

"Camel's Needle," 125–26, 190
Caner, Daniel, 232–33n23, 247n24
cannibalism, accusations of, 157–59
Capdocian Church Fathers, 246n19
Cephas, 144, 147
charismata (spiritual gifts), "love chapter" and, 167–71
charitable giving. *see also* love, charity, and forgiveness in ancient thought; love, charity, and forgiveness in Jesus's teachings
  almsgiving, 121, 210, 235n7
  among early church fathers, 187–89
  Anthony of Egypt and monastic movement, 191–94
  atonement and forgiveness in early church, 209–12
  Basil the Great and coenobitic monks, 193–95
  Basil the Great and invention of public charities, 195–97
  charitable giving in ancient Rome, 64–69
  Christianity and impact on, 3, 250n3
  Clement of Alexandria and, 189–91, 211
  and economic disparity in ancient Greece and Rome, 61–64
  interpersonal forgiveness and, 212–14
  Jesus's resurrection and effect on, 199–209
  Jesus's teaching about forgiveness based on repentance, 198–99
  in Jesus's teachings, 120–27
  Luke's writings on charity, 185–87
  Paul and collection for Jerusalem, 183–85
  as response to calamity, 181–83

253

charitable giving *(cont.)*
   Roman patronage system and, 197–98
Charity (Anderson), 239n21
Charmides (Xenophon's character), 65
"chosen ones," 79
Christ. *see* Jesus of Nazareth
Christ, Matthew, 22
Christian apologetics, 43, 155–62
Christianity. *see also* ethics taught by followers of Jesus; Jesus of Nazareth; New Testament; *individual Gospel entries*
   altruism and impact of, 3, 219–22, 250n3
   ancient thought and influence on, 31, 40–41
   baptism, 146–47, 209
   forgiveness concept as changed by, 76
   Lord's Prayer, 131–32, 134, 147, 151, 212, 214
   Old and New Testaments as Scriptural "authority" in, 15
   Old Testament (*see* Hebrew Bible)
   rise of, after Jesus's death, 139–41, 240nn1—2
   as Roman Empire's state religion, 2–3
   Trinity, doctrine of, 246n19
"Christ poem" of Philippians (Paul), 172–73
Church History (Eusebius), 178
"church," terminology for, 249–50n47
Clement, 177, 189–91, 211, 244n10
The Clouds (Aristophanes), 53
Colossians (New Testament), 151–52, 242n16
Commodus, 159

Confucius, 82
Constantine (Roman Emperor), 179, 193
Constantius II (Roman Emperor), 179
Corinthians, 142–48, 167–71, 177, 183–84, 240n31, 244n8, 244n10, 245n5
Crislip, Andrew, 196
cultic laws, defined, 79
Cynics and Cynicism, 23, 25–26, 29, 37–40
Cyprian, 211, 212

Daniel, book of, 87, 235n10
Darwin, Charles, 9–10
David (King of Israel), 109, 112, 204, 238n12
Dawkins, Richard, 10
Dead Sea Scrolls, 106–8, 237n7
Decius (Roman Emperor), 211
Deuteronomy (book of Hebrew Bible), 78, 100, 111, 116, 146
Devil concept, 86
Didache of the Twelve Apostles, 154–55, 210
Diocletian (Roman Emperor), 192–93
Diogenes (Cynic), 23, 29, 38–39, 40
Diogenes Laertius, 23, 25, 28–29, 39
Dionysius (bishop), 177–78
Dionysus (Greek god), 50
Diotima, 55, 57
disaster, charity as response to, 1–2, 181–83, 245n3. *see also* charitable giving
The Discourses (Epictetus), 34–35, 39–40
dominance, ideology of, 45–47

Eastern religions, influence of, 3
effective altruism movement, 223n2

INDEX

egoism
- altruism vs., 5, 8
- "love your neighbor as yourself" concept and, 59–60
- motivation as, 11–12

Ehrman, Bart
- education of, 5, 13, 48, 149, 228–29n21
- faith of, 13–14, 43–44
- runaway car example, 5–8

empathy, 37

Enlightenment, rationalism and, 11

Epictetus
- *The Discourses*, 34–35, 39–40
- Stoicism and influence of, 31, 32
- on worldly goods, 127–28

Epicurus, 25–30, 32, 36, 198–99, 227n16

Eros (Greek god), 51

eros (passionate love), 49–57, 102, 166–67

Essenes
- apocalypticism and, 84
- historical context of Jesus's teachings and, 106–8, 110, 237n7

ethics
- ethical laws, defined, 79
- helping strangers in need as impulse, 10
- motivation and, 8–12, 16–17, 96–97
- principles of, shared by human societies, 43–45

ethics and happiness in ancient thought, 13–41. *see also eudaimonia*
- altruism in ancient Greece, 21–23
- Cynicism and, 23, 25–26, 29, 37–40
- Epicurus and, 25–32, 36, 198–99, 227n16
- ethics among Greek and Roman philosophers, 17–21
- ethics and ancient religion, 14–17
- ethics and faith as connected, 13–14
- ethics in ancient Rome, at time of Jesus's birth, 23–25
- Stoicism and, 25–26, 30–37

ethics in Jesus's teachings, 77–97
- almsgiving, 121, 210, 235n7
- altruism and egoism in ethics of Jesus, 96–97
- apocalypticism and, 84–88, 91–93
- as divisive in his time, 91
- followers' divergent interpretations of, 77
- Golden Rule and, 82
- historical records of Jesus and, 88–93
- Jesus's ideology of service, 93–95
- Jewish ethical teachings as context for, 82–84
- Jewish law and, 78–81
- Judaism and contemporary Christian misunderstanding/bias, 77–78

ethics taught by followers of Jesus, 137–62
- Christianity's rise after Jesus's death, 139–41
- "objective" morality argument and, 137–39, 150
- Paul's followers and communal ethics, 150–54
- Paul's writings on ethics, 141–50
- shift in ethics between Jesus and Paul, 145–50
- in written works after New Testament, 154–62

255

eudaimonia
  charity and, 62
  Cynicism on, 40
  defined, 17–21
  Epicurus on ethics and, 28–32, 36
  Jesus on, 41
  love and, 54–57
  Roman thought on, 23–25
  sacrifice in Jesus's teachings vs. concept of, 96–97
  serving others vs., 175
  Stoicism on, 33–37, 127–28
euergetism ("doing good"), 67, 129
Eusebius, 178
evangelical Christians, on ethics and faith as connected, 14
evolution, altruism and, 9–10, 223n1
The Existence of God (Swinburne), 229n1
Exodus (book of Hebrew Bible)
  abortion reference in, 242–43n3
  Law of Moses in, 78, 79
Ezekiel, 80

false teachers, letter to Colassians on, 151
forgiveness. *see also* love, charity, and forgiveness in ancient thought; love, charity, and forgiveness in Jesus's teachings
  atonement vs., 71–72
  Christianity and changed concept of, 72, 76
  concept of restoring relationships with, 69–74
  in Hebrew Bible, 130–31
  Jesus "died for our sins" concept and, 69, 203–9

  in Jesus's teachings, 3, 129–30, 131–36
  letter to Colassians on, 151
  steps needed for, 70–71
friendly love *(philia)*, 48, 50, 57–61, 102, 166–67
Fronto, 157

Galatians, 143
"Galileans," 180
gender
  androgyne concept in ancient Greece, 53–54
  hierarchy of, letter to Colassians on, 152
  Musonius Rufus (Stoic) on education and, 228n19
  Paul on men's hair, 149–50
  Paul on women's roles and head covering, 144, 148–50, 241–42n13
  pederasty in ancient Greece and, 51–55
Genesis (book of Hebrew Bible), 78
Genesis 1 (Greek version), 228n20
God. *see also* Kingdom of God, inheriting
  Christ and (*see* Jesus of Nazareth)
  Gospel of John on Logos (divine being), 32–33, 228n20
  Holy of Holies and Jewish temple, 105–6
  "moral argument" for existence of, 43–44
  Yahweh, 206, 249n39
Golden Rule, 82
Good Samaritan parable, 116–18, 185
Gospel(s)
  on "church" term, 249–50n47
  Gospel, defined, 90

INDEX

"teachings of Jesus" (historical Jesus) vs. writings about Jesus, 201
Gospel of John
  agapē in, 153–54
  Christ as model of *agapē* in, 171
  First Epistle of John and, 176
  Jesus's ethical teachings as interpreted by, 77, 90, 175–76, 236n14
  as last canonical Gospel, 153–54
  Logos (divine being) in, 32–33, 228n20
  love concepts in, 48, 167, 175–76
  on Mary Magdelene, 206
Gospel of Luke
  charitable giving concept and, 44, 185–87, 201, 207
  on forgiveness, 201
  Herod mentioned in, 164
  inner-communal relations in Christian ethical discourse and, 153
  Jesus's ethical teachings as interpreted by, 77, 83, 90, 176
  on Jesus's teachings about love, 102, 111, 116, 118, 122–23, 129, 132, 134, 136, 235n13, 238n15, 238n18, 239n23, 239n24, 240n29
  love in Christian teachings after Jesus, 167
Gospel of Mark
  charitable giving concept and, 40, 190, 201, 202, 204–9
  Jesus's ethical teachings as interpreted by, 77, 83, 87, 88, 90, 92, 94, 95, 97, 176, 236n14
  on Jesus's opposition to temple, 249n39
  on Jesus's teachings about love, 102, 110–17, 124, 126, 129, 167, 238n15, 239n24
Gospel of Matthew
  charitable giving concept and, 40, 185, 192, 194, 195, 199, 201, 205–7, 212–13
  Jesus's ethical teachings as interpreted by, 82, 83, 90, 95, 176
  on Jesus's teachings about love, 102, 104, 111, 115, 116, 118, 121–23, 126, 129, 132–34, 167, 238n13, 239n24
  on Mary Magdelene, 206
  on Pharisees, 104–5
  Sheep and Goats parable, 118–19, 195
Gospel of Thomas, 153, 236n12
Graham, Billy, 88
"Great Persecution," 192–93
Griswold, Charles, 70

happiness, ancient thought about. *see* ethics and happiness in ancient thought
Harris, William, 68
health care, monastic system of, 196–97
heaven and hell concepts of early Christians, 140–41
Hebrew Bible. *see also* Leviticus
  Amos, 120
  Daniel, 87, 235n10
  Deuteronomy, 78, 100, 111, 116, 146
  Exodus, 78, 79, 242–43n3
  Genesis, 78
  Isaiah, 80, 81, 120, 185
  Jacob, 106
  Jesus's teachings based on, 2
  Job, 86
  Joshua, 112, 138

Hebrew Bible (*cont.*)
  love and wrath as central themes in, 99–102
  on love of others and God's love, 171
  Numbers, 78, 112, 243n3
  Old Testament as Scriptural "authority" in Christianity, 15
  Pentateuch (Five Books of Moses), 78
  prophets on God's commands as disobeyed, 80–81
  Psalm 51, 131
  Tobit, 121
  Torah, 15, 78–79, 103–6, 110, 111, 207
  Yahweh, 206, 249n39
Hebrew people. *see* Judaism
Hebrews (book of New Testament), 141, 202–3, 210
Helvidius Priscus, 35
Hermas, 187–89
Herod, 164
Herodotus, 82
Hillel (rabbi), 82, 110
History (Herodotus), 82
Hobbes, Thomas, 11
Holy of Holies, 105–6
homosexuality, 230n10, 236n1
Hosea, 80
Hume, David, 17

ideology of dominance
  defined, 45–47
  Jesus's ideology of service vs., 93–95
immortality, 55–57
incest, accusations of, 157–59
individuals
  altruism and, 22
  eudaimonia and, 19–21, 24

infanticide, accusations of, 157–59
interpersonal forgiveness concept, 212–14. *see also* charitable giving
Isaiah, 80, 81, 120, 185
Isocrates, 235n6
Israel
  Jesus and Galilee, 2
  Judah (nation), 85
  Judea and Samaria locations in contemporary Israel, 118
  as Promised Land, 108–10
I Will Tear Down My Barns (Basil the Great), 194, 195

Jacob, 106
James, book of, 213–14
James (disciple), 94
Jeremiah, 80
Jericho, Joshua (book) on, 138
"Jesus and the Rich Man," 122–26, 190–91, 192, 194
Jesus of Nazareth. *see also* ethics in Jesus's teachings; love, charity, and forgiveness in Jesus's teachings; *individual Gospels*
  Beatitudes, 123, 185
  Christ as model of *agapē* in, 171–73
  "cleansing of the temple" by, 208, 249n41
  ethical thought of ancient Roman, at time of birth, 23–25
  on forgiveness based on repentance, 198–99
  Gospel of John on Logos (divine being), 32–33, 228n20
  historical records of, 88–93
  interpretation of teachings of (*see* ethics taught by followers of Jesus)

Jewish context of ethics of (*see* ethics in Jesus's teachings; Judaism)
love, charity, and forgiveness concepts and, 48–49, 60, 68, 69, 72, 74, 76
as messiah, 142, 185, 203–9
Paul on baptism and "body of Christ," 146–47
resurrection of, and changed view of charitable giving, 199–209
Roman trial and crucifixion of, 91, 110, 164, 204
as self-proclaimed "king of the Jews," 91, 109, 204
Sermon on the Mount, 60, 82, 115–16, 121–22, 154
"teachings of Jesus," defined, 201
Western moral conscience and influence of, 1–3, 8
Jesus son of Sirach (Ben Sira), 82–84, 110, 120
Jewish Bible. *see* Hebrew Bible
Job, book of, 86
John (disciple), 94. *see also* Gospel of John
John the Baptist, 84, 91
Jonathan, 112, 238n12
Josephus, 106, 108, 118
Joshua, book of, 112, 138
Joshua (Jewish leader), 108
Judah (nation), 85
Judaism. *see also* Hebrew Bible; temple (Jerusalem); Torah; *individual names of leaders and prophets*
anti-Semitism, 77–78, 99–100, 164
apocalypticism and, 84–88, 91
contemporary Christian misunderstanding/bias of, 77–78, 99–100
Day of Atonement, 106, 130, 207
ethical teachings of, in Jesus's time, 82–84
on forgiveness, 234n34
Golden Rule and, 82
Jesus's followers as primarily gentiles vs. Jews, 139–41, 240n1
Jesus's teachings about love and historical context of, 103–10
Jesus's teachings based on, 2, 82–84
Jewish law and Jesus's teachings, 78–81, 103–5
Jewish law and Paul's teachings, 142–43
on messiah, 80, 109, 204
Mishnah and Talmud of, 104
Passover, 91, 106, 205, 208
Paul and collection for Jerusalem, 183–85
Psalm 51, 131
ritual purity laws, 106–8, 116, 234n3
Shema, 111
Torah as Scriptural "authority" in, 15
"Welcome the stranger" concept of, 165, 221
Judas Iscariot, 205, 237n2, 243n5
judgment, time of. *see* apocalypticism
Julian the Apostate (Roman Emperor), 179–80
Justin of Rome (Justin Martyr), 159, 187

Kant, Immanuel, 17
Kingdom of God, inheriting
Jesus on ethics for, 83, 87–88, 91, 92, 95, 96

INDEX

Kingdom of God, inheriting *(cont.)*
  Jesus on love for, 115, 122, 123, 125, 239–40n25
Konstan, David, 70, 73, 74

Law of Moses, historical context of Jesus's teachings and, 78–81, 99, 103–5, 146. *see also* Hebrew Bible
Lazarus and the Rich Man parable, 122–26, 185, 190
lepers, 196–97
Letter 43 (Seneca), 36–37
letters of Paul. *see* Paul (apostle)
Levi and the Levites, 106
Leviticus (book of Hebrew Bible)
  on Day of Atonement, 130
  Law of Moses in, 78
  on sacrifice, 106
  "Welcome the stranger" in, 165
  "You shall love your neighbor as yourself" in, 100, 111–12, 116
Lewis, C. S., 43–44
Life of Anthony (Athanasius), 191–92
The Lives of Eminent Philosophers (Diogenes Laertius), 23, 25, 28–29, 39
logos (logic) and Logos (divine being), 32–33, 228n20
Loisy, Alfred, 250n47
Lord's Prayer, 131–32, 134, 147, 151, 212, 214
love. *see also agapē* (active love); love, charity, and forgiveness in ancient thought; love, charity, and forgiveness in Jesus's teachings; love taught by followers of Jesus
  eros (passionate love), 49–57, 102, 166–67

  philia (friendly love), 48, 50, 57–61, 102, 166–67
  stergō, 49, 166–67
love, charity, and forgiveness in ancient thought, 43–76
  agapē (active love) and ancient thought, 48
  altruism as "tribal," 47, 74–76
  charitable giving in ancient Rome, 64–69
  charity and economic disparity in ancient Greece and Rome, 61–64
  eros (passionate love), 49–57, 102, 166–67
  ethical principles shared by human societies, 43–45
  forgiveness in ancient Greece and Rome, 69–74
  ideology of dominance and, 45–47
  love concepts in ancient Greece and Rome, overview, 47–50
  philia (friendly love), 48, 50, 57–61, 102
  Plato's and Aristotle's influence in time of Jesus, 60–61
love, charity, and forgiveness in Jesus's teachings, 99–136
  charity in Jesus's teachings, 120–27
  forgiveness in Hebrew Bible, 130–31
  forgiveness in Jesus's teachings, 129–30, 131–36
  Good Samaritan parable and, 116–18
  Judaism and historical context of, 103–10
  love and Ten Commandments in Jesus's teachings, 110–15
  love and Ten Commandments in Paul's teachings, 145–46

INDEX

love and wrath as central themes in Hebrew Bible and New Testament, 99–102
love concept in Jesus's Sermon on the Mount, 115–16, 121–22
love concept in Jesus's teachings, 102–3
  on "sell everything you have and give to the poor," 40–41, 125, 141, 183, 188, 190
  Sheep and Goats parable, 118–20, 195
  voluntary poverty in Jesus's teachings vs. Roman thought, 127–29
love taught by followers of Jesus, 163–80
  Christ as model of *agapē* in, 171–73
  Christ's true servant, Paul's self-portrayal as, 173–75
  love and its different connotations, 166–67
  Paul's "love chapter" in Corinthians, 167–71
  politics and misuse of Jesus's teaching, 163–66
  self-sacrificing ethic, outside Church, 179–80
  self-sacrificing ethic outside New Testament, 176–79
  in written works after Paul, 175–76
"love your neighbor as yourself." *see also* others
  egoism and concept of, 59–60
  in Leviticus, 100, 111–12, 116
  Paul on, 142–43
Lucilius, 36–37
Lucretius, 227nn16–17
Luke. *see* Gospel of Luke

Maccabean Revolt, 85
Marcus Aurelius (Roman Emperor), 31, 157, 159
marital ceremony, "love chapter" and, 167–71
Mark. *see* Gospel of Mark
Mary Magdalene, 206
Mary (mother of Jesus), 185
Matthew. *see* Gospel of Matthew
Mendez, Hugo, 244n9
men's roles. *see* gender
Mere Christianity (Lewis), 43–44
messiah
  Jesus as, 142, 185, 203–9, 248n34
  Judaism on, 80, 109, 204
"might makes right," dominance ideology and, 45–47
Minucius Felix, 157–59
monastic movement
  anchorite monasticism, 192
  Anthony of Egypt and, 191–94
  coenobitic monks, 193–95
Moody Bible Institute, 5, 13, 149
"moral purpose" *(prohairesis)*, 34, 229n22
Morgan, Teresa, 226n7
Moses. *see* Law of Moses
motivation
  for altruism, 8–12
  ethical standards and paganism, 16–17
  Jesus's ethical teachings, altruism and egoism in, 96–97
  mustard seed parable, 92–93
"mystery cults," 225n6

Nero (Roman Emperor), 64, 245n2
New Deal, 217–18

INDEX

New Testament. *see also* Paul (apostle); *individual books in New Testament; individual epistles; individual Gospel entries*
   Apocalypse of John (book of Revelation), 77, 99, 100, 230n5
   Gospel of John as last canonical Gospel, 153
   Gospels as source material about Jesus, 90
   Hebrews, book of, 141, 202–3, 210
   love and wrath as central themes in, 99–102
Nicomachean Ethics (Aristotle), 18, 57–60, 231n13
Numbers (book of Hebrew Bible), 78, 112, 243n3
Nussbaum, Martha, 70, 231n13

"objective" morality argument, 137–39, 150
Octavius (Minucius Felix), 157–59
Of Consolation to Marcia (Seneca), 37
Old Testament. *see* Hebrew Bible
On Benefits (Seneca), 64
On the Happy Life (Seneca), 64, 65
"On the Lapsed" (Cyprian), 212
On the Nature of Things (Lucretius), 227nn16–17
On the Origin of Species (Darwin), 9–10
On Works and Alms (Cyprian), 211
Origen of Alexandria, 159
others
   altruism as moral obligation to strangers, 1–3
   altruism toward others in ancient Greece, 21–23

   contemporary hostility toward, 3, 224n6
   Golden Rule and, 82
   grotesque accusations in polemical texts, 158–59
   "love your neighbor as yourself," 59–60, 100, 111–12, 116, 142–43
   Luke on charity for, 185

paganism
   of ancient Rome, 74, 179–80
   Jesus's followers and conversion from, 139–41, 240n1
   Octavius (Minucius Felix) and criticism of Christianity, 157–59
   Paul on pagan gods, 144
   polytheism of ancient Greece and Rome, 14–17
Parable of the Unforgiving Slave, 133–34
Passover, 91, 106, 205, 208
"pathos" (suffering), 37
Paul (apostle)
   on "atoning sacrifice," 200, 247n29
   charitable giving concept and, 183–85, 199–201, 203, 206, 209–10
   "Christ poem" of Philippians, 172–73
   collection for Jerusalem by, 183–85
   communal ethics following time of, 150–54
   Corinthians, 142–48, 150, 155, 177, 183–84, 244n8, 245n3
   Corinthians, "love chapter" in, 167–71
   disputed letters of, 242n16
   early life of, 142, 203, 241n5
   ethics in writing by, 141–50
   forgiveness and, 240n31
   Galatians, 124, 142–43, 148

Jesus's ethical teachings as interpreted by, 77, 85
Romans (book), 124, 141–44, 183
self-portrayal by, as Christ's true servant, 173–75
Thessalonians, 148, 209, 242n15
timing of Gospel of John and death of, 175
on wrath in New Testament, 100
Pausanias, 52
pederasty, 51–55, 155
Peloponnesian War (Thucydides), 46
Pentateuch (Five Books of Moses), 78
Peter (apostle), 48–49, 126, 133, 156, 186, 206, 236n14, 248n36
Petition for the Christians (Athenagoras), 159–62
Phaedrus, 52
Pharisees
  apocalypticism and, 84
  historical context of Jesus's teachings and, 104–5, 107, 110
philia (friendly love), 48, 50, 57–61, 102, 166–67
Philo of Alexandria, 106
Pilate, Pontius, 91, 106, 109–10, 164, 205
Plato
  Aristotle and, 57
  ethics and influence of, 17, 18, 23, 27, 31, 39
  on heaven and hell concepts, 141
  influence of, in time of Jesus, 60–61
  The Symposium, 50–54, 155, 230–31n13
Pliny the Elder, 106–7, 245n3
Plutarch, 64
polis (city), 20, 23
Politics (Aristotle), 20

politics (contemporary)
  altruism perspective in, 217–19
  misuse of Jesus's teaching in, 163–66
Polycarp, 214
polytheism, 14–17
Popular Morality in the Early Roman Empire (Morgan), 226n7
Poverty and Leadership in the Later Roman Empire (Brown), 233–34n33
poverty and wealth. see also charitable giving
  ancient attitudes toward, 61–64, 232–33n23
  charity in Jesus's teachings, 120–27
  euergetism ("doing good"), 67, 129
  grain doles for impoverished, 68, 232n18
  voluntary poverty in Jesus's teachings vs. Roman thought, 127–29
Prodigal Son parable, 134–36, 185
prohairesis ("moral purpose"), 34, 229n22
Promised Land, 108–10
Proverbs, 112, 120, 129
Psalm 51 (Hebrew Bible), 131

Reimarus, Hermann Samuel, 237–38n8
religion. see also Christianity; Judaism; paganism
  ethics and, as contemporary concept, 13–14
  "mystery cults," 225n6
  polytheism of ancient Greece and Rome, 14–17
repentance
  Gospel of John and absence of, 153–54

repentance *(cont.)*
  Jesus's teaching about forgiveness based on, 93, 198–99
  love in teachings of Jesus and concept of, 102, 110, 113, 129–31, 135–36
resurrection
  Athenagoras on, 161
  Jesus's resurrection and effect on charity, 199–209
Revelation, book of (Apocalypse of John), 77, 99, 100, 230n5
Rhee, Helen, 247n28
The Rich and the Pure (Caner), 232–33n23
Rich Man and Lazarus parable, 122–26, 190
ritual purity laws (Judaism), 106–8, 116, 234n3
Roman Empire. *see also individual names of emperors*
  apostasy in, 211
  calamity and response by, 1–2, 182–83, 245n3
  Christianity as state religion of, 2–3, 84
  "Great Persecution," 192–93
  Jesus's trial and crucifixion by, 91, 110, 164, 204
  Julian the Apostate, 179–80
  paganism and religion of, 74, 179–80
  patronage system, 197–98
Romans (book), 124, 141–44, 183
Roosevelt, Franklin Delano, 217–18
runaway car example, 5–8

sacrifice, Paul on "atoning sacrifice," 200, 247n29

sacrifice of animals. *see* animal sacrifice
Sadducees, 106, 107, 110
salvation
  charitable giving and concept of, 199–203
  Jesus on salvation for whole world, 93, 119
  Paul on, 143, 241n7
Satan concept, 86
"selfish gene," 10
self-sacrificing ethic
  altruism and motivation for, 9–10, 96–97
  in Christian writings outside New Testament, 176–79
  evidence of, outside Church, 179–80
Seneca, 31, 36–37, 64, 65, 229n23, 233n23
Sermon on the Mount (Jesus), 60, 82, 115–16, 121–22, 132, 154
sexual morality arguments
  Christian apologetics' response to pagans' criticism, 155–62
  "Corinthinize," 144
  homosexuality, 138, 230n10, 236n1
  letter to Colassians on, 151
  Paul's teachings on prostitution and, 145–48
Shabbat (Babylonian Talmud), 82
Sheep and Goats parable, 118–20, 195
Shema (Jewish prayer), 111
Shepherd of Hermas (Hermas), 187–89
Social Security Act of 1935, 217–18
Socrates
  ethics and influence of, 18, 27, 39
  on love, 50, 51, 53–55, 57
  The Symposium (Plato) on, 50–55, 230–31n13
  The Symposium (Xenophon) on, 65

Solomon (King of Israel), 105
Son of Man, 87, 109, 118–19, 207
"speaking in tongues," 140, 144, 145, 169–70
spiritual gifts, "love chapter" and, 167–71
Stanford Encyclopedia of Philosophy, 11
stergō, 49, 166–67
Stoicism
  on altruism, 231–32n16
  Epictetus, 31, 32, 34–35, 39–40, 127–28
  on ethics and happiness, 25–26, 30–37
  logos (logic) concept and, 32–33, 228n20
  Musonius Rufus, 228n19
  Seneca, 31, 36–37, 64, 65, 229n23, 233n23
  on worldly goods, 127–28
strangers. *see* others
suggnome/sungnōmē (forgiveness), 73, 133
Swinburne, Richard, 229n1
sympathy, 37
The Symposium (Plato), 50–55, 155, 230–31n13
The Symposium (Xenophon), 65

temple (Jerusalem)
  Babylonian destruction of, 82, 85, 105, 109
  "cleansing of the temple" by Jesus, 208, 249n41
  historical context of Jesus's teachings, 105–6
Ten Commandments
  "love commandment" in Jesus's teachings, 110–15

"love commandment" in Paul's teachings, 145–46
on Sabbath observance, 103
Tertullian of North Africa, 159, 187
Thessalonians (New Testament), 148, 209, 242n15
Thomas, Gospel of, 153, 236n12
Thucydides, 46
Timothy (Paul's companion), 151
Tobit, book of, 121
Torah. *see also* Deuteronomy; Exodus; Genesis; Leviticus; Numbers
  on atonement, 207
  Jesus's teachings and historical context of, 103–4, 105–6, 110, 111, 124
  as Jewish Scriptural "authority," 15
  Law of Moses in, 78–79
To the Rich (Basil the Great), 194–95
tragedy, charity as response to, 1–2, 181–83, 245n3. *see also* charitable giving
Trinity, doctrine of, 246n19

Unforgiving Slave parable, 133–34

Valerian (Roman Emperor), 211
Vespasian (Roman emperor), 35, 89
Veyne, Paul, 66–67
violence
  charity as prevention of, 68
  Jesus's opposition to, 109, 237–38n8, 248n33
virtue (*aretē*), 21, 32, 52, 58–61

wealth. *see* poverty and wealth
weddings, "love chapter" and, 167–71

Who Is the Rich Man Who Can Be Saved? (Clement), 189–91
The Wisdom of Jesus Son of Sirach (Jesus son of Sirach/Ben Sira), 82–84, 120
women's roles. *see* gender
wrath, as central theme in Hebrew Bible and New Testament, 99–102

Xenophon, 65

Yahweh, 206, 249n39

Zacchaeus, 185
Zealots, 108–9
Zeno, 30
Zeus (Greek god), 32, 53–54, 160

ABOUT THE AUTHOR

BART D. EHRMAN is a leading authority on the New Testament and the history of early Christianity. A distinguished professor of religious studies at the University of North Carolina at Chapel Hill, he is the author of six *New York Times* bestsellers, including *Misquoting Jesus*, *How Jesus Became God*, and *The Triumph of Christianity*. He has also created nine popular audio and video courses for The Great Courses. His books have been translated into twenty-seven languages, with over 2 million copies and courses sold.